C000216689

LOTTIE GROSS

DOG-FRIENDLY WEEKENDS

50 BREAKS IN BRITAIN FOR YOU AND YOUR DOG

Happy travels from Arty

Bradt GUIDES

Bradt Guides Ltd, UK
Globe Pequot Press Inc, USA

COVID-19

Please note that research for this guide was carried out during the Covid-19 pandemic. Because of the impact of the crisis on tourism, some businesses or services listed in the text may change their hours or their protocols, others may change their dog-friendly policies and others may no longer operate. We will post any information we have about these on ⌀ bradtguides.com/updates. And we'd of course be grateful for any updates you can send us during your own travels, which we will add to that page for the benefit of future travellers.

First edition published May 2022
Bradt Guides Ltd
31a High Street, Chesham, Buckinghamshire, HP5 1BW, England
www.bradtguides.com
Print edition published in the USA by The Globe Pequot Press Inc,
PO Box 480, Guilford, Connecticut 06437-0480

Text copyright © 2022 Bradt Guides Ltd
Map copyright © 2022 Bradt Guides Ltd; includes map data © OpenStreetMap contributors
Photographs copyright © 2022 Individual photographers (see below)
Project Manager: Anna Moores
Editor: Samantha Cook
Cover research: Ian Spick

ISBN: 9781784778774

British Library Cataloguing in Publication Data
A catalogue record for this book is available from the British Library

Photographs Photographers credited beside images & also those from libraries and other sources credited as follows: Dreamstime.com (DT); Lottie Gross (LG); Shutterstock.com (S); SuperStock (SS)
Front cover Top: Walkers at Buttermere, Cumbria (Tim Mannakee/4Corners); Bottom: Arty at Caerphilly Castle (LG)
Back cover Taking a dip in the Scottish Borders (Jennie Routley/S)
Title page Arty at Whitby Abbey (LG)

Maps David McCutcheon FBCart.S

Typeset by Ian Spick, Bradt Guides
Production managed by Zenith Media; printed in the UK
Digital conversion by www.dataworks.co.in

ABOUT THE AUTHOR

Lottie Gross is a travel writer and dog lover who has spent a number of years dragging her dogs along on adventures for work. Joining her on everything from light aircraft flights to the Isles of Scilly to city breaks in Lincoln, her dogs are almost as well travelled as she is. Lottie has penned dog-related travel articles for the likes of *The Telegraph*, *The Times*, *woman&home* and *Woman*.

During her trips, she has noticed a marked difference between hotels and attractions that claim they are dog-friendly and those that actually are; plenty of places will allow your dog inside, but not everywhere really welcomes them. That's why she has made finding Britain's truly dog-friendly destinations her mission.

ACKNOWLEDGEMENTS

My first thanks have to go to Milo – this book exists because of that weird little Manchester terrier and these pages are dedicated to all the adventures we never got to have. Thanks to my mum and her cavapoochon Izzy for putting up with our frenzied travels in 2021 – you've been the finest companions and I'm just sorry about all the rain. Thanks to Dad for always being a willing dog-sitter, and to Steph Dyson for being a spectacular stepmother to my neurotic animal. Huge thanks to Erin Hickey at VisitScotland for always being supportive, and to Zoe Poulton at Four Communications and Nikki Nichol at the Caravan and Motorhome Club for being so understanding about the bumps on the road (I hope you managed to fix the motorhome). Claire Thorburn, you were instrumental in helping me kick my book research off in Northumberland, and for that I'll be eternally grateful. I need to thank Bronya Oldfield and Kate O'Rourke for being top dog-walking companions, and Simon Willmore for the introduction to Bradt that started this all off. Thanks to Claire Strange, Anna Moores and Samantha Cook for your amazing work on the book, and to Helen Ochyra for always being a source of career inspiration. Alex Frith, I owe you thanks for helping the project get off the ground, and finally I have to thank Arty, the dog who has helped road test so much of what's gone into the finished book. He is the finest travel buddy, even if he does bark at almost everyone.

CONTENTS

INTRODUCTION ix
TRAVELLING RESPONSIBILY x
DOGS ON TOUR: THE ESSENTIALS xiii
USING THIS GUIDE xvii

1 Isles of Scilly 2
A blissful island-hopping escape
2 Roseland Heritage Coast 10
A seaside jaunt on a quiet Cornish coastline
3 Dartmoor National Park 18
A wild weekend on the moors
4 Weymouth 26
A classic south coast seaside break packed with Victorian charm
5 Isle of Wight 28
An island adventure for young & old
6 Hastings 32
A family holiday at the seaside
7 Portsmouth 34
Retail therapy meets naval history
8 New Forest National Park 36
A family foray in the forest
9 Midhurst 40
Country pursuits in the South Downs
10 Clovelly 48
A picture-perfect seaside escape
11 Winchester 50
An enticing Slow city break in the former English capital
12 Salisbury 52
A medieval city break with a cracking cathedral
13 Royal Tunbridge Wells..54
A right royal escape with wonderful walks
14 Wells & Glastonbury 56
A bohemian break in rural Somerset
15 Bath 62
A regal city break with a Roman twist
16 London 64
A bright lights, big city break

17 Cardiff 72
A cosmopolitan city break in the Welsh capital

18 Pangbourne-Wallingford Thames Path..................78
A riverside adventure with literary leanings

19 Pembrokeshire National Park................................84
A spectacular beach break with wildlife-watching trips

20 Wye Valley AONB & Forest of Dean.......................92
A riverside romp on the English-Welsh border

21 North Cotswolds 96
A chocolate-box weekend in the countryside

22 Brecon Beacons National Park...........................104
Towering mountains & subterranean sights

23 Aldeburgh 108
Art & history by the beach

24 Stratford-upon-Avon 110
Time travel with the Tudors

25 Bury St Edmunds...112
Simple pleasures in Suffolk

26 Ludlow 114
A hill-walking adventure with a touch of history

27 Rutland 118
An underrated foodie feast

28 Holkham & Wells...124
A coastal jaunt with countryside fun

29 Nottingham...128
A spirited city break resounding in legend

30 Snowdonia National Park 130
A mountain adventure with mining heritage

31 Lincoln 138
A city break steeped in history

32 Anglesey 144
An easy island adventure

33 The southern Peak District 148
An adventure on - & in - the rocks

34 Liverpool 156
A city break with industrial heritage & fantastic food

35 Beverley...158
A slow escape to a Yorkshire market town

36 Nidderdale AONB 160
Art meets nature in the Yorkshire Dales

← Grasmere, Lake District. (and_cut/S)

37 North York Moors 164
Hiking & heritage in a national park
38 Ullswater 170
A lakeside adventure for all ages
39 Corbridge & Northumberland National Park...........174
An adventure through Roman Britain
40 Galloway Forest Park 178
A birdwatching adventure in the forest
41 Northern Northumberland 180
Huge castles, tiny islands & never-ending sands
42 Tweed Valley..188
Slow travel on the Scottish Borders
43 Edinburgh 192
Fun & festivities in a creative city
44 Loch Lomond & The Trossachs National Park 198
An active adventure in a Scottish wilderness
45 Dundee 202
A family-focused city break by the sea
46 Isle of Mull 204
A wild island getaway with fabulous food
47 Glencoe & the Nevis Range 210
Magical mountains & glorious glens
48 Cairngorms National Park 212
Mountain adventures big & small
49 Aberdeen 220
Striking architecture by the sea
50 Loch Ness 222
A lochside escape with waterfalls & wild legends

INDEX...227
INDEX OF ADVERTISERS 231

INTRODUCTION

This book has been written at an unprecedented time. Not because of the pandemic-induced restrictions that have made researching it quite the challenge, but because this is an unprecedented time for dogs. According to the Pet Food Manufacturing Association, in the 12 months following March 2020, over 3.2 million pets were welcomed into homes across Britain, many of which were dogs. By 2021, 12.5 million dogs were living with their owners, who make up 33% of British households. Right now, it feels like there are more dogs in Britain than ever before.

Of course, we've always been a nation of dog lovers. We don't call them man's best friend for nothing. But not everybody loves dogs, nor does everyone understand the needs of dog owners. I learned this the hard way when travelling with my first dog, Milo – a particularly highly strung Manchester terrier with perfectly folded ears and puppyish eyes that could melt the hardest of hearts. He'd often come with me on trips when I was on assignment for my job as a travel writer, and so he got to stay in some of the best hotels in the country. We quickly found, though, that not every dog-friendly hotel was actually that friendly to dogs at all. Some, in fact, made your life as a dog owner so much harder it was hardly worth bringing them along.

We stayed in one property in Dorset that gave me a double-sided A4 sheet of paper listing the 'House Rules for Dogs', which included not letting Milo on

↑ Arty at Merrivale, Dartmoor National Park. (LG)

the furniture in the bedroom even if I was not in the room (I never did master telepathic discipline) and a zero-tolerance policy on barking. Of course nobody wants an incessantly barking dog next door on their holiday, but there's bound to be the occasional woof and a zero-tolerance policy is simply unsustainable – they're animals, after all, and barking is often instinctive.

Another favourite was the London hotel which asked dog owners to never leave their animal alone in the room, but also didn't allow the dog into the restaurant or breakfast room. I asked management which policy they prefer I'd break, and they suggested I eat in the next-door café instead, or pay extra to have breakfast brought up to the room. Hardly a dog-friendly policy. Fortunately, they've changed it now and feature as one of the best dog-friendly hotels in this book.

But on our adventures around Cornwall, Sussex, East Yorkshire and the Cotswolds, I also learned that not all dogs travel well. Our first ever big trip together was to the Isles of Scilly. We took the night train from London to Penzance, on which Milo slept in his crate in the guard's carriage while I had a lovely sleeper bunk, and then flew to the archipelago on a tiny ten-seater plane. I was animated with excitement, but the dog was less than impressed. The swaying of the train made him sick in bed, the twists of the Cornish roads on the drive to the airport had him panting and drooling, and then the noisy ten-seater aeroplane had him barking all the way to St Mary's. Needless to say, he was a terrible traveller.

And so all of this is why this book exists. It might feel like sometimes it's just easier to leave the dog at home or in kennels, but there *are* genuinely dog-friendly places out there and by taking your dog away with you, you strengthen your bond, improve their mental health and make memories without leaving anybody – dog or human – behind.

This book is your practical and, I hope, inspirational guide to travelling in Britain with your dog. From beach breaks on our vast and varied shoreline to mountainous adventures and cultural getaways you can enjoy with the dog by your side, there are 50 excellent dog-friendly weekends covered within these pages, each one personally curated by me and my newest companion, Arty.

So, go forth and wander with your dog. Try foraging in Oxfordshire (see page 80), hire canoes in the Cairngorms (see page 214) or pound the streets of Britain's biggest city (see page 64). Just don't forget to send me a postcard.

TRAVELLING RESPONSIBLY

When you're holidaying with a dog, responsible travel isn't just about being climate conscious and choosing sustainable options. The very presence of your pet alters your overall impact on the environment around you and it means you need to be far more aware than if you were without them. Responsible dog owners consider others first – be it other people, other dogs or even other animals – and ensure their dog leaves no trace.

FOLLOW THE COUNTRYSIDE CODE

The Countryside Code (⊘ gov.uk) is your guide to enjoying time in rural spaces safely and responsibly. It covers everything from parking to following local byways, but the most important advice for dog owners is to keep your dog under control and in sight. That means if your dog's recall isn't consistent, they're better off on the lead. This protects them from any unexpected dangers, such as electric fences or farm traffic in fields, and it protects local wildlife and farm animals from being disturbed.

It is illegal for dogs to worry livestock such as sheep, and farmers have the right to shoot your animal if they are causing harm or stress. Keeping them on the lead is the best option for all. The only situation in which you might let them off lead around farm animals is if you find yourself surrounded by overly curious or, in rare cases, aggressive cows. People have been seriously injured and killed by bulls or cows when trying to protect their dogs, so it's always best to let them off the lead so they can run away, therefore removing the threat and hopefully allowing you safe passage.

The second most important piece of advice in the Countryside Code is about dog poo. It must be bagged and binned wherever you are, even if it's a muddy field full of other animal faeces. While some local authorities also encourage the 'stick and flick' method, it's still best to pick it up where possible. This is because dog mess is a toxic pollutant and can cause harm to natural habitats and other animals. Bags of dog mess hung in trees or on bushes are also a blight on our landscapes and an even worse pollutant, so no matter how far you are from a bin, take it with you and dispose of it correctly. Don't want to carry it for hours on your long walk? Grab yourself a Dicky Bag (⊘ dickybag.com; see also page xv).

FEEDBACK REQUEST

At Bradt Guides we're aware that guidebooks start to go out of date on the day they're published – and that you, our readers, are out there in the field doing research of your own. You'll find out before us when a fine new family-run hotel opens or a favourite restaurant changes hands and goes downhill. So why not tell us about your experiences? Contact us on ✆ 01753 893444 or ✉ info@bradtguides.com. We will forward emails to the author who may post updates on the Bradt website at ⊘ bradtguides.com/updates. Alternatively, you can add a review of the book to Amazon, or share your adventures with us on social:

f BradtGuides **𝕏** @BradtGuides & @lottiecgross **⊙** @bradtguides

BE AWARE OF WILDLIFE It pays to know what wildlife is likely to be around in whichever season you're travelling in. The UK is home to ground-nesting birds from March until August, whether it's puffins on the coast or skylarks in the countryside. If your dog disturbs them, they could abandon their young out of fear and the chicks might die. Similarly, find out in advance if you are likely to come across seals on the coast and keep your dog well away from colonies on beaches.

USE A MAP A map isn't only essential to avoid getting lost, it's also important to ensure you don't trespass – plenty of landowners don't take kindly to bumbling tourists turning up on their patch, especially if they're accompanied by a dog. Use a physical OS Map or the digital version on your phone (⌀ osmaps.ordnancesurvey.co.uk) to find your way around, and consult websites like ⌀ gps-routes.co.uk, ⌀ alltrails.com or ⌀ walkhighlands.co.uk (Scotland only) for inspiration for great walks for all abilities.

↑ Canoeing, Symonds Yat. (Ceri Breeze/S)

MASTER THESE BASIC COMMANDS My personal dog trainer, Kate O'Rourke, has been my stress-free travel saviour while researching this book, helping to train my young Manchester terrier, Arty, for all manner of situations. Here are her top commands for dogs that travel:

Come back: Recall is the single most important thing you can teach your dog. It can help get them out of unsavoury or dangerous situations and will mean you can walk them with confidence in all kinds of environments. Choose a word that's distinctive (I use 'hustle') and instil it into your dog's psyche with the best treats you've got.

Sit/lie down and stay: Unless you're self-catering all weekend, your dog needs to learn some pub etiquette. Teaching them to lie down under a table or picnic bench will mean you can have a stress-free meal out and they won't disturb other diners. You can build this up at home by asking them to sit or lie down and wait beneath your dining table or on the floor next to the sofa while you have a cup of tea. A practice run at your local pub is a good excuse for a night out before you go away, too.

Leave it: This one is essential for busy beaches or parks – the last thing you want is for your dog to snaffle the sausage rolls from someone else's picnic. Ensure they know what 'leave it' means, and you'll be able to walk past myriad picnic blankets without worry.

Not sure how to teach your dog these commands? Watch some of the excellent videos on the Zak George's Dog Training Revolution YouTube channel (⌀youtube.com) or find your local force-free dog trainer.

DOGS ON TOUR: THE ESSENTIALS

(P)ETIQUETTE ON THE ROAD Our trusted partner, ⌀ PetsPyjamas.com (see ad, page 1), was co-founded by Denise Elphick in 2011. Denise has travelled to hundreds of hotels across the UK and Europe with her various dogs throughout the years, testing out their dog friendliness and searching for the best properties for the PetsPyjamas portfolio. From lovely little B&Bs to five-star resorts, she has seen it all, and her dogs are now well versed in travel etiquette. Here are a few tips from Denise to make sure you'll be welcomed back…

- When you arrive at a hotel make sure your dog has a little stroll around the grounds before coming in to meet the reception team. This will calm your dog down as they rush to get out of the car and give them a chance to familiarise themselves with their new surroundings – and have a little loo break.
- Ensure your dog is a good guest by always taking them outside first thing in the morning and after meals, and for a walk last thing at night.
- Make sure you give your dogs plenty of walks so that they are calm when they're indoors.
- Take a towel out with you to dry muddy paws before returning to the property, and definitely don't let your dog get up on the hotel's sofas or chairs – even if that's what they're used to at home.

STAYING SAFE It's easy to get carried away with the fun of a holiday and forget that the same dangers exist everywhere, not just at home. It's possible there will be new dangers, too, like steep cliff edges or parasites and diseases you are unlikely to come across if you live in a city. Keeping your dog safe is the key to having a relaxing holiday, so remember the following rules for a stress-free break…

- Ensure your dog's vaccinations are up to date. Parvovirus and leptospirosis can be deadly and are present all over Britain.
- Always restrain them in the car, either with a travel crate or harness and seat belt mechanism. Remember: you can be fined for having an unrestrained dog in your vehicle.
- Avoid walking in extreme temperatures – that means both hot and cold – and check the temperature of the pavement before you step out. If you can't bear it on your wrist for 10 seconds, it's not safe for your dog's paws; salt and grit are also dangerous for their feet, so avoid it or buy them some winter booties.
- Never leave your dog in a car during hot weather – not even for five minutes. Vehicles heat up incredibly quickly and heat exhaustion kills dogs fast.
- Check your dog for grass seeds during spring and summer. These have the potential to cause serious harm if stuck in between toes or if they penetrate the skin.
- If you're travelling in winter, a fluorescent collar, reflective coat or flashing light is essential in case your dog runs off in the dark.
- Don't let them swim unless you absolutely know it's safe. Some water might look calm, but rivers, straits and coastal areas can have strong currents.

TRAVEL SICKNESS Got a dog that doesn't travel well? I've been there. Try travel sickness medication from your local pet shop or Queezibics (⏴ queeziebics.com) anti-sickness snacks. If all that fails, ensure they've got plenty of water available in the car and avoid feeding them in the four hours before your journey.

BUILDING YOUR PET FIRST AID KIT You probably wouldn't bother travelling with a first aid kit for humans on a quick weekend away, or even a week-long holiday, but it's worth travelling with a dog-friendly first aid kit no matter how long you're away from home, as accidents big and small can happen any time. You can buy first aid kits for animals online or put your own together, but whatever you pack, vet and animal welfare campaigner Marc Abraham OBE says you still need to seek veterinary advice if your animal is in an accident or appears ill.

'A first aid kit isn't for self-treating,' he told me. 'It's for biding your time, stopping any bleeding and keeping things clean before you get to the vet. You should always get your dog seen by a professional, regardless of what you can do at home.' Here's what Marc puts in his animal first aid kit:

- Soft bandages for covering wounds and preventing contamination
- Hibiscrub or similar antibacterial wound cleaner
- Clippers to cut the hair around a wound
- Large syringes for flushing wounds with saline or warm water
- Tweezers for removing thorns or grass seeds
- Antihistamine for allergies and insect stings
- Tick hook/remover
- Muzzle to prevent your dog licking its wound or biting you while you tend to it

WHAT TO PACK

- Bedding, including a travel crate if your dog usually sleeps in a cage or your own sheets if they usually sleep on your bed
- A travel crate or seatbelt with a harness for the car
- Toys to keep them entertained in the room if you need to leave them for a short time
- Long-lasting chews such as yak bars, antlers or pizzle sticks to keep them busy in pubs or restaurants
- Poo bags and, for longer walks where you're unlikely to see bins, a Dicky Bag (⏴ dickybag.com; see ad, page 1) which can attach to any bag or belt loop and will contain your dog mess until you reach a disposal point

- Plenty of their usual food, plus a little extra just in case
- A variety of treats for any essential bribery or training reinforcement
- Spare towels for soggy days out
- Insurance details for your dog's policy in case of emergency vet visits

BOOKING TIPS

- Book direct with hotels so you can tell them you're bringing a dog and confirm their dog-friendly policy
- Don't be afraid to ask if you need a more secluded room for anxious dogs, or if you would like direct access to outside space
- Call ahead to pubs or restaurants to ensure there's space for the dog; some places have limited areas for dog owners
- Book through an established dog-friendly provider like our preferred partner, PetsPyjamas.com (see page xiii), which has one of the largest selections of dog-friendly hotels and cottages available to book online

OTHER USEFUL RESOURCES

bluecross.org.uk/pet-advice/dog-laws-uk Essential legal knowledge
countrysidedogwalks.co.uk To purchase helpful walking guides
petspyjamas.com This book has been independently researched, but is in partnership with PetsPyjamas which has exclusive packages for many of the properties listed. Where this is the case, we have listed PetsPyjamas instead of the property's own web address.
rspca.org.uk/adviceandwelfare General advice
Thekennelclub.org.uk/health-and-dog-care General advice

↑ Arty enjoying a hotel stay at the White Hart, Salisbury. (LG)

USING THIS GUIDE

This book details 50 different well-rounded weekends away in Britain, ordered geographically from south to north. Each chapter is focused on a different destination and provides ideas for things to do, where to stay and what to eat, as well as veterinary services nearby and pet supplies stores.

Some chapters are shorter than others and offer a whirlwind tour of the chosen destination, while others have descriptive introductions followed by longer listings sections. Some cover a single city, while others might cover an entire national park or region. In those larger areas, it's unlikely you'll be able to do everything listed within a single weekend, so consider these for longer trips, or choose a base as suggested in that chapter and keep your explorations local.

KEY TO SYMBOLS

Maximum number of dogs allowed in accommodation. Where this symbol is missing, there is no formal policy on the number of dogs you can bring with you, but it's always best to call ahead to check.

This indicates locations where it is usually safe to have your dog off the lead. Use common sense and be aware of your surroundings. If any local signage indicates otherwise, keep your dog on the lead.

Indicates activities suitable for rainy days. Finding things to do with the dog on a soggy afternoon can be tricky, especially with young kids who might not want to spend hours sitting in the pub, so look out for this if you want a wet-weather-friendly trip.

OPENING TIMES The opening times given for attractions, pubs and restaurants are an indication of the establishment's core hours during high season or in the months indicated in the 'when' line at the beginning of each chapter. Opening times are notoriously changeable, however, so it's always best to check online before setting out.

PRICES Where a hotel or attraction charges entry for a dog, the price has been stated in the listing. Where no price for dogs is given, it's safe to assume there is no charge for bringing your pet along.

WHICH DESTINATION IS BEST FOR YOU?

BEST FOR BEACHES...

Anglesey page 144
Cornwall page 2 & page 10
Holkham page 124
Isle of Mull page 204
North Northumberland page 180

BEST FOR BOAT TRIPS...

Edinburgh page 192
Isle of Mull page 204
Thames Path page 78
Ullswater page 170
Wye Valley & Forest of Dean 92

BEST FOR BOOKWORMS...

Edinburgh page 192
Stratford-upon-Avon page 110
Thames Path page 78
Tweed Valley page 188
Winchester page 50

BEST FOR CAR-FREE TRAVELLERS...

Cardiff page 72
Edinburgh page 192
London page 64
Thames Path page 78
Weymouth page 26

BEST FOR A CITY BREAK...

Aberdeen page 220
Cardiff page 72
Edinburgh page 192
Lincoln page 138
London page 64

BEST FOR DARK SKIES...

Anglesey page 144
Brecon Beacons page 104
Dartmoor National Park page 18
Galloway Forest Park page 178
Nidderdale AONB page 160

↑ Enjoying the beach in Anglesey. (LG)

BEST FOR (YOUNG) FAMILIES...

Dundee page 202
Hastings page 32
Isle of Wight page 28
New Forest page 36
Pembrokeshire page 84

BEST FOR FOODIES...

Isle of Mull page 204
Isles of Scilly page 2
Liverpool page 156
Pembrokeshire page 84
Rutland page 118

BEST FOR HIKERS...

Glencoe & the Nevis Range page 210
Nidderdale AONB page 160
Peak District page 148
Snowdonia National Park page 130
Ullswater page 170

BEST FOR HILLS & MOUNTAINS...

Cairngorms National Park page 212
Glencoe & the Nevis Range page 210
Glastonbury & Wells page 56
Ludlow page 114
Snowdonia National Park page 130

BEST FOR HISTORY BUFFS...

Corbridge page 174
Dartmoor page 18
Lincoln page 138
Stratford-upon-Avon page 110
Winchester page 50

BEST FOR TRAIN (& FUNICULAR) LOVERS...

Glencoe & the Nevis Range page 210
Hastings page 32
Isle of Wight page 28
North York Moors page 164
Snowdonia National Park page 130

↑ Shopping in Cardiff. (Portia Jones)

CharleyChau
Beautiful bedding for dogs

1 A BLISSFUL ISLAND-HOPPING ESCAPE

WHERE	Isles of Scilly, Cornwall
WHEN	May–Oct
HIGHLIGHTS	White-sand beaches for lazy days in the sun, thrilling wildlife and abundant local seafood.

The Isles of Scilly are Britain's little bit of paradise. Much is said about the microclimate here – these low-lying islands, 55km off the Cornish coast, enjoy warmer, more reliable weather than the rest of the nation thanks to their location on the Gulf Stream – but they're spectacular in any conditions. As long as you've got waterproofs and sunscreen, you can't go wrong with a weekend (or even a week) in this enchanting archipelago.

There are five inhabited islands in the Scillies, none bigger than 15km^2 and each with its own appeal, and every one is incredibly welcoming for dogs. St Mary's is the main isle; its airport, and a harbour for arrivals on the *Scillonian III* ferry, make it the entry point for most. Hugh Town, its 'capital', is a hive of activity with plenty of dog-friendly pubs and cafés, and neighbouring island Tresco is a popular place to head for tropical gardens and excellent walks. But the best way to experience these islands is to seek out remoteness – which is not difficult to find, even on a weekend break.

On St Martin's, even in the height of summer, you could find you're the only people on the white-sand beach by the quay. There's very little to do here beyond eat, walk, sleep and gaze at the astonishingly blue sea with a glass of wine from the local vineyard. Bryher, the smallest island, has excellent walking and swimming and seal-spotting opportunities from its many bays and beaches, while St Agnes is one of the wilder isles. The footpaths here skirt around rocky bays and across lush green pasture from the local Troytown Farm (don't miss a taste of the Troytown ice cream, served throughout the archipelago).

← Pelistry Beach. (James LePage/S) ↑ Pretty houses in Hugh Town. (Andrew Roland/DT)

It's easy to eat well in the Scillies. With such remoteness comes self-sufficiency, and you can't walk far without coming across an honesty box, perhaps selling fresh fish from the morning's boats, meat from a local farm, fruit and vegetables from allotments or flowers and plants all cultivated on Scilly soil. Production and creativity come naturally here, it seems, and you'll meet artists of all kinds, their studios open for people (and often dogs, too) to pop inside and see their work, be it jewellery made from beachcombed plastic or paintings of the Scillies' myriad seabirds.

The wildlife is particularly exciting: Atlantic grey seals, Manx shearwaters, puffins and petrels can all be seen on boat trips that travel out as far as Bishop Rock, the southernmost point of the UK. Hop on board with the dog with the St Mary's Boatmen's Association (The Quay, Hugh Town, St Mary's TR21 0HU ⚓ scillyboating.co.uk ⊖ daily departures; £20) or St Agnes Boating (The Quay, St Agnes TR22 0PL ⚓ stagnesboating.co.uk ⊖ Wed; £20) for guided excursions in partnership with the Isles of Scilly Wildlife Trust.

Getting around the Scillies is half the fun – the small ferries that run between the islands are adventures in themselves – and you can easily nip from one island to another for day trips. Any of the islands make a reasonable base but St Mary's offers the most flexibility; from there you will be able to enjoy all the activities suggested below. Up four times a year – usually in spring and late summer – you won't need a boat at all to travel between Tresco and Bryher. Instead, you'll be able to join a party on the sand, as the two islands come together for a short but sweet seafood and music festival on the sea floor. A unique event for a unique and beguiling archipelago.

GARRISON WALLS & WOOLPACK BATTERIES (St Mary's TR21 0LT
⌀ english-heritage.org.uk ✈) On a headland on the western edge of St Mary's, accessible from the top of Garrison Hill just 100m from the north end of Hugh Street in Hugh Town, the Garrison Walls and Woolpack Batteries are a fascinating

↑ Overlooking Hugh Town Quay on St Mary's. (Andrew Roland/S)

and well-preserved piece of military history that make a spectacular walk with the dog. The oldest parts are around the Star Castle Hotel at its northern end, dating back to the late 1500s, and you can follow the 17th-century curtain wall which encloses the entire headland. Footpaths run through the site, offering access to various Victorian batteries, and on a clear day the views to St Agnes are wonderful.

PELISTRY BEACH (St Mary's TR21 0NX 🐕) The three beaches closest to Hugh Town (Porthmellon, Town Beach and Porthcressa) are dog-friendly only from November through March, but Pelistry, around 3km from town on the northeast corner of the island, welcomes off-lead dogs year-round. This idyllic little stretch has soft white sand and shallow, clear waters perfect for paddling; the beach itself lacks facilities, but there's a tea room at the top of the hill leading down to the sand. Walk a kilometre or so north and you'll find some Bronze Age burial mounds overlooking the sea.

TRESCO ABBEY GARDEN (Carn Near Rd, Tresco TR24 0QQ ⌂ tresco.co.uk ⊙ 10.00–16.00 daily; adult/child £15/£5) Tresco's fabulous gardens are a 30-minute stroll from the quays at both New and Old Grimsby, on the west and east side of the island respectively. Over 20,000 plants thrive in the microclimate here, hailing from some 80 countries. There are bristling palms and unusual succulents, and brilliant views out to that ever-present blue sea. Don't miss the on-site Valhalla Museum, which showcases intricately carved figureheads from ships wrecked hereabouts.

KING CHARLES'S & CROMWELL'S CASTLES (Tresco TR24 0QE ⌂ english-heritage.org.uk) On the northeastern side of Tresco, a stunning 3km walk from the Abbey Garden, lies a pair of astonishingly well-preserved coastal castles. The first, northernmost, castle sits on higher ground above the coastline and was built during the mid-1500s by forces under King Edward VI. Its set-back position meant it was eventually abandoned, being rendered useless for defence, and was partly dismantled to create Cromwell's Castle, closer to the sea. This round tower of a fortress, a rare relic of Cromwell's time, was built in 1651 and enjoyed a far better defensive position, keeping this side of Tresco safe from a Dutch fleet seeking repatriations from the Royalists on land.

ST MARTIN'S VINEYARD (Higher Town, St Martin's TR25 0QL ⌂ stmartinsvineyard.co.uk ⊙ see website; adult/child £10/£1) Take a self-guided tour of this beautiful vineyard, which sits just 500m from the pontoon at Higher Town Bay, to learn about what goes into producing their bottles of white and rosé. Tours include a tasting, but if you'd rather just enjoy the wine you can try a flight from £6 before (or perhaps best after) a wander around the coastal path.

↑ Cromwell's Castle, Tresco. (Neil Duggan/S) ← Tresco Abbey Garden. (Gardens by Design/S)

LET'S GO

GETTING THERE

You can't take your car to the Isles of Scilly, but if you drive down to Cornwall you can leave it at your departure point. There are two main ways to reach the islands: the *Scillonian III* ferry departs Penzance daily, while small Skybus aeroplanes leave daily from Newquay, Exeter or Land's End airports (islesofscilly-travel.co.uk); buses and taxis are available from Penzance station to Land's End Airport. The overnight train from London to Penzance (gwr.com) is a lovely way to reach the ferry; you can book seats or a two-berth cabin, but the dog must travel in a crate in the guard's carriage.

Getting around each island is best done on foot or, if on St Mary's which has some slightly longer distances, by taxi. Ferries sail between the islands; times are posted daily on quay blackboards and within hotels. Most hotels will offer a pick-up service from the nearest quay where necessary.

EATING

✕ **Adam's Fish & Chips** Highertown, St Martin's TR25 0QN adamsfishandchips.co.uk 18.00–20.30 Tue, Thu & Sat. Line-caught and cooked by Adam himself, the pollock (and chips) here might just be the best you'll ever taste. The lobster scampi is also sublime, its batter gloriously crisp, and there are sausages from their own farm and veggie burgers for those who prefer not to eat from the sea. Dog-friendly seating is outside, under cover.

✕ **The Atlantic** Hugh St, Hugh Town, St Mary's TR21 0PL atlanticinnscilly.co.uk 11.00–23.00 daily. An excellent pub serving hearty meals and zingy Cornish cider, with a terrace out back offering great views over the harbour.

✕ **The Beach** Porthmellon Beach, Hugh Town, St Mary's TR21 0JY scillybeach.com noon–21.00 daily. Chunky burgers with smoky bacon and cheese and loaded fries with short rib make this an ideal departure from the ubiquitous fish menus. It's right on Porthmellon Beach, and the views alone are enough to please.

✕ **Island Fish** Newpark, Bryher TR23 0PR islandfish.co.uk 09.00–17.30 Mon-Sat. This long-running family business offers some of the best lobster and crab on the islands. The father and son duo go out fishing each morning, and the catch is served up in simple dishes like fish pie or quiche with salad.

✕ **Juliet's Garden** Seaways/Porthlow, St Mary's TR21 0NF julietsgardenrestaurant. co.uk 10.00–21.00 daily. Exceptional crab sandwiches are the highlight here, but the menu also includes cream teas and a hearty ploughman's lunch. The views steal the show, though, with tables outside on the terrace overlooking Hugh Town harbour.

✕ **Ruin Beach Café** Back Ln, Old Grimsby, Tresco TR24 0PU tresco.co.uk 09.00–20.30 daily. Tea, coffee, seafood sharing platters and wood-fired pizzas served right on the beach.

✕ **The Turks Head** The Quay, St Agnes TR22 0PL turksheadscilly.co.uk 10.00–18.00 Tue, 13.00–18.00 Wed, 10.00–21.30 Thu–Mon. This old boozer has real character inside, but the outdoor terrace overlooking the sandbar that connects St Agnes to the tiny island of Gugh is the main draw. Order a Cornish cider with fish and chips and stare out at the azure waters before taking a dip.

SLEEPING

🏠 **Hell Bay Hotel** Bryher TR23 0PR hellbay. co.uk 🐾 2. The ground-floor rooms are all dog-friendly, some offering sea views and most with direct access to the gardens. The restaurant-bar area allows dogs, and there's a gorgeous terrace for alfresco drinks. *From £190/night B&B; dogs from £15/night.*

🏠 **Karma St Martin's** Lower Town, St Martin's TR25 0QW ⌂ petspyjamas.com 🐾 **1**; see ad, page 236. The premier luxury hotel in the islands sits right on the beach. Dogs are allowed throughout, including in the restaurant, which serves beautifully presented local fish and has a 'canine menu'. Pet-sitting is available. *From £214/night B&B.*

🏠 **Star Castle Hotel** Garrison Walls, Hugh Town, St Mary's TR21 0JA ⌂ star-castle.co.uk 🐾 **2**. The oldest hotel in the archipelago, inside a 16th-century star fort. Its lovely garden rooms are dog-friendly, and some come with their own sea-view veranda. *From £300/night B&B.*

OTHER PRACTICALITIES

Tourist information centre Porthcressa Bank, Hugh Town, St Mary's TR21 0LW ⌂ visitislesofscilly. com ⊙ 08.30–18.00 Mon–Sat, 09.00–14.00 Sun. **Pet supplies** Islands Homeware (Garrison Ln, Hugh Town, St Marys TR21 0JJ ⌂ islandhomehardware. co.uk ⊙ 09.00–17.00 Mon–Sat) has a small selection of dog accessories and food.

Veterinary practices IOS Veterinary Practice (Launceston Cl, Old Town, St Mary's TR21 0NJ ✆ 01720 423667) is the only vet's in the archipelago and can fly your pet to the mainland in emergencies.

↑ Great Bay, St Martin's Island. (James LePage/S)

2 A SEASIDE JAUNT ON A QUIET CORNISH COASTLINE

WHERE	Roseland Heritage Coast, Cornwall
WHEN	Year-round
HIGHLIGHTS	Soft, sandy beaches hugged by a dramatic coastal path; glorious castles and gardens with secrets to discover.

With the Atlantic on its eastern flank and a vein-like network of rivers and creeks to the west, the Roseland Peninsula is a wonderfully remote stretch of Cornwall's southern coast. Thanks to its dearth of major roads and large towns, it doesn't see the same thronging crowds and maddening traffic jams as other areas of this popular beach-break county. This makes it an ideal place to bring the dog for coastal hikes, lazy beach days and, of course, seafood sampling in the many seaside cafés and restaurants that dot its craggy coastline.

The Roseland's main area begins just south of St Austell, around Porthpean, and stretches south to St Mawes, overlooking the Carrick Roads estuary, around 34km away. Along its shores lie towering cliffs, undulating fields dotted with grazing cattle, and some of the finest stretches of soft white sand in the county – most importantly, the majority of its beaches are dog friendly year-round. Keep your pet on a lead when it's busy with picnicking families, but at quiet times feel free to let them

↑ Arty on Carne Beach. (LG)

run around Polstreath Beach (📍PL26 6TH) or Vault Beach (📍PL26 6JS) in the north, or Porthcurnick (📍TR2 5EW) to the south.

The long-distance South West Coast Path (🖉 southwestcoastpath.org.uk) tracks along the peninsula, climbing high on to the cliffs and plunging down into tiny fishing villages like Portscatho, Portloe and Gorran Haven, where cafés and weathered old pubs will refuel you after long rambles along the trail. Some of the best views are in the south, around Carne Bay and St Anthony Head, so if you're a keen hiker, base yourself in or around St Mawes for wonderful routes from your doorstep.

The northern half of the Roseland is better for those who aren't so enamoured with long coastal walks, and if you've got kids this is the place to stay. Overnight in or near Mevagissey and you'll be within short driving distance of attractions like the Lost Gardens of Heligan, with their compelling tale of loss and restoration, and the handsome historic harbour at Charlestown, which featured in the BBC's *Poldark* series and regularly sees tall ships docking between its 18th-century walls. There's a great little shipwreck museum in Charlestown, and the vast and enthralling Eden Project is just a 10-minute drive inland.

No matter where you stay, though, the Roseland is relatively compact so you're rarely more than a 45-minute journey away from any of the main sights. And anything you miss will serve as an excellent excuse to return – this is not the kind of place you can keep away from for too long.

THE EDEN PROJECT (Bodelva PL24 2SG ⌀ edenproject.com ⊙ 09.30–18.00 daily; adult/child £35/£10) It's hard to imagine that this 13ha site of gardens, landscaped terraces and bulbous biomes was once a bleak, industrial china clay pit, but that's exactly what it was until 1998. Now transformed by hundreds of gardeners, the Eden Project, around a 20-minute drive north of Mevagissey, is a spectacularly green and pleasant patch of land – the size of around 35 football pitches – with footpaths snaking around beautiful seasonal borders and plant-based exhibitions. Dogs are allowed everywhere except inside the mammoth biomes (it's well worth taking turns to explore them if you're travelling in a group, or you could leave the dog in the car for an hour if it's not too hot; there's under-cover parking available, ask the attendant when you arrive). There's a covered seating area at the café for a dog-friendly lunch stop, too.

SHIPWRECK TREASURE MUSEUM (Quay Rd, Charlestown PL25 3NJ ⌀ shipwreckcharlestown.co.uk ⊙ 10.00–20.00 daily; adult/child £10/£8 ⬈) Sitting right on Charlestown's harbour, just a 15-minute drive north of Mevagissey, this engaging little museum charts the history of wreck diving and explores the

↑ The Eden Project. (Nicole Kwiatkowski/S)

unusual objects found beneath the sea from more than 150 shipwrecks. Don't miss a stroll around the beautiful harbour afterwards.

THE LOST GARDENS OF HELIGAN (B3273, Pentewan PL26 6EN ⊘ heligan.com ⊙ 10.00–17.00 daily; adult/child £17.50/£8.50) On the outskirts of Mevagissey, this 80ha site, comprising green fields, kitchen gardens and jungle, could consume an entire day of a weekend break. Once a 400ha estate, the garden was effectively abandoned in the early 20th century when many of its gardeners went off to war. With the house used as a convalescence hospital in World War I and the garden left to ruin, it was reclaimed by the undergrowth and only rediscovered in the 1990s, after which direct descendants of the garden's original creators, the Tremayne family, began a huge restoration project. Today, you can walk among its Italian gardens, see Victorian pineapple houses and stroll down to the thick, wild jungle which has one of the oldest and tallest tree ferns in Britain. The enormous, centuries-old rhododendrons are particularly impressive, and there are moving tales about the gardeners who never returned from the Great War. For families there's a playground, zip line and farm animals to see, and you can bring the dog along to all areas, including the café and shop.

↑ The Lost Gardens of Heligan. (khd/S)

CAERHAYS CASTLE (Gorran Churchtown PL26 6LY ⌀ visit.caerhays.co.uk ⊙ Feb–Jun 10.00–17.00 daily; adult/child £10/£5) For a walk with a difference, head to the grounds of this courtly 19th-century castle just 15 minutes south of Mevagissey. Still used as a private home by the Williams family, the castle opens its gardens to the public every spring when you can walk among spectacular flowering rhododendrons, magnolias and camellias. Spend some time on lovely Porthluney Bay beach afterwards.

ST ANTHONY HEAD (Military Rd, TR2 5HA ⌀ nationaltrust.org.uk) On the tip of the Roseland Peninsula, this headland offers some of the finest views of the south Cornwall coast. Take the circular 1½km walk from the car park, and in addition to those Falmouth Bay vistas you'll see a number of old military buildings, including a paraffin store and a battery dating to the early 1900s. You might spot seabirds such as fulmars gliding by the cliffs, too, and in spring and summer kestrels and greenfinches can be seen on land.

ST MAWES CASTLE (Castle Drive, St Mawes TR2 5DE ⌀ english-heritage. org.uk ⊙ 10.00–17.00 daily; adult/child £6.90/£4.10) Perched on the cliffs of St Mawes on the southern edge of the Roseland, this is one of many coastal fortresses built by Henry VIII that can be found across the Cornish coast. Dating to 1539, it is a superbly preserved piece of military history, with fascinating exhibits on how the building would have been manned. See a replica gun station overlooking the Atlantic and look out for the glass-covered oubliette, where prisoners or rebellious soldiers would have been locked away. Dogs are allowed in all areas of the castle and its grounds.

↑ Caerhays Castle. (Massimiliano Finzi/S)

↑ St Anthony Head. (Mick Blakey/S)

LET'S GO

GETTING THERE

The Roseland is difficult to reach and explore by public transport so it's best visited in your own vehicle. The A390 is the closest main road to the peninsula, offering access from the north. Take the A3078 to St Mawes or the B3273 for Mevagissey; a network of single-track lanes connects the coastal villages.

EATING

✕ **Harbourside** Charlestown PL25 3NJ ⌂ harboursideinncharlestown.co.uk ⊙ noon–21.00 daily. A St Austell Brewery-owned pub on the harbour in Charlestown, serving pies and fish and chips, or deep-fried banana blossom for vegan diners.

✕ **The Hidden Hut** New Rd, Portscatho TR2 5HR ⌂ hiddenhut.co.uk ⊙ 11.00–15.00 daily. On the shores of Porthcurnick Beach, this friendly café serves fresh salads with ingredients from their allotment, homemade pasties, and grilled mackerel from the local fishing vessels. There are freshly baked cakes to help you on your way along the coast path, too.

✕ **The Sharksfin** The Quay, Mevagissey PL26 6QU ⌂ thesharksfin.co.uk ⊙ 10.30–23.00 daily. Outstanding fresh fish dishes with views over Mevagissey's harbour, including a blackened cod burger, moules marinière and shrimp tacos.

✕ **The Thirstea Co** Porth Farm, St Anthony TR2 5EX ⌂ thethirsteacompany.co.uk ⊙ 10.00–17.00 daily. Set inside an old farm building just steps away from Towan Beach, not far from St Anthony Head, this lovely husband-and-wife-run café has excellent coffee, sandwiches and pasties – perfect for post coast-path walk treats.

SLEEPING

⌂ **Edgcumbe** Penare PL26 6NY ⌂ nationaltrust. org.uk 🐾 1. This National Trust cottage, which sleeps up to four people, is a cosy stone bolthole in a tiny hamlet 6½km south of Mevagissey. There's an enclosed garden for the dog and an open fire for cosy nights in. *From £100/night.*

⛺ **Merrose Farm Caravan and Motorhome Club Site** Portscatho, TR2 5EL ⌂ caravanclub. co.uk. Tents and touring pitches are available

at this leafy campsite just 2km north from Porthcurnick Beach. There's a dog exercise area on site and plenty of footpaths to romp around nearby, and families will welcome the adventure playground. *From £15.50/night.*

🏠 **The Nare** Carne Beach TR2 5PF 🖱 narehotel. co.uk 🐾 1. Overlooking Carne Bay, this country house-style hotel is stunning. At the time of writing, due to pandemic protocols, dogs weren't allowed in the restaurant, but once normal seating resumes it's expected they'll be allowed to dine with you in the Quarterdeck, which serves the same exceptionally high-quality, beautifully presented food as in the main dining room. You can also have dinner and breakfast delivered to your room. Dogs get towels and a chef-prepared dinner on request and room rates include daily afternoon tea with scones and cake on the terrace. Don't miss a massage or swim in the outdoor heated pool. *From £328/night B&B; dogs from £19/night.*

🏠 **The Rosevine** Portscatho TR2 5EW 🖱 petspyjamas.com 🐾 2. A really lovely apart-hotel overlooking Gerrans Bay (15 minutes from St Mawes in the south), the Rosevine has a dog-friendly dining lounge for dinner and breakfast, and the gorgeous Porthcurnick Beach is just down the road. The modern and stylish studios include kitchenettes, and there's an indoor pool and a garden with a huge lawn. *From £210/night B&B.*

🏠 **St Mawes Hotel** Harbourside, St Mawes TR2 5DN 🖱 stmaweshotel.com 🐾 1. Right in the centre of St Mawes, overlooking the ferry terminal, this hotel provides dog beds, towels and bowls for your pet, and the restaurant and bar are also dog-friendly. Rooms are bright and airy with blue and white seaside décor *From £190/night B&B; dogs £30/stay.*

OTHER PRACTICALITIES

Tourist information Roseland Visitor Centre, St Mawes, Truro TR2 5AG 🖱 stmawesandtheroseland. co.uk 🕐 10.00–13.00 Mon–Fri.

Pet supplies Pets at Home (Pentewan Rd Retail Park, St Austell PL25 5BU 🖱 petsathome.com 🕐 09.00–18.00 Mon–Sat, 10.00–16.00 Sun) is a 15-minute drive from Mevagissey.

Veterinary practices Vets4Pets, inside Pets at Home (see above), has a 24-hour emergency line (📞 01726 626820).

↓ St Mawes Castle. (Andy333/S)

3 A WILD WEEKEND ON THE MOORS

WHERE	Dartmoor National Park, Devon
WHEN	Mar–Oct
HIGHLIGHTS	Great hikes with wild swimming, towering waterfalls and astonishing ancient sites.

It's hard not to be affected by the beauty of Dartmoor, a national park that stretches almost 1,000km² across the south Devon countryside. It doesn't matter when you come or for how long, this landscape of high moorland and lush river valleys is just beguiling. In spring and summer yellow gorse and pink heather coat its perfectly curved moors, then come autumn it all turns to brown and amber, lending the landscape the look of a vintage photograph. The sun brings out the vivid colours, but the rain – and the notoriously fast-descending mist – creates an atmosphere you experience in few other places. Dartmoor in a downpour becomes moody and brooding, with a palpable sense of mystery.

Mystery is in fact a dominant feature here – alongside the region's strong folklore and enduring traditions are the physical remains of ancient civilisations we're still making discoveries about today. An astonishing number of early human settlements are strewn across the moors, with stone circles and 3,500-year-old roundhouses amid the grasses, making this not just a spectacular dog walking location, but a living history lesson, too.

↑ Bellever Tor. (LG)

You can witness this at the prehistoric settlement on the moorland around Bellever Tor, in the heart of the national park, or 5km north at the Grimspound Bronze Age village. The most intriguing remains are in the western side of the park in Merrivale, where a pair of stone rows lie adjacent to the main road: to this day, historians don't know their purpose, though theories abound. It can be tricky for the untrained eye to understand the significance of much of this, so the best way to explore is to join zealous local guide Emma Cunis (dartmoorsdaughter.com; from £15) and her dog, Skye, on a guided walk to get a better understanding of what life was like on Dartmoor thousands of years ago.

Walking is, naturally, the main attraction for many – a qualified guide is essential if you're not confident with a map and compass – but Dartmoor is also famously wet, so it's fortunate that there are several excellent indoor attractions to keep adults, children and dogs entertained. Base yourself in the centre of the park, around the villages of Princetown or Two Bridges, and you'll have easy access to top walking spots and great indoor attractions. You could head south to take a scenic steam train journey from the town of Buckfastleigh, or go east to play with the marble runs at House of Marbles in Bovey Tracey, a small town that's a thriving hub in peak season. Princetown itself has the park's main visitor centre, where an excellent five-room exhibition charts local geology and explores the varied wildlife that thrives here.

Tucked between vast swathes of moorland are lovely towns and villages with shops selling local crafts, and ample cosy pubs and cafés for indulging in Devonshire cream teas or homemade game pie. Chagford, in the north, around 25 minutes from Princetown, is particularly charming – pick up a local tipple in Jaded Palates Wines (42 The Square, TQ13 8AH ⚲ jadedpalates.com ◻ 10.00–18.00 Mon–Sat) – while the quaint village of Widecombe-in-the-Moor, between Princetown and Bovey Tracey, is home to a striking 14th-century church with an imposing 36m tower.

Due to the wildlife and grazing animals throughout Dartmoor, dogs are best kept on the lead and, at the time of writing, local bye-laws were being rewritten in a consultation that aimed to make it a legal requirement (check ⚲ dartmoor.gov.uk). If yours needs to run off some steam, try the secure fields at Haytor Mutt Mayhem (⚲ TQ13 7TY ⚲ haytormuttmayhem.com ◻ 07.00–21.00 daily; £12/hour) near Ilsington, or Dartmoor Dog Walking Field (⚲ TQ13 7TY ⚲ dartmoordogwalkingfield.uk ◻ 06.00–21.00 daily; £8/hour) just outside Bellever Forest.

BELLEVER TOR (⚲ PL20 6TU 🐾)

In the heart of the national park, around 11km northeast of Princetown, Bellever Tor (442m) rises gently above the managed pine forest of the same name and commands 360-degree views of the surrounding moorland. It's a gentle 5km walk from the Forestry Commission car park nearest Postbridge to the tor; once you've made it through the woods, the landscape opens out on to a moor where Bronze Age stone circles and remnants of ancient thatched roundhouses can be found along with the bilberry (or whortleberry, as it is known in Devon) bushes and heather that blushes pink in summer. It's beautiful at any time of year and in any weather – rain and wind only add atmosphere and are easily forgotten in the warm embrace of the nearby Warren House Inn (see page 24).

SPITCHWICK (⚲ TQ13 7NT)

Spitchwick is a picturesque common on the banks of the River Dart, around 16km east of Princetown and a 25-minute drive south of Bellever. Follow the path under the bridge and over a steep mound and you'll come to an open area right by the water, idyllic for long lazy picnics and wild swims. This beauty spot gets incredibly busy in summer, when parking is a nightmare, so it's usually best avoided when the crowds descend on Dartmoor in July and August.

SOUTH DEVON RAILWAY (⚲ TQ11 0DZ ⚲ southdevonrailway.co.uk

◻ 09.00–17.30 daily; adult/child £11.50/ £7, dogs £1 ☂) Take a ride in vintage train carriages that date back as far as the 1930s, pulled along by steam engines. Departing Buckfastleigh, on the southeastern edge of the park (15 minutes south of Spitchwick), you'll travel through the Dart Valley, following the river for 11km along a line built in 1872. It's a slow and scenic 30-minute trip, passing through woodland and past grazing pasture; you can explore the market town of Totnes and grab a hot drink, or take a walk along the towpath next to the winding River Dart, before hopping back aboard for the return.

↑ South Devon Railway. (Chris Jenner/S)   → Canonteign Falls. (Tom Meaker/S)

↑ Haytor. (Andyfox0co0uk/DT)

HOUSE OF MARBLES (Pottery Rd, Bovey Tracey TQ13 9DS ⚲ houseofmarbles. com ⊙ 10.00–17.00 daily; free ☂) On the eastern edge of the national park, just outside Bovey Tracey and around 20km north of Buckfastleigh, this industrial building features a pottery museum, marble museum, glass-blowing factory and department store selling women's clothing, handmade wooden furniture and children's toys. Kids will love the giant marble run above the stairs and the games garden, and you can all – including the dog – enjoy hot lunches in the restaurant.

CANONTEIGN FALLS (♀ EX6 7RH ⚲ canonteignfalls.co.uk ⊙ 10.30–16.00 daily; adult/child £8.50/£6.50) A 15-minute drive north of Bovey Tracey, rushing over the edge of a vertiginous, 67m-high cliff, Canonteign is one of England's highest waterfalls and the 30-minute walk to its top makes a deeply enjoyable hike. Follow the trail that wends its way up the cliff over a Victorian-built stone staircase and a handful of wooden bridges, and you'll enjoy numerous views of the falls as you go. From Buzzard's View, at the top, where the water spills over

LET'S GO

GETTING THERE

Dartmoor sits just beyond the end of the M5 at Exeter, from where the A30, A386 and A38 skirt around the edges of the national park. In 2021, a new train line opened to connect Okehampton (Station Rd, EX20 1EJ), in the north of the region, to Exeter. Getting around by public transport is less easy.

EATING

✖ **Birdcage** 11 The Square, Chagford TQ13 8AA ✆ 01647 433883 ⊙ 09.00–15.00 Mon–Tue & Thu–Sat. Gorgeous cakes, loose-leaf teas and excellent coffee, plus light lunches such as soups and paninis, in the heart of Chagford. Dog biscuits are available on the bar and there's water outside the front door.

✖ **The Little Farm Shed** Merrivale PL20 6ST ⚲ eversfieldorganic.co.uk ⊙ 10.00–18.00 daily. Cakes, beers, wines and dog-friendly ice creams are sold from a tiny shed next to the Dartmoor Inn

(see opposite), with outdoor picnic benches under cover for those rainy days.

✖ **The Rugglestone Inn** Widecombe-in-the-Moor TQ13 7TF ⚲ rugglestoneinn.co.uk ⊙ 11.30–15.00 & 17.00–22.00 Mon–Fri, 11.30–22.30 Sat–Sun. Splendid traditional inn with a big beer garden and cosy bar. Classic comfort food, and local ales on cask.

✖ **Ullacombe Farm Shop & Cafe** Ullacombe Farm, Haytor Rd, Bovey Tracey TQ13 9LL ⚲ ullacombefarm.com ⊙ 09.00–17.00 daily. Less than 10 minutes from Bovey Tracey, this rustic café is the place to go for cream teas, hearty hot lunches and proper fry-ups. Stock up on goodies from the farm shop before you leave. There are swings and a tractor for the kids to play on.

✖ **Warren House Inn** B3212, Postbridge PL20 6TA ⚲ warrenhouseinn.co.uk ⊙ 11.00–22.00 Mon–Sat, noon–21.30 Sun. With two roaring fires – supposedly kept burning for 175 years – in the bar, this is the perfect pre- or post-walk pub.

the edge, you can see the bucolic patchwork of grazing fields beyond the 36ha estate. There are sculpture and dinosaur trails for kids along the route. Once you've descended, stop at the dog-friendly café, which serves hot food, cakes and dog-friendly frozen yoghurt next to an adventure playground.

Outdoor tables overlooking the moor are the top spot in warm weather; in colder months the homemade rabbit pie is top choice.

SLEEPING

🏠 **Dartmoor Inn** Merrivale PL20 6ST ⊘ eversfieldorganic.co.uk 🐾 **1**. A delightful pub with rooms, run by local Eversfield Organic Farm, just a few kilometres from Princetown. The simple but cosy bedrooms are a perfect hideaway and dogs can join you in the main restaurant for meals. *From £80/night B&B; dogs £25/stay.*

🏠 **New Park Cottage** Widecombe-in-the-Moor TQ13 7TF ⊘ widecombecottage.com 🐾 **2**. This handsome stone cottage sleeps up to six people (two doubles, one twin). There's a gorgeous lawned garden for games of fetch and an Aga for warming up after walks. Muddy paws must be cleaned before dogs are allowed upstairs. *From £600/week.*

🏠 **Two Bridges Inn** Two Bridges PL20 6SW ⊘ twobridges.co.uk. Just a few kilometres from Princetown, this beautiful 18th-century inn on the banks of the West Dart and Cowsic rivers, attracts returning guests each year. Towels are provided at the front door for muddy paws and there's a residents' lounge where you can dine with the dog (the food is excellent). Other bonuses include the lawns at the front for late-night loo trips and a lovely hour-long there-and-back walk to gorgeous Wistman's Wood. *From £129/night B&B; dogs £15/night.*

OTHER PRACTICALITIES

Tourist information centre Tavistock Rd, Princetown PL20 6QF ⊘ dartmoor.gov.uk ⊙ 10.00–17.00 daily.

Pet supplies Ron's Pet Supplies (5 W Devon Business Park, Tavistock PL19 9DP ⊘ ronspets. co.uk ⊙ 09.00–17.00 Mon–Sat) has all the essentials, including collars, harnesses and a good range of natural chews and handmade treats.

Veterinary practices Moorgate Veterinary Group (Station Rd, Bovey Tracey TQ13 9AL ⊘ 01626 833023) has a few practices around the national park and an emergency line (⊘ 01647 440441).

↑ Swimming in the River Lyd. (Peter Turner Photography/S)

4 A CLASSIC SOUTH COAST SEASIDE BREAK PACKED WITH VICTORIAN CHARM

WHERE	Weymouth, Dorset
WHEN	May–Sep
HIGHLIGHTS	Good old-fashioned seaside fun with a sprinkling of military history and irresistible fish and chips.

Traditional seaside family fun abounds in Weymouth, a former Victorian resort on Dorset's Jurassic coast. Elegant townhouses line the seafront, but the main draw is the **beach** (♥ DT4 8DQ), a huge sweep of soft golden sand that is dog-friendly at its southern end and ideal for lazy summer days and messing about on the water with bodyboards or inflatables. At this end of the beach you'll find families fishing for crabs with buckets and string on the adjacent Esplanade, and **The Boat** (41 The Esplanade, DT4 8DH ✆ 01305 784274 ☉ 08.00–19.30 daily), a take-away café that serves ice cream and fish and chips.

Get your twopence coins out for a game in **Alexandra Gardens amusements** (The Esplanade, DT4 8DL ✆ alexandra-gardens.edan.io ☉ 10.00–21.30 daily ☂) at the beach's southern tip, or simply stroll around the attractive harbour a few

↑ Weymouth's harbour at sunset. (Pozdeyev Vitaly/S)

minutes' walk further south, nipping in and out of its lovely pubs for pints of local Badger ale – the **Ship Inn** (Custom House Quay, DT4 8BE ⊘ shipweymouth.co.uk ⊙ 11.00–23.00 daily) has the most character, and sells dog ice cream.

For anyone with an interest in history, Weymouth offers plenty beyond its Victorian waterfront. From the harbour, walk the 1km over Town Bridge and along Nothe Parade to **Nothe Fort** (Barrack Rd, DT4 8UF ⊘ nothefort.org.uk ⊙ 11.00–16.00 daily; adult/child £9.50/£4 ⛱). This historic sea fort not only offers excellent views over to Weymouth and beyond, but also has fascinating exhibits illustrating how it was used by the armed forces before being abandoned in the 1950s. From its ramparts you'll see the rocky Isle of Portland, around 5km away, and its man-made harbour, where **Adventure4All** (Portland Marina, DT5 1DX ⊘ adventure4all.co.uk ⊙ 09.00–18.00 daily; from £15) rents out kayaks and paddleboards – well-behaved dogs can sit on top.

Portland, on the **South West Coast Path** (⊘ southwestcoastpath.org.uk), is fantastic walking territory, so make time to drive across the causeway (around 20 minutes from Weymouth centre) to explore its wild, blustery cliffs; striking **Portland Bill Lighthouse** (Old Coastguard Cottages, DT5 2JT) is the highlight on the tip of the island, while remote **Church Ope Cove** (📍 DT5 1HT), on the eastern edge, is a delightful dog-friendly pebble beach.

LET'S GO

Weymouth, at the end of the A35 and A37, is easy to reach by car. Weymouth train station (Ranelagh Rd, DT4 7BN) has direct connections to London Waterloo, Bristol and Bournemouth.

For hearty Italian food with a view, try Art Deco **Al Molo** (Pier Bandstand, DT4 7RN ⊘ almolo. co.uk ⊙ 18.00–22.00 Wed–Mon, noon–14.30 Sat–Sun) on the beach, where the owners will fuss over the dog, and for the town centre's best seafood, book **Rockfish Weymouth** (48–49 The Esplanade, DT4 8DQ ⊘ therockfish.co.uk ⊙ 17.00–21.00 Mon, noon–21.00 Tue–Sat, noon–16.30 Sun) – one of the few fish and chips restaurants to allow dogs inside. Out towards Portland, don't miss the **Crab House Café** (Ferrymans Way, Portland Rd, DT4 9YU ⊘ crabhousecafe.co.uk ⊙ noon–14.30 & 18.00– 21.00 Wed–Sat, noon–15.00 Sun), where local oysters, crab and scallops are expertly prepared, and dogs are offered water on arrival.

Parents with young children will love **Moonfleet Manor** (Fleet Rd, DT3 4ED ⊘ moonfleetmanorhotel.co.uk 🐾 2; £140/night B&B, dogs from £15/night) which has a pool, indoor play area and dog-friendly lounge for dining. For a more subdued break, try Portland's **Cove Park** (Pennsylvania Rd, DT5 1HU ⊘ thepennestate.co.uk; £97/night), which has ten pet-friendly lodges and static caravans on the cliffs above Church Ope Cove.

For supplies, there's a **Pets at Home** (Jubliee Close Retail Park, Jubilee Cl, DT4 7BG ⊘ petsathome. com ⊙ 08.00–20.00 Mon–Fri, 09.00–19.00 Sat, 10.00–16.00 Sun); **Medivet** (South Walks Rd, Dorchester DT1 1DU ✆ 01305 262913), 13km north of Weymouth, offers 24-hour support.

5 AN ISLAND ADVENTURE FOR YOUNG & OLD

WHERE	Isle of Wight, Hampshire
WHEN	May–Oct
HIGHLIGHTS	Boat trips with brilliant views of towering chalky cliffs, and traditional seaside fun for all the family.

Queen Victoria's favourite holiday destination still has plenty of appeal. This sand-fringed island, 6½km off the south coast of mainland Britain, is home to kitsch seaside towns like Ventnor in the south and Ryde on the north coast, where amusement arcades back the beaches and fish and chips are obligatory. On the southeast coast, Shanklin makes a quaint seaside base, while neighbouring Sandown is another classic resort. The footpaths that criss-cross the island's green centre are ideal for long walks with the dog and, with its UNESCO Biosphere Reserve classification, you can almost guarantee you'll see some of Britain's most exciting wildlife, from red squirrels to water voles.

The Isle of Wight makes a fantastic family holiday destination, and its relatively small size means you're rarely more than a 40-minute drive from anywhere. In a single day, for example, you can visit Osborne House, the famous royal palace that Queen Victoria loved, before heading south to walk through the leafy gorge of Shanklin Chine (3 Chine Ave, Shanklin PO37 6BW ⌂ shanklinchine.co.uk ☺ 10.00–20.00 daily; adult/child £6.95/£5.30) or go fossil hunting on the year-round dog-friendly beach at Brook Bay (♀ PO30 4HA) on the west coast. On the way, stop in at the Isle of Wight Pearl (Military Rd, Brighstone PO30 4DD ⌂ iowpearl.co.uk ☺ 10.30–16.00 daily) to browse jewellery made with local pearls and indulge in cream tea at the on-site café.

↑ Alum Bay. (visitisleofwight.co.uk)

Most beaches are dog-friendly, and with 40km of coastline the island has plenty to choose from. And quite apart from outdoor pursuits there are enough attractions across the island to entertain everyone. The Isle of Wight Steam Railway will get the kids excited, as will Blackgang Chine amusement park (Ventnor PO38 2HN ⟋ blackgangchine.com ⊘ 10.00–17.00 daily; £26), while adults might prefer sedate strolls around the Osborne House estate and a piquant lunch at the popular Garlic Farm (**Mersley Ln, Newchurch PO36 0NR** ⟋ thegarlicfarm.co.uk ⊘ 09.00–17.30 daily). Don't let the dog miss a taste of the local Rex's Range ice cream for animals, which is sold across the island.

OSBORNE HOUSE (York Ave, East Cowes PO32 6JX ⟋ english-heritage. org.uk ⊘ 10.00–18.00 daily; adult/child £19/£11.40) Queen Victoria said it was 'impossible to imagine a prettier spot' and she was not wrong – her summer house, on the north coast near the yachting town of Cowes, is in a gorgeous setting. The Italianate building sits within 143ha of formal landscaped gardens and parkland overlooking the sea, ideal for sedate dog walks. You can explore the terraces for fine views, stroll among the seasonal flowerbeds that sing with different seasonal colours, or wander along the rhododendron walk down to the beach, but to see the ornate state rooms you'll need to leave the dog outside with a member of your party.

NEEDLES PLEASURE CRUISES (Cobblers, Bouldnor Rd, Yarmouth PO41 0UR ⟋ needlespleasurecruises.co.uk ⊘ daily from 10.30; adult/child £7/£4; see ad, page 235) Around 20km west of Osborne House, the iconic Needles, towering

↑ Osborne House. (Garry Basnett/S)

chalk stacks that jut out of the sea, are best seen from the water. On the 20-minute slow cruise around Alum Bay you'll get up close to these 30m-high natural towers and enjoy spectacular views back towards the island's bright white chalk cliffs. There's plenty of space in the open-deck boat for the dog lie down while you cruise.

CARISBROOKE CASTLE (Castle Hill, Newport PO30 1XY ⊘ english-heritage. org.uk ⊙ 10.00–16.00 daily; adult/child £11.30/£6.80) A 20-minute drive east of Yarmouth to bustling Newport, in the island's centre, brings you to this mighty fortress. Growing from a modest hill fort in the 11th century to a vast castle bristling with towers, turrets and keeps, its walls have seen a lot in its 1,000 years of existence. Explore with the dog, climbing the wall walk or visiting the Edwardian-style garden. Kids will love the small herd of donkeys that work on the treadwheel to bring water up from the castle well.

ISLE OF WIGHT STEAM RAILWAY (Main Rd, Havenstreet, Ryde PO33 4DS ⊘ iwsteamrailway.co.uk ⊙ 10.00–17.00 daily; adult/child £14.50/£7.25, dogs £3 ⛱) Running along a 15km track around 6km from Newport, this heritage railway is a great family activity and staff love to see your pets on board. The route begins in 1940s-style Havenstreet Station, in the middle of the line, where you'll find a railway museum, a woodland walk and a play area, and heads out to Smallbrook before chugging the full length of the track back towards Wootton and ending up in Havenstreet again. The trip takes around one hour and you'll travel in Edwardian- or Victorian-style carriages.

↑ Isle of Wight Steam Railway. (Liz Miller/S) → Shanklin. (Loz Baker/S)

LET'S GO

GETTING THERE

Car ferries and hovercraft run from Lymington, Southampton and Portsmouth to Yarmouth, Ryde, Fishbourne and Cowes on the north coast. Cross-Solent travel providers Hovertravel (⌂ hovertravel.co.uk), Wightlink (⌂ wightlink. co.uk) and Red Funnel (⌂ redfunnel.co.uk) offer free carriage for dogs; the latter two have designated pet lounges, too.

EATING

✕ **Chocolate Apothecary** 7 Esplanade, Ryde PO33 2DY ⌂ chocolateapothecary.co.uk ⌚ 10.00–17.00 Mon–Sat, 10.00–16.00 Sun. Head here for the mightiest hot chocolate you've ever tasted – they come in varying flavours and are made with real melted chocolate – and pick up a box of treats to take home.

✕ **The Lifeboat** Britannia Way, East Cowes PO32 6UB ⌂ thelifeboatcowes.co.uk ⌚ 10.00–23.00 Mon–Sat, 10.00–22.00 Sun. A smart riverside restaurant with dog treats on the bar and a menu packed with local produce in dishes from blue cheese salads to vegan burgers.

✕ **The Waterfront Inn** 19 Esplanade, Shanklin PO37 6BN ⌂ waterfront-inn.co.uk ⌚ 09.00–22.00 daily. Fry-ups, Sunday roasts and seafood platters with a sea view. There's a great kids' menu and the desserts are irresistible.

SLEEPING

⌂ **Luccombe Manor** 11 Popham Rd, Shanklin PO37 6RG ⌂ luccombemanor.co.uk 🐾 1. On the coast in charming Shanklin, sea views and an outdoor pool are the highlights here. It's very welcoming for dogs, who get a sausage at breakfast in the pet-friendly restaurant. Rylstone Gardens, opposite, is a good location for morning loo trips. *From £120/night B&B; dogs £10/night.*

⌂ **Scout Hall** Church Pl, Chale PO38 2HB ⌂ theshacks.co.uk. Stay in the old village scout hall in the lovely village of Chale, near Ventnor, for self-catering with a difference. There's an enclosed garden, a barbecue and quirky, artistic décor. *From £165/night; dogs from £30/stay.*

⌂ **Southland** Winford Rd, Newchurch, Sandown PO36 0LZ ⌂ experiencefreedom.co.uk. Between Newport and Shanklin, this beautifully landscaped Caravan and Motorhome Club site has a handful of dog-friendly safari tents which sleep up to five people in real beds. They have a small kitchen and barbecue outside, plus enclosed decking for alfresco meals. *From £60/night.*

OTHER PRACTICALITIES

Tourist information centre East Cowes Heritage Centre, 8 Clarence Rd, PO32 6EP ⌂ visitisleofwight. co.uk ⌚ 10.00–13.00 daily.

Pet supplies Jollyes (River Way Industrial Estate, Hurstake Rd, Newport PO30 5BP ⌂ jollyes.co.uk ⌚ 08.30–18.00 Mon–Sat, 10.00–16.00 Sun) has essentials and accessories.

Veterinary practices The Isle of Wight Emergency Vet (2 Bishops Way, Newport PO30 5WT ✆ 01983 550135) is your best bet for medical issues; for non-emergencies try the Mobile Vet (✆ 01983 212999).

6 A FAMILY HOLIDAY AT THE SEASIDE

WHERE	Hastings, East Sussex
WHEN	Year-round
HIGHLIGHTS	A vast pier, pebbly beach and arcades – the classic seaside holiday with a side of fishing industry charm.

Sitting on the East Sussex coast, Hastings is a town of two halves – the old and the new. From its central railway station, the new town spreads out south to a long shingle beach, a kitschy seafront and, to the west, a striking, RIBA-award-winning 280m-long **pier**. A dog-friendly section of beach stretches from the pier to Warrior Square Gardens in arty, on-the-up St Leonards, 500m to the east, while the seafront lures visitors with classic amusement arcades and family-friendly attractions. For horrible histories of the not-so distant past, head for the **True Crime Museum** (Palace Court, White Rock, TN34 1JP ⌂truecrimemuseum. co.uk ☉ 10.00–17.00 daily; adult/child £9.50/£7.50 🐾). With hands-on games and gruesome exhibitions, it promises a gory, entertaining afternoon – even dogs can get their mugshots taken.

Less than 1km east, you can take one of the town's two 19th-century funicular railways, the **West Hill Lift** (43 George St, TN34 3EA ✆ 01424 451111 ☉ 10.00–

↑ Hastings beach. (Andrew Fletcher/S)

17.30 daily; adult/child return £4/£2.50), up to the clifftops backing the seafront, or play a round at the seaside **Hastings Adventure Golf complex** (Pelham Pl, TN34 3AJ ⌂ hastingsadventuregolf.com ⊙ 08.30–22.00 daily; adult/child £7.75/£3.85).

East again lies Hastings' old town, a time capsule of 1,000 years of fishing history, its cluster of narrow streets dotted with quirky shops and restaurants. On the beach, working boats sit crooked on the shingle and tall, black fishermen's huts make a distinctive sight. Kids (and small/medium dogs) will love a short but sweet ride on the **Hastings Miniature Railway** (Rock-a-Nore Rd, TN34 3DW ✆ 01424 451111 ⊙ 10.30–18.30 Mon–Fri, 10.30–19.30 Sat–Sun; £2.50 return). Snack on fresh fish sandwiches from one of the huts, or take the **East Hill Lift** (Rock-a-Nore Rd, TN34 3DW ⊙ 10.00–17.30 daily; adult/child return £4/£2.50) for views over the old town's jumble of houses and a walk on the gentle green slopes of **Hastings Country Park**.

Hastings is also a brilliant base for exploring inland East Sussex. A 20-minute drive northwest, or a 30-minute train journey (alight at Battle), takes you to the **1066 Battlefields and Abbey** (High St, Battle TN33 0AE ⌂ english-heritage. org.uk ⊙ 10.00–17.00 daily; adult/child £13.90/£8.40), where King Harold and William the Conqueror fought for England's future. Alternatively, sample some Sussex wine and tour the vines at **Sedlescombe Organic Vineyard** (♀ TN32 5SA ⌂ sedlescombeorganic.com ⊙ 10.00–17.00 daily), a 20-minute drive north of Hastings, or **Carr Taylor Wines** (♀ TN35 4SG ⌂ carr-taylor.co.uk ⊙ 10.00–17.00 daily), a 15-minute journey from town.

LET'S GO

Hastings is well connected by road and its railway station (Havelock Rd, TN34 1BA) has direct trains from London Bridge, Brighton and Ashford International. Its main access roads are the A259 to the east and west, and A21 from the north.

Take-away fish sandwiches and seafood chowder rarely come fresher than from **Maggie's at the Boat** (17 Rock-a-Nore Rd, TN34 3DW ⌂ maggiesfishandchips.co.uk ⊙ 12.00–16.00 Fri–Sun), but for indoor dining, try **The Crown** (All Saints' St, TN34 3BN ⌂ thecrownhastings. co.uk ⊙ 11.00–23.00 Mon–Sat, 11.00–22.30 Sun) – a gastropub with a good selection of local beers and English wine. **Ruby's Rooms** (54 Eversfield Pl, TN37 6DB ⌂ rubysrooms.com; from £105/night) is a beautifully furnished B&B right on the seafront opposite the dog-friendly section of the beach. For self-catering, try **The Lookout** (St Leonards on Sea ⌂ caninecottages. co.uk 🐾 1; from £500/week) – a modern two-bed property with sea views and an enclosed patio.

Pet Express (28–29 Queens Rd, TN34 1QY ✆ 01424 430021 ⊙ 09.00–17.30 Mon–Sat, 11.00–15.00 Sun) has a good selection of food and accessories. For medical queries **Sussex Coast Vets** (103–105 London Rd, TN37 6AT ✆ 01424 424870) is convenient; their out-of-hours service is in Bexhill (✆ 01424 224818), a 15-minute drive west of Hastings.

7 RETAIL THERAPY MEETS NAVAL HISTORY

WHERE   Portsmouth, Hampshire
WHEN   Year-round
HIGHLIGHTS   Harbour cruises, dog-friendly shops and blustery coastal walks.

An island city and an important naval base, Portsmouth is famous for its **Historic Dockyard**, which draws thousands of visitors to its shores each year. Dogs, unfortunately, aren't allowed to step foot within the dockyard itself, which is home to gargantuan modern warships, huge submarines and the remains of Henry VIII's wooden warship, the *Mary Rose*. But don't be disheartened: you can see many of the impressive vessels from the water on a cruise with **Portsmouth Boat Trips** (♥ PO1 3TZ ✐ 01983 564602 ⌀ portsmouth-boat-trips.co.uk ☉ daily sailings vary, call ahead; adult/child £10/£6 ☂). Hop aboard at Gunwharf Quays (see opposite), 1km west of the town centre, and you'll sail right by the dockyard, getting arguably better views of the moored ships than from within the site itself

↑ View towards Portsmouth. (Ricky Howitt/S)

– you might even catch a glimpse of British Navy sailors going about their day on board a military craft. An excellent commentary offers insight into modern navy life and the history of the area, and as you return to Gunwharf Quays you can enjoy spectacular views of the 170m-tall, spire-like Spinnaker Tower.

For shoppers, **Gunwharf Quays** (♀ PO1 3TZ ⏣ gunwharf-quays.com ☉ 10.00–20.00 Mon–Fri, 09.00–20.00 Sat, 10.00–18.00 Sun) is the highlight, with more than 90 of its stores welcoming dogs and many restaurants offering outdoor seating for alfresco lunches. From here, you can take a pleasant 5km walk along the seafront, across Southsea Common and all the way down to **Southsea Beach**, where dogs can run off-lead year-round on the stretch outside the Royal Marines Museum (Eastney Esplanade, PO4 9PX 🐾).

Exclusions on the rest of the beach are in place from March through September, but you can still enjoy the sea views from **Southsea Beach Cafe** (Eastney Esplanade, PO4 0SP ⏣ southseabeachcafe.co.uk ☉ 09.00–18.00 Mon–Fri, 08.00–18.00 Sat–Sun) which serves hearty breakfasts and moreish fish and chips. A few minutes' walk east along Eastney Esplanade, **Southsea Model Village** (Lumps Fort, PO4 9RU ⏣ southseamodelvillage.biz ☉ 10.30–16.30 daily; adult/child £5/£4) will entertain young families.

Beyond Portsmouth itself lies a fantastic coastline worth exploring on foot: drive 30 minutes east to the beautiful walking territory of **Chichester Harbour AONB** and **West Wittering beach** (♀ PO20 8AJ), which has a year-round dog-friendly area to the west of groyne 18. A 20-minute drive inland up the A3 lies the vast **Queen Elizabeth Country Park** (S Downs Way, PO8 0QE 🐾), where you can hike through kilometres of forest or play fetch in the open fields.

LET'S GO

Portsmouth, served by the M27 and A27, which connects to the A3(M), is easy to reach from the north, east or west by car. Portsmouth Harbour station (The Hard Interchange, PO1 3EB), next to Gunwharf Quays, has direct connections with London Waterloo, Cardiff and Bristol.

For dinner with a view, head to **The Still & West** (Bath Sq, PO1 2JL ⏣ stillandwest.co.uk ☉ noon–23.00 Mon–Sat, noon–22.30 Sun) on Portsmouth Point; **The Dolphin** (41 High St, PO1 2LU ⏣ greatukpubs.co.uk ☉ noon–23.00 Sun–Thu, noon–midnight Fri–Sat) claims to be the oldest pub in town and serves American-style fast food.

Portsmouth's top dog-friendly hotel is Georgian townhouse **Becketts of Southsea** (11 Bellevue Tce, PO5 3AT ⏣ beckettssouthsea.co.uk; from £155/night, dogs from £25/stay), whose restaurant serves seriously good Saturday brunches and legendary Sunday roasts with great veg options.

For pet supplies, head to **Jollyes** (Portsmouth Retail Park, PO6 4FB ⏣ jollyes.co.uk ☉ 09.00–18.00 Mon–Sat, 10.00–16.00 Sun), while **Harbour Veterinary Group** (17 Villiers Rd, PO3 5HG ✆ 023 9282 7014) can provide medical help.

8 A FAMILY FORAY IN THE FOREST

WHERE	New Forest National Park, Hampshire/Wiltshire
WHEN	Mar–Oct
HIGHLIGHTS	Walks where wild-spirited ponies roam and regal estates with family-friendly fun.

Straddling the border between Hampshire and Wiltshire, the New Forest is Britain's second-smallest national park and one of its youngest – it only officially received the accolade in 2005 – but it's also one of the most diverse destinations for a holiday in the UK. Despite its relatively small size – it covers just 580km² – it has an astonishing array of things to see and do, and a surprisingly varied landscape. While there is indeed plenty of woodland here, with oak, ash and beech making up most of its treescape, it also features pasture, moorland and shingle beaches.

That means long woodland walks in the dappled shade of ancient oaks are just a short drive away from lazy days on the beach or coastal castle explorations. If glorious gardens take your fancy, head to Exbury; if you're more of a history fan, Lyndhurst's New Forest Heritage Centre will offer brilliant insights. Of course, there are also those famous free-roaming New Forest ponies, not quite wild but still notoriously tenacious if you've got snacks. They can be seen all over the park, but you can almost guarantee a herd will be grazing on the pasture at Beachern Wood (📍 SO42 7QD) near Brockenhurst; keep dogs on leads.

The park's size also means that you can base yourself almost anywhere and be within reach of the main attractions. The 'capital' of the New Forest is Lyndhurst, in the centre of the park on the A337, which dissects the region from north to south. Here you'll find cosy cafés and cute shops, including the rabbit warren that is Lyndhurst Antiques Centre (19–21 High St, SO43 7BB 🖱 lyndhurstantiques.co.uk ⊙ 10.00–17.00

↑ Bolderwood Arboretum. (Helen Hotson/S)

daily) where you can browse with the dog. A short drive to the south is Brockenhurst, a lovely village with plenty of pub appeal and excellent walking on its doorstep. Beaulieu makes a great base if you're keen to get on the river or explore the village's Victorian estate, while on the south coast, places like Milford on Sea and Lymington offer access to the South West Coast Path (southwestcoastpath.org.uk).

NEW FOREST HERITAGE CENTRE (Main Car Park, Lyndhurst SO43 7NY newforestheritage.org.uk 10.00–16.00 daily) This visitor information centre in Lyndhurst, in the centre of the national park, boasts a small but excellent museum. Exhibits chart the region's history, explore its ecology and explain how the New Forest ponies came to be here. There are displays about the wartime era in this rural region, plenty of hands-on activities for kids, and a dog-friendly café on site.

THE BEAULIEU ESTATE (Beaulieu SO42 7ZN beaulieu.co.uk 10.00–17.00 daily; adult/child £23/£12) More like a theme park than a country estate, Beaulieu – a 15-minute drive southeast of Lyndhurst – started out as an impressive Victorian home surrounded by beautiful gardens and grounds. Those gardens are still a lovely place to stroll with the dog – the Millpond Walk by the tidal river is most picturesque – and you can explore the Victorian kitchen gardens and flower beds with your pet on a lead, not to mention enjoy glorious views of the gothic Palace House. While dogs can't enter the indoor areas – including the National Motor Museum, World of Top Gear, and a museum about the estate's role as a school for undercover agents during World War II – there is a designated space for tying them up if you're happy to do so; alternatively, take it in turns to head inside.

NEW FOREST ACTIVITIES (Beaulieu SO42 7WA ⊘ newforestactivities.co.uk ⊙ daily; adult/child £34/£25 for two hours) See the New Forest from an alternative perspective on a guided canoeing trip along the Beaulieu River. You can bring the dog in canoes for up to four people, and your guide will offer commentary on the local flora and fauna, as well as the history of the area.

EXBURY GARDENS & STEAM RAILWAY (Exbury SO45 1AZ ⊘ exbury. co.uk ⊙ 10.00–17.30 daily; adult/child £13/£4.50) With over 35km of footpaths to pound, Exbury is a superb spot for a dog walk. Just 10 minutes southeast of Beaulieu and set on the banks of the Beaulieu River, this vast garden has a brilliant collection of tropical plants, colourful rhododendrons and elegant wisteria, depending on the time of year. There's also a fun little steam train that trundles along a narrow-gauge railway through woodland, around a small pond, over a bridge and through a tunnel – a great activity for kids (and dogs) with weary feet.

HURST CASTLE (♀ SO41 0TP ⊘ hurstcastle.co.uk ⊙ 10.00–17.30 daily; adult/ child £4/£2 🗼) Perched on the end of a coastal spit near the village of Milford on

LET'S GO

GETTING THERE

Sitting at the end of the M3 and M27 and criss-crossed by A-roads, the New Forest is simple to reach by car. Brockenhurst train station (Station Approach, SO42 7TW) is most convenient and has direct connections with London Waterloo, Weymouth, Poole and Bournemouth.

EATING

🗡 **The Forage** 39 High St, Lyndhurst SO43 7BE ⊘ the-forage.co.uk ⊙ 08.30–22.00 daily. A café by day, with big cooked breakfasts, brilliant eggy brunches, afternoon teas and excellent coffee, this place becomes a lovely restaurant after 5pm. Expect pizzas, pasta and a few fish and meat mains, plus tempting cakes for dessert.

🗡 **The Foresters Arms** 10 Brookley Rd, Brockenhurst SO42 7RR ⊘ forestersarms-brockenhurst.co.uk ⊙ 11.00–22.00 daily. People rave about the pies at this lovely village pub, but they also offer local mussels, lamb shank and barbecued ribs, plus a great veggie and vegan selection.

🗡 **The Lighthouse** Hurst Rd, Milford on Sea SO41 0PY ⊘ thelighthousemilford.co.uk ⊙ 09.00–22.00 daily. Local fish is the highlight here; try the dressed crab and haddock with chips. There's a good cocktail selection and brilliant views over the beach.

SLEEPING

🏠 **Balmer Lawn** Lyndhurst Rd, Brockenhurst SO42 7ZB ⊘ balmerlawnhotel.com 🐾 2. On the

Sea, around a 20-minute drive southwest of Beaulieu, this fortress was established by Henry VIII and added to extensively during the 19th and 20th centuries. It was key in defending the area during the Napoleonic Wars and World War II, and today you can visit for spectacular ocean views and an insight into Victorian defence systems. You can't drive out to the castle, so park in Milford on Sea and walk the 3km along the spit, or take the ferry from nearby Keyhaven.

edge of Brockenhurst, Balmer Lawn makes a good base, with an outdoor pool, plenty of nearby walks and a great dog-friendly restaurant. *From £135/ night B&B; dogs from £20/night.*

🏠 **Green Hill Holiday Park** New Rd, Landford SP5 2AZ ⌖ lovatparks.com 🐾 2. Dog-friendly accommodation in stylish lodges (sleeping six) and cool safari tents (sleeping four) on the northern edge of the forest, around 20 minutes north of Lyndhurst. You could spend an entire weekend just here, as you can hire normal and electric bikes (with dog buggies), go axe throwing in the woods (dogs on leads), or simply head out on to the nearby common for long walks amid ancient trees. There's a dog-friendly café, too. *From £185/night.*

🏠 **The Montagu Arms** Palace Ln, Beaulieu SO42 7ZL ⌖ montaguarmshotel.co.uk. A luxurious hotel with stylish rooms and a cosy pub for drinks and dinner. The handsome grounds were inspired by horticulturalist Gertrude Jekyll and the Hay Loft Suites come with a complimentary decanter of seasonal gin. Excellent dog-focused packages include a doggy hamper with treats and toys. *From £421/night.*

OTHER PRACTICALITIES

Tourist information centre New Forest Heritage Centre (see page 37).

Pet supplies Karen's Pet Market (9 St Thomas St, Lymington SO41 9NA ✆ 01590 676886 ⏱ 09.00– 17.00 Mon–Sat) sells natural dog treats, food and accessories.

Veterinary practices Midforest Veterinary Practice (Beechen Ln, Lyndhurst SO43 7DD ✆ 023 8028 2358) is the New Forest's most central surgery and has an emergency line.

↑ Hurst Castle. (Ian Woolcock/S)

9 COUNTRY PURSUITS IN THE SOUTH DOWNS

WHERE	Midhurst, West Sussex
WHEN	Mar–Oct
HIGHLIGHTS	Fantastic walking, with welcome pit stops at vineyards, ruins and a couple of brilliant museums.

Hiking is the name of the game in the South Downs National Park, which, sprawling between Winchester in Hampshire and Eastbourne in East Sussex on the south coast, encompasses chalk downland, wooded ridges and ecologically rich heathland that rolls right down to the sea. You could explore this varied landscape on the 161km South Downs Way, the only long-distance trail in the UK that runs entirely through a national park: whether you want easy hill walking, a meander through nature reserves or a riverside stroll, the South Downs offers it all. In fair weather, its bright green pastures and patchwork of crop fields makes an idyllic setting for walking with the dog, while a handful of peaceful market towns and quintessentially English villages offer alternative activities year-round for those who prefer not to spend all day tramping the trails.

Right at the park's heart is the market town of Midhurst, where centuries-old timber-framed buildings creak side-by-side on Church Hill. The town has played host to important monarchs and military men, including Oliver Cromwell and Queen Elizabeth I – today, you can sleep in the very same coaching inn they stopped at all those centuries ago. From here, walk to the impressive ruins of a Tudor home at nearby Cowdray, or travel back in time at the Weald and Downland Living Museum around 9km to the south.

You've also got easy access from Midhurst to other pretty towns and villages, including Amberley, Cocking and Petworth. The last is home to a huge National Trust-run estate where you can roam with the dog off-lead, and its town centre has a smattering of lovely antique shops to rummage in for unusual sculptures, old drawings and quirky furniture – Petworth Antiques Market (East St, GU28 0AB 🖉 petworthantiquesmarket.com ⊙ 10.00–17.00 Mon–Sat, 11.00–16.00 Sun) is a dog-friendly favourite. Just 12km to the south, another great Sussex estate, Goodwood (📍 PO18 0PX 🖉 goodwood.com) – owned by the 11th Duke of Richmond – offers good walking among elegant lawns, pristine cricket pitches and regal Lebanese cedar woodland.

Midhurst is an ideal base from which to explore the viticulture that's been quietly burgeoning in West Sussex since the 1970s and 80s. Within half an hour's drive of town, Nyetimber (Gay St, West Chiltlington RH20 2HH 🖉 nyetimber.com; ⊙ tours summer 11.00 Fri–Sat; £35) and Blackdown Ridge (Lurgashall GU27 3BT 🖉 blackdownridge.co.uk ⊙ tours summer 11.00 Fri–Sat; £15) produce award-winning sparkling wines and offer occasional tours and tastings, while smaller producers like the Tinwood Estate (Halnaker, Chichester PO18 0NE 🖉 tinwoodestate.com; ⊙ tours noon & 15.00 Sat, 15.00 Sun–Fri; from £18) welcome visitors year-round for tours or afternoon teas. Sip a Blanc de Blanc as the sun goes down over the vines and you could find yourself transported to the Continent.

Nature steals the show within this national park and one of the highlights is Iping and Stedham Commons (📍 GU29 0PB 🖉 sussexwildlifetrust.org.uk 🏃), just a 5-minute drive from Midhurst. Heather and gorse were once farmed here, and its grassy pasture used by the people for grazing cattle. Today Scots pines and beech forest are invading in an attempt to reclaim the land and a substantial rhododendron forest has sprung up, which is spectacular when in flower. Views of the Downs to the south are spectacular and, despite being so close to town, it can feel a world away from civilisation as you stare out on to a landscape with little sign of human activity.

COWDRAY ESTATE (♥ GU29 0AJ ♂ cowdray.co.uk 🐎) A 15-minute walk from the centre of Midhurst, the Cowdray Estate is an expansive landscape encompassing working farmland, managed woodland with roaming deer, and sporting fields where polo tournaments take place. You could stroll for hours along its trails and footpaths (maps are available in the farm shop) and, providing there's no deer in sight, the dog can race around the fields off the lead. Most enticingly, though, the estate is home to an imposing, fire-ravaged ruined Tudor home that can be found less than half a kilometre's walk along the River Rother from Midhurst. Spend a morning wandering around the ruins and the estate, then finish up with a coffee and cake or locally sourced lunch outside the lovely Farm Shop Café (🕐 08.00–17.00 Mon–Sat, 09.00–17.00 Sun).

WEALD & DOWNLAND LIVING MUSEUM (Town Lane, Singleton PO18 0EU ♂ wealddown.co.uk 🕐 10.00–16.00 daily; adult/child £14/£6.50 ☂) Just a 10-minute drive south of Midhurst, this excellent open-air museum, set across 16ha, is a compelling place to learn about rural life in the region. Among its many historic structures, you might recognise the thatched barn from the BBC series *The Repair Shop* and kids will love playing traditional games in the Hambrook Barn. Expect to see Tudor cooking demonstrations, meet traditional working farm animals and stroll on the many walking trails. Dogs are allowed in almost all the buildings except the watermill, Winkhurst Tudor Kitchen and Newdigate bakehouse. The on-site café is also dog friendly.

PETWORTH HOUSE & PARK (♥ GU28 9LR ♂ nationaltrust.org.uk 🐎) Around 15 minutes east of Midhurst, Petworth House is one of those grand estates that never fails to make you feel a little bit fancy as you walk past its regal façade, all sash windows and Portland stone. Set within a handsomely landscaped 285ha estate, with a deer park and Capability Brown-designed pleasure garden that inspired a number of Turner paintings, it's a prime location for a long walk with the dog. Unusually for a National Trust property, dogs are allowed off lead – but do keep them under close control, especially around the deer.

AMBERLEY MUSEUM (New Barn Rd, BN18 9LT ♂ amberleymuseum.co.uk 🕐 10.00–16.30 Wed–Sun; adult/child £14/£6.50) A fantastic family day out, this part indoor, part outdoor museum in Amberley (around 30 minutes' drive southeast of Midhurst) is packed with artefacts and scenes from recent history.

↑ Cowdray Estate. (Greg Salmon/S) → Weald & Downland Living Museum. (Chon Kit Leong/DT)

↑ Sunrise over Iping Common. (Julian Gazzard/S)

See old motorcars and buses, a handful of vintage red telephone boxes and an impressive mock-up of an old radio station. The ancient craft village hosts live demonstrations of blacksmithing, woodworking and pottery. Dogs are allowed in all the exhibition buildings and on the lovely nature trails around the site.

PIED-A-TERRE ADVENTURES (⊘ patadventures.com; from £65) Delve deeper into the landscape of the South Downs on a hike with Pied-a-Terre Adventures, whose highly knowledgeable and mountain-trained guides can offer unparalleled insight into the geological and botanical aspects of the area. Dogs can join you on their 'Hills, Heath, Hops & Hampers' group walk, which explores the highest region in the South Downs, Black Down, and includes a locally sourced picnic with fine Sussex cheeses. Alternatively, you can book a private guided hike (from £250 per day; multi-day hikes with dog-friendly accommodation also an option).

↑ Fallow deer in Petworth Park. (Brian Clifford/S)

LET'S GO

GETTING THERE

Midhurst sits conveniently on the A272, just 16km from the A3 at Petersfield. Rail connections aren't hugely convenient, but the closest train station, Petersfield (Station Rd, GU32 3EE), has connections with London Waterloo and Portsmouth. The 92 bus runs from Petersfield train station to Midhurst around once per hour; it takes around 30 minutes.

EATING

⚔ The Angel Inn Angel St, Petworth GU28 0BG ⟨⟩ angelinnpetworth.co.uk ⊙ 08.00–23.00 daily. Mammoth burgers, excellent fry-ups and roast dinners with head-sized Yorkshire puddings – this excellent pub doesn't do things by halves. Expect local ales on draught and a good gin selection.

⚔ Fitzcane's North St, Midhurst GU29 9DJ ⟨⟩ fitzcanes.com ⊙ 08.30–17.00 Mon–Fri, 09.00–17.00 Sat–Sun. Great breakfasts, sandwiches, soups and coffees, plus tempting waffles and cakes. The garden is a suntrap when the weather's right.

⚔ The Hollist Arms Lodsworth GU28 9BZ ⟨⟩ thehollistarms.com ⊙ noon–22.30 Wed–Sun; kitchen noon–14.30 & 18.00–21.00. You can walk to this excellent country pub, just 5km northeast of Midhurst, across the Cowdray Estate. Game meats and indulgent desserts are the highlights.

SLEEPING

⌂ Benbow Holiday Cottages Cowdray Park GU28 9BX ⟨⟩ cowdray.co.uk 🐾 **2**. By far the best location in the area for a self-catering break, these three cottages on the Cowdray Estate are luxurious and perfectly placed for long walks with the dog. A welcome pack of Cowdray goodies awaits you on arrival. *From £120/night.*

⌂ Goodwood Hotel Chichester PO18 0QX ⟨⟩ goodwood.com. A modern country hotel that makes a great standalone weekend break. The Farmer, Butcher, Chef restaurant serves exceptionally good dinners sourced from within a 40km radius, you can play a round of golf or have lessons with the dog by your side, and walks on the estate are stunning. Dog beds, bowls and treats are included in the room; mini fridges are available on request for food storage. *From £120/ night B&B; dogs £30/stay.*

⌂ The Spread Eagle South St, Midhurst GU29 9NH ⟨⟩ hshotels.co.uk 🐾 **2**. The area's most enchanting hotel, this historic property is one of the oldest coaching inns in England. All creaky floors and blackened wood beams, plus bedrooms with antique furniture and the only 15th-century wig closet still in existence, it's an atmospheric place to stop overnight – eminent guests have included Elizabeth I, Oliver Cromwell and Charles I. The bar and conservatory are dog-friendly for mealtimes and their Muddy Paws package (from £329) includes a welcome kit for the dogs, a drying coat to take home, and dinner, bed and breakfast. *From £149/night B&B; dogs £20/night.*

OTHER PRACTICALITIES

Tourist information centre North St, Midhurst GU29 9DH ⟨⟩ southdowns.gov.uk ⊙ 09.00–14.00 Mon–Fri, 09.00–14.30 Sat.

Pet supplies Farringdons Pet Care Centre (16c Chapel St, Petersfield GU32 3DS ⟨⟩ 01730 710091 ⊙ 09.00–17.00 Mon–Sat) has food, treats and accessories.

Veterinary practices Springfield Vet Surgery (Lamberts Lane, Midhurst GU29 9EA ⟨⟩ 01730 816833) is a reliable practice with an out-of-hours and emergency service.

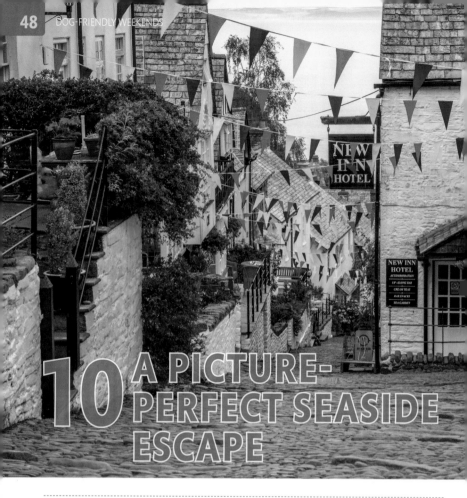

10 A PICTURE-PERFECT SEASIDE ESCAPE

WHERE	Clovelly, Devon
WHEN	May–Sep
HIGHLIGHTS	A dramatic Devon landscape of fishing heritage, literary links and spectacular coastal walks.

Huddled inside a deep ravine that cuts through 120m-high cliffs and winds down to the sea, Clovelly is a unique, privately owned little village on the north Devon coast. The estate, which comprises woodland and around 800ha of farmland beyond the village itself, was originally owned by William the Conqueror and has changed hands just a few times since. Today, it belongs to descendants of the Hamlyns family, who have kept it since the 18th century.

The village, all cobbled streets, stone houses and timber-framed buildings, is only accessible on foot and has just one way in and out. This means visiting comes at a cost – Clovelly charges an entrance fee (adult/child £8.25/£4.80), which is put towards the upkeep of the estate. You get decent bang for your buck, though, with

↑ Clovelly. (chrisdorney/S)

entrance to a handful of museums and – of course – those priceless sea views. For dogs, it's almost easier to explain where they can't go rather than where they can, as Clovelly welcomes pets with open arms in almost all its museums and venues.

Park at the **visitor centre** (♀ EX39 5TA ⊘ clovelly.co.uk ⊙ 09.00–17.00 daily) and take the 300m winding path through the forest to get to the steep High Street, where the sea views will tempt you downhill along the same narrow road where the famous Clovelly donkeys once hauled the fishermen's fresh herring catch. After a couple of minutes walking, around halfway down, you'll find the **Fisherman's Cottage** (⊙ 09.00–17.00 daily) – an interesting small museum showing how the village's most important residents used to live – and the **Kingsley Museum** (⊙ 09.00–17.00 daily), dedicated to Victorian writer Charles Kingsley who visited the area regularly. Pop in to hear a recorded recital of his most famous poem, *The Three Fishers*.

At the bottom of the hill lies the historic **Clovelly Quay** and the **beach** (no restrictions for dogs). For a good walk, head back up towards the visitor centre and hit the **South West Coast Path** (⊘ southwestcoastpath.org.uk) near the donkey stables – there's a great 8km circular route from here that takes in Mouthmill Beach and nearby Brownsham Woods.

Families can check out the **Milky Way Adventure Park** (Bideford EX39 5RY ⊘ themilkyway.co.uk ⊙ 10.30–16.30 daily; adults/under 3s £14.95/£7.95) around a 10-minute drive inland. A 20-minute drive west takes you to the elegant 18th-century **Hartland Abbey** (Hartland EX39 6DT ⊘ hartlandabbey.com ⊙ 11.00–17.00 Sun–Thu), a lovely spot for a walk through woodland and gardens; the tea room (14.00–16.00) has outdoor seating for dog owners.

LET'S GO

Clovelly lies off the A39 on the north Devon coast. The nearest railway station is Barnstaple (Sticklepath EX31 2BD) which has direct trains from Exeter Central, and is connected to the visitor centre by the 319 Stagecoach South West bus, which leaves a few times daily and takes around an hour (⊘ stagecoachbus.com).

The village has two pubs with rooms: **The New Inn** (93 High St, EX39 5TQ ⊘ thenewinnclovelly.co.uk; £80/night, dogs £10/night) is a great little B&B with a breakfast room that turns into a fish-and-chip lounge later in the day, while **The Red Lion** (48 The Quay, EX39 5TF ⊘ redlion-clovelly.co.uk; from £125/night, dogs £10/night) is an 18th-century inn in a prime location overlooking the quay. Three of its 17 rooms are dog-friendly; all have spectacular sea views. The staff adore dogs, so prepare for a fuss, and don't miss dining on the freshest fish and seafood, from local lobster to crab, herring and seabass, in the bar (noon–16.00 & 17.00–20.00 daily).

Supplies are available at **Pets at Home** in Barnstaple (Barnstaple Retail Park, EX31 2AU ⊘ petsathome.com ⊙ 09.00–20.00 Mon–Fri, 09.00–19.00 Sat, 10.00–16.00 Sun) and **Vets4Pets** (⊘ 01271 335520) are located on the same site.

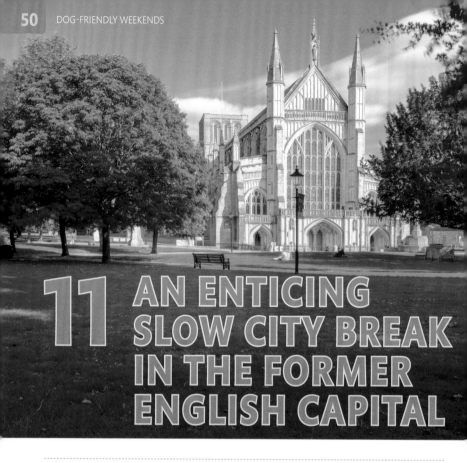

11 AN ENTICING SLOW CITY BREAK IN THE FORMER ENGLISH CAPITAL

WHERE	Winchester, Hampshire
WHEN	Year-round
HIGHLIGHTS	Enchanting architecture so pretty it inspired Keats, plus heritage railway adventures and charming old pubs.

It's all about the architecture in Winchester. This exceptionally attractive city, formerly the capital of England, has some of the finest Elizabethan and Regency buildings around and, with a dramatic Gothic cathedral at its heart, it's a truly captivating place. So captivating, in fact, that poet John Keats penned his ode *To Autumn* after a stay here in 1819. Follow in his footsteps on the **Keats' Walk** (maps from the Tourist Information Centre, Guildhall, High St, SO23 9GH ⊘ visitwinchester.co.uk ☉ 10.00–16.00 Mon–Fri, 09.00–17.00 Sat, 10.00–15.00 Sun), a 3km route that the poet is said to have walked daily. It starts at King Alfred's statue on The Broadway, heads east past the cathedral and Deanery, then takes in Cheyney Court with its 15th-century timber-framed buildings. You'll pass Kingsgate – one of only two surviving medieval gates in the city – and the house where Jane Austen finished her last novel, *Persuasion*.

↑ Winchester Cathedral. (Julian Gazzard/S)

The trail passes through **Wolvesey Castle** (College St, SO23 9NB ⊘ english-heritage.org.uk ☉ 10.00–16.00 daily), where you can walk among the ruins of a 12th-century palace that was once home to the Bishops of Winchester; download the audio tour from the English Heritage website to learn more. You then proceed south through Winchester's beautiful water meadows, with the option to climb the 67m-high St Catherine's Hill before finishing at the medieval **Hospital of St Cross** (St Cross Back St, SO23 9SD), England's oldest charitable institution, which you can admire from the outside. Stop for lunch or a drink at the nearby **Bell Inn** (83 St Cross Rd, SO23 9RE ⊘ thebellstcross.co.uk ☉ 11.00–15.00 Mon, noon–21.00 Tues–Sat, 11.00–20.00 Sun) before walking back into town along St Cross Road.

Time could easily be passed pleasantly by popping in and out of Winchester's dog-friendly pubs and cafés, but there are out-of-town day trips to enjoy, too. For a scenic steam train journey, take a 90-minute return trip on the **Watercress Line** (Railway Station, Alresford SO24 9JG ⊘ watercressline.co.uk ☉ Feb–Oct daily; adult/child £18/£9 🎫) from the picturesque Georgian town of Alresford, just 12km away. Following an old railway track once used to transport the region's most important crop – you guessed it, watercress – the train offers bucolic Hampshire views and stops at the market town of Alton for 40 minutes where you can take a stroll around King's Pond (♥ GU34 2PQ) before hopping back on for the return.

An easy 25-minute drive southeast of Winchester takes you to the ruined **Bishop's Waltham Palace** (3 Station Rd, Bishop's Waltham SO32 1DH ⊘ english-heritage.org.uk ☉ 10.00–16.00 daily, museum noon–16.00 Sat–Sun), one of the grandest bishop's palaces in Britain. See it in its prime at the small but insightful museum.

LET'S GO

Winchester Railway Station (Station Rd, SO23 8TJ) has excellent connections with London Waterloo, Portsmouth Harbour, Poole and Bournemouth. The city sits just off the M3 and at the end of the A34, making it simple to reach by road.

For excellent food and drink, dine in the bar at **The Old Vine** (8 Great Minster St, SO23 9HA ⊘ oldvinewinchester.com ☉ 11.00–23.00 daily) or head to upmarket wine bar and bistro **Greens** (4 Jewry St, SO23 8RZ ⊘ greensbarandkitchen.co.uk ☉ 08.30–22.30 daily).

The central **Wykeham Arms** (75 Kingsgate St, SO23 9PE ⊘ wykehamarmswinchester.co.uk 🐾 2; from £160/night B&B, dogs £15/night) has two rustic rooms for dog owners. A 15-minute drive northwest of town is **Lainston House** (Woodman Ln, Sparsholt SO21 2LT ⊘ exclusive.co.uk 🐾 2; from £265/night B&B, dogs £40/stay), a stunning 17th-century estate with regal rooms, an afternoon tea terrace and an extensive estate for long walks.

Pet supplies are sold at **Pet Pantry** (65b High St, SO23 9DA ⊘ petpantrywinchester.co.uk ☉ 09.30–17.00 Mon–Sat, 10.00–16.00 Sun), while **Stable Close Vets** (St Cross Rd, SO23 9PR ✆ 01962 410041) will help in medical emergencies.

12 A MEDIEVAL CITY BREAK WITH A CRACKING CATHEDRAL

WHERE	Salisbury, Wiltshire
WHEN	Year-round
HIGHLIGHTS	Streets packed with historic buildings, ancient hill forts to climb – oh, and that world-famous cathedral.

Salisbury is a city that doesn't feel much like a city at all. Its medieval centre is so small you can walk around it in just 15 minutes and, aside from the splendid Gothic cathedral that dominates the skyline to the south, there's little sign that it's more than just a lovely market town.

The best way to begin any trip is a walking tour with one of the brilliant Blue Badge guides at **Salisbury City Guides** (Fish Row, SP1 1EJ ⌂ salisburycityguides. co.uk ⊙ 11.00 daily; adult/child £10/£5). You will explore the oak courtroom in the **Guildhall** (Market Pl, SP1 1JH), see stunningly preserved medieval murals at **St Thomas Church** (St Thomas Sq, SP1 1BA) and end up at magnificent **Salisbury Cathedral** (♀ SP1 2EJ ⌂ salisburycathedral.org.uk ⊙ 09.30–16.00 daily; adults £9/ under 13s free), where you can head inside with the dog to see the spectacular vaulted ceilings reflected in the free-flowing font.

From the cathedral, an excellent circular 4km walk takes you through the beautiful **Water Meadows**. Head south from the cathedral entrance down to De Vaux Place, along St Nicholas Road and then westward along New Harnham Road until you reach Harnham Cricket Pitch, where you can cut across the lawns towards an old mill. From here you enter the Water Meadows; take the Town Path north towards the centre and enjoy lovely views of the sheep fields and cathedral spire.

A 10-minute drive north of Salisbury takes you to **Old Sarum** (Castle Rd, SP1 3SD ⌂ english-heritage.org.uk ⊙ 10.00–16.00 daily; adult/child £5.90/£3.50), the

↑ View over Salisbury. (Alexey Fedorenko/S)

site of an Iron Age fort, a Roman settlement, a medieval castle and Salisbury's first cathedral. Today it's all ruins and a walk around its ancient ramparts offers fabulous views of the Wiltshire plains. Aviation enthusiasts will love the **Boscombe Down Aviation Collection** (Hangar 1 South, Old Sarum Airfield, SP4 6DZ ⊘ boscombedownaviationcollection.co.uk ⊙ 10.00–17.00 Tue–Sun; adult/child £9.50/£6.50), a 5-minute drive from Old Sarum, where you can sit in the cockpits of hundreds of jets and fighter planes.

LET'S GO

Salisbury is at the centre of a network of A-roads, including the A30, A36 and A338, making it easily accessible from Southampton, Bath and London. A well-connected, central train station (South Western Rd, SP2 7RL) offers direct rail links to London Waterloo, Portsmouth Harbour, Cardiff and Exeter St David's.

The best hotel is the **Mercure White Hart Hotel** (1 St John St, SP1 2SD ⊘ all.accor.com; from £70/night, dogs £10/night. It's conveniently central, with spacious, stylish rooms, and your dog can join you for breakfast in the restaurant. There's also a leafy courtyard out back. For self-catering, try **Meadow Cottage** (Harnham SP2 8LP ⊘ petspyjamas.com; from £360/night), 2½km southwest of Salisbury city centre and a few minutes' walk west of the

Water Meadows. It sleeps up to six and has an enclosed garden.

Salisbury is packed with characterful pubs, but **Haunch of Venison** (1 Minster St, SP1 1TB ⊘ haunchpub.co.uk ⊙ 11.00–23.00 Thu–Tue) must be its finest: the food – especially the venison – is excellent, hearty stuff.

For fry-ups, solid lunches and good gluten-free, vegan and vegetarian options, try **Greengages** (31 Catherine St, SP1 2DQ ⊘ greengagessalisbury. co.uk ⊙ 08.30–16.00 Mon–Sat).

Clearway Pets (4 Winchester St, SP1 1HB ⊘ clearwaypets.co.uk ⊙ 09.00–17.00 Mon–Sat, 10.00–14.00 Sun) sells food, toys and treats. **The Vets** (123 Exeter St, SP1 2SG ⊘ 01722 337117; out of hours ⊘ 01722 238079) is reliable for medical queries.

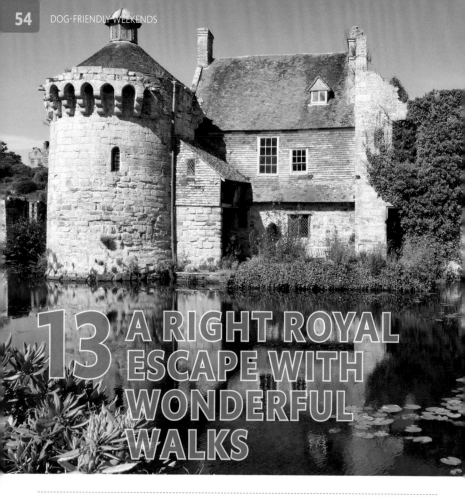

13 A RIGHT ROYAL ESCAPE WITH WONDERFUL WALKS

WHERE	Royal Tunbridge Wells, Kent
WHEN	Year-round
HIGHLIGHTS	Long walks on the Weald, mooching in independent boutiques and exploring amazing castles.

Kent's High Weald AONB has some of the best dog-walking territory in all of Britain. This landscape of rolling hills garnished with woodland and rocky sandstone outcrops has 2,395km of footpaths and bridleways to romp across. The best time to enjoy it is during September's **High Weald Walking Festival** (⌀ highwealdwalks.org.uk), when you can bring the dog along on guided hikes throughout the region. It's just as easy to explore alone if you're capable with an OS Map or similar, though.

Base yourself in Tunbridge Wells, a well-to-do Royal spa town where dogs are almost as common as humans on the high street and cafés spill on to the pavement around The Pantiles, a leafy pedestrianised shopping street lined

↑ Scotney Castle makes a good day trip from Tunbridge Wells. (Rusana Krasteva/S)

with handsome colonnades and wrought-iron balconies. It's a great place to fuel up for a day of walking: **The Pantiles Café & Bar** (42 The Pantiles, TN2 5TN ⌀ thepantilescafe.co.uk ⊙ 09.00–16.00 Thu–Tue) serves mighty breakfasts and light lunches, while **Framptons** (2 The Pantiles, TN2 5TJ ⌀ framptonsbar.co.uk ⊙ 10.00–23.00 Mon–Sat, 10.00–19.00 Sun) offers roast dinners, brunch pancakes and excellent cocktails. If you're feeling flush and want to spoil your pet, head for **Collared** (9 The Pantiles, TN2 5TE ⌀ collared.co.uk ⊙ 10.30–16.30 daily) which sells luxurious dog accessories.

From The Pantiles, you've got easy access to one of the top circular walking routes in the High Weald: the **Tunbridge Wells Circular** (⌀ explorekent.org) – a nearly 44km waymarked path that circles around the town. Take in the pleasant 9km section from Pembury village, just 10 minutes' drive northeast of town (download the route from ⌀ gps-routes.co.uk), which meanders along the outskirts of the village through woodland, across farmland and through orchards. More excellent walking territory can be found east of Tunbridge Wells at **Dunorlan Park** (♥ TN2 3QN 🐾), a former Victorian estate with landscaped gardens, a Grecian temple and a boating lake, or on **Tunbridge Wells Common** (♥ TN4 8BX 🐾) in the west, where you can see some of the area's distinctive sandstone outcrops.

Day trips beyond Tunbridge Wells are plentiful, with the romantic **Scotney Castle** (Lamberhurst TN3 8JN ⌀ nationaltrust.org.uk ⊙ 10.00–16.00 daily) just 20 minutes' drive southeast of town and **Hever Castle** (Hever, Edenbridge TN8 7NG ⌀ hevercastle.co.uk; adult/child £15.80/£9.95) 25 minutes northwest. Bring a picnic and hang out outside the grand, old double-moated childhood home of Anne Boleyn, or eat alfresco at either of the on-site restaurants, then walk among the Italianate gardens, the Tudor topiaries and the rose plantings.

LET'S GO

Tunbridge Wells train station (Mount Pleasant Rd, TN1 1BT) has direct connections with London and Hastings. The town sits on the A26 around 20km south of the M25.

Most pubs here allow dogs in their bar at least; the **White Bear** (84 High St, TN1 1YB ⌀ the-white-bear.co.uk ⊙ noon–22.00 daily) is a local favourite for their charcoal-grilled meats. If you take the Pembury Circular, stop in at the **Black Horse** (12 High St, Pembury TN2 4NY ⌀ blackhorsepembury.co.uk ⊙ 11.00–22.00 Mon–Sat, noon–21.30 Sun) for a real ale and hearty restorative home-cooked pie.

The top accommodation is **Royal Wells Hotel** (59 Mount Ephraim, TN4 8BE ⌀ royalwells.co.uk 🐾 2; from £80/night, dogs £10/night) which has cosy rooms with minimalist vibes.

Wolfit Pet Shop (14 Monson Rd, TN1 1ND ⌀ wolfit.co.uk ⊙ 09.00–17.30 Mon–Sat) sells supplies, while **Companion Care** (Fountains Retail Park, Dowding Way, TN2 3FB ☎ 01892 500050) has a 24-hour phone line for medical emergencies.

14 A BOHEMIAN BREAK IN RURAL SOMERSET

WHERE	Wells & Glastonbury, Somerset
WHEN	Year-round
HIGHLIGHTS	Channel your inner flower child atop mystical hills, browse quirky shops and visit England's smallest city.

Sitting in northeast Somerset, separated by just a 25-minute drive along the A39, Wells and Glastonbury make a bewitching pairing for a weekend away in rural southwest England. Think superb cider on tap, gorgeous walks in the dramatic Mendip Hills, and mystical history that'll capture the imaginations of kids and adults alike.

Wells might be England's smallest city but it has one big attraction that'll entice you away from its buzzy central shopping streets and Saturday market: a cathedral so grandiose you'll wonder how it ended up in this quiet little corner of Somerset. The building – which dates to 1175 and was the first in Britain to be built in this imposing Gothic style – lords over the northeast corner of town at the end of the High Street and welcomes friendly dogs to walk beneath its vaulted ceilings and spectacular stained-glass windows. The neighbouring Bishop's Palace and Gardens is a lovely spot for a stroll or picnic, while off-lead fun can be had at Wells Recreation Ground across the road.

Homeware shoppers and antiques collectors will enjoy the Wells Reclamation Co (Wells Rd, BA5 1RQ ⊘ wellsreclamation.com ⊙ 08.30–17.00 Mon–Fri, 09.00–16.00 Sat), on the southern edge of town, where thousands of unusual pieces of furniture are littered across its yards and warehouses, but it's in Glastonbury where the shopping gets really quirky.

Glastonbury is most famous for its connections with the music festival that takes over nearby Worthy Farm almost every year. Its town centre is now something of an extension of the festival's famously hippyish Green Fields, with shops selling healing crystals, tarot cards and Tibetan singing bowls. But while it's all a bit incense and tie-dye these days, Glastonbury does have some genuine mystical connections. It's said this was the Isle of Avalon, where King Arthur's famous sword was forged, and one story tells that Jesus Christ visited Glastonbury as a boy with a travelling merchant. All that, along with a modern population of pagans, hippies and Druids, and it's hardly surprising this place has such a unique atmosphere.

EBBOR GORGE & WOOKEY HOLE (♀ BA5 1BA ⊘ mendiphillsaonb.org.uk 🐕) Just 4km northwest of Wells, the village of Wookey Hole is the gateway to the southern Mendips – an Area of Outstanding Natural Beauty. From here, you can follow a 6½km circular trail that takes in the dramatic limestone Ebbor Gorge and affords fantastic views across the Somerset Levels and Glastonbury Tor. There are a few steep climbs involved but it's well worth it. Dogs will love sniffing among the wild flowers at Ebbor Wood, and they'll find water in the streams you'll cross along the way.

WELLS CATHEDRAL (Cathedral Green, BA5 2UE ⊘ wellscathedral.org.uk ⊙ 07.00–19.00 daily; adult/child £6/£4 donation 🐕) A 12th-century Gothic marvel, fronted by manicured lawns and blessed with three tall towers, this

← Glastonbury Tor. (chrisdorney/S)

Wells Cathedral. (Reimar/S)

arresting cathedral lies hidden behind a walled compound at the end of Wells' High Street. Look out for its clock, said to be the second oldest in the country, on which a pair of jousting knights mark its strike every 15 minutes. You can bring dogs inside and, providing the group and guide approve, take them on the insightful outdoor tours.

BISHOP'S PALACE & GARDENS (♀ BA5 2PD ⊘ bishopspalace.org.uk ⊙ 10.00–18.00 daily; adult/child £15/£7.50) Easy strolls can be had in the gardens

LET'S GO

GETTING THERE

Located on the A39, Glastonbury and Wells are around 21km off the M5 and 35km off the M4. The most convenient train station is Bristol Temple Meads (Redcliffe, BS1 6QF), 41km north, from where you can catch the local 376 Mendip Explorer bus to both towns (every 30mins; around 1hr 20mins).

EATING

✖ **Hundred Monkeys** 52 High St, Glastonbury BA6 9DY ⊘ hundredmonkeyscafe.com ⊙ 10.30–16.30 Wed–Sun. With an emphasis on sustainable food and small-scale producers, this quirky café offers great vegetarian and vegan options – including wraps, salads, curries and filo pies. A lovely patio at the back is great for dogs who need a bit more space.

✖ **LOAF** 38 Market St, Wells BA5 2DS ⊘ loafisbaking.co.uk ⊙ 08.30–17.00 Mon–Wed, 08.30–22.00 Thu–Sat, 09.00–15.00 Sun. Gorgeous little café hidden just off Market Street in Wells town centre, serving ludicrously sticky buns and lovely brunches.

✖ **Queen of Cups** 10–12 Northload St, Glastonbury BA6 9JJ ⊘ queenofcups.co.uk ⊙ 17.30–23.00 Mon & Thu, noon–23.00 Fri–Sat, noon–18.00 Sun. This exceptionally friendly restaurant has its own 'pupwatch' board pinned with Polaroids of visiting dogs. The small plates menu is unusually varied, including Japanese and

↑ The Bishop's Palace, Wells. (Adrian Baker/S)

at the Bishop's Palace, which sits next to the cathedral. Set within its medieval walls are 5½ha of wide lawns, mulberry and Indian bean trees, and beautiful plantings with colourful borders that come alive in summer. You can't take the dog inside the palace itself, but if you're keen to see it take turns to explore the 800-year-old interior, where you can visit the impressive Long Gallery and chapel.

GLASTONBURY ABBEY (Magdalene St, BA6 9EL ⊘ glastonburyabbey.com ⊙ 10.00–18.00 daily; adult/child £11/£6.60) Legend has it that followers of Christ came to Glastonbury in the 1st century and built a wooden church on this sacred ground. No evidence remains of such things, but there is evidence of a Saxon church constructed in AD700. The serene 10th-century ruins you can walk among today sit in the centre of Glastonbury town, surrounded by lush lawns and leafy gardens.

GLASTONBURY TOR (♀ BA6 8BG ⊘ nationaltrust.org.uk) Glastonbury's Tor is unmissable: a curiously conical 158m hill which rises strikingly out of the Somerset Levels and is topped with a tower that belonged to the 14th-century church of St Michael. A circular walking route from St Dunstan's Car Park (Magdalene St, BA6 9EH; see tourist information board for directions) takes you along the High Street and to a public footpath which crosses the fields towards the Tor. The climb can be steep, but the views are so fabulous you won't be short of excuses to stop and look back as you ascend. Allow at least an hour.

Middle Eastern dishes; all are brilliantly executed. Local beers on tap and great cocktails, too.

SLEEPING

🏠 **Middlewick Holiday Cottages** Wick BA6 8JW ⊘ middlewickholidaycottages.co.uk. You can stay in cottages, glamping dens and cabins at this gorgeous farm on the outskirts of Glastonbury, just a 30-minute walk from the tor. The farm shop is a highlight (dogs are allowed inside), there's a shepherd's hut spa with reasonably priced treatments, and in summer there's an outdoor café. Dogs must be on leads due to the farm animals, but there's usually a dedicated field for off-lead exercise. *From £90/night; dogs £15/stay.*

🏠 **White Hart Hotel** 19–21 Sadler St, Wells BA5 2RR ⊘ petspyjamas.com 🐾 1. A 15th-century inn with simple, comfortable rooms opposite the Cathedral Green. Dogs can sit with you in the lounge area while you dine and the hotel's resident pet, Camber, offers an enthusiastic welcoming committee. *From £76.50/night B&B.*

OTHER PRACTICALITIES

Tourist information centre 1 Magdalene St, Glastonbury BA6 9EW ⊘ glastonbury.uk ⊙ 10.00–15.00 daily.
Pet supplies Pets Corner (Princes Rd, Wells BA5 2DT ⊘ petscorner.co.uk ⊙ 09.00–18.00 Mon–Sat, 10.00–16.00 Sun) has all the essentials.
Veterinary practices Orchard Vets (Wirral Park Roundabout, Glastonbury BA6 9XE ☎ 01458 832972; emergency line ☎ 01223 849784) is a reliable independent practice.

15 A REGAL CITY BREAK WITH A ROMAN TWIST

WHERE	Bath, Somerset
WHEN	Year-round
HIGHLIGHTS	Elegant architecture meets Roman remains, and scenic river cruises take in the city's wilder landscapes.

Sitting on edge of the southern Cotswolds, Bath is one of England's prettiest cities, world-famous for its Georgian architecture and the subterranean hot springs that have made this a spa town since Roman times. It's thanks to this rich Roman history, most dramatically seen in the (unfortunately not dog-friendly) Roman bathhouse, that it now enjoys UNESCO World Heritage status. Bath's layout was very much influenced by the Roman settlement here and its city walls originate from that period and, being relatively compact, it's a joy to walk around with the dog.

Download an **audio walking tour** from **Visit Bath** (⊘ visitbath.co.uk) to explore the highlights. The UNESCO-themed tour, which takes around 90 minutes, starts at the 16th-century abbey and takes in Queen Square, the iconic Royal

↑ Pulteney Bridge, Bath. (Billy Stock/S)

Crescent and Pulteney Bridge – one of only four bridges in the world to have buildings all the way across it. Alternatively, choose the Jane Austen tour (60 mins) to follow in the footsteps of Bath's most famous resident. **Photo Tours in Bath** (⊘ phototoursinbath.co.uk; from £75), meanwhile, will let the dog join you on a private photography tour of the city.

Running through the city centre is the River Avon, which in its more rural stretches is a haven for wildlife such as kingfishers and otters. It doesn't take long to escape the city on the water – join **Pulteney Cruisers** (Forester Rd, BA2 6QE ⊘ pulteneycruisers.com ⊙ 10.00–17.00 daily; adult/child £10/£5 ☂) for an hour-long boat trip and you'll sail towards Bathampton to the north, passing under Pulteney Bridge and into the bucolic Avon Valley. Keep an eye out for flashes of blue flitting between the riverbanks.

Green spaces aren't in short supply in town, either. **Royal Victoria Park** (Marlborough Ln, BA1 2NQ 🐾) is a great place to let the dog run free, but the 10km **Skyline trail** (⊘ nationaltrust.org.uk 🐾) is a must-do; follow the yellow arrows from Cleveland Walk (📍 BA2 6JP), 1½km east of Bath centre, and enjoy an aerial perspective on the city as you climb into the hills beyond. Another excellent long walk runs 15km along the Kennet and Avon Canal towpath to the picturesque stone town of **Bradford-on-Avon**, from where regular trains run back to Bath.

LET'S GO

Bath, around 12km south of the M4, sits at the point where the A36 meets the A4 and A46. The well-connected Bath Spa railway station (Railway Pl, BA1 1SU) sees direct services to London Paddington, Portsmouth Harbour, Bristol Parkway and Weston Super Mare.

Eating and drinking in Bath is a pleasure, and plenty of its pubs let dogs in the bar at least. For beer lovers, **BeerCraft of Bath** (3 Argyle St, BA2 4BA ⊘ beercraftbath.com ⊙ noon–21.00 Fri–Sat, noon–19.00 Sun–Thu) is an essential stop, while anyone seeking a sugar hit should head to **Sweet Little Things** (6 Lower Borough Walls, BA1 1QR ⊘ sltbath.co.uk ⊙ 09.00–17.30 daily), a cutesy tea room with reasonably priced afternoon teas.

Abbey Hotel (North Pde, BA1 1LF ⊘ petspyjamas.co.uk 🐾1; from £210/night) is a standout among the city centre's many excellent hotels. For easy access to green spaces, stay at the colourful **The Bird, Bath** (Pulteney Rd, BA2 4EZ ⊘ petspyjamas.com.🐾2; from £204), which sits next to a recreation ground.

If you fancy visiting the Roman Baths, Becky at Pawsitively Happy Dogs (⊘ pawsitivelyhappydogs. com; £12) can take the dog for a walk or sit with them in your accommodation. **Guildhall Pet Supplies** (Stall 33 Guildhall Market, BA2 4AW ⊘ bathpetsupplies.co.uk ⊙ 09.00–17.00 Mon–Sat) sells food, treats and accessories; for health concerns, call city-centre **Ashman Jones Vets** (5 Widcombe Pde, BA2 4JT ☏ 01225 807510) or Trowbridge-based **MiNightVet** (6 Paxcroft Way, BA14 7DG ☏ 01225 710770) for out-of-hours emergencies.

16 A BRIGHT LIGHTS, BIG CITY BREAK

WHERE	London
WHEN	Year-round
HIGHLIGHTS	Take in huge green spaces and big city views – and feast on exciting international cuisine.

L ondon is a dog-loving city, there's no doubt about it. It's a well-known fact that if you get on the London Underground with your dog, someone's day will be made infinitely better just by the sight of your pet swaying to the gentle rumble of the train. Crowds in tube stations part for oncoming animals like the Red Sea parted for Moses, and you'll likely spot more than one delighted commuter as you make your way to the platform. With the dog by your side, London transforms from the antisocial, unsmiling city it's often portrayed to be, and instead becomes a warm, welcoming, chatty place where strangers will smile at you (and the dog) and strike up conversations about your animal wherever you are. Travelling with the dog makes any exploration of London that little bit more joyful.

And there is plenty of joy for the taking in London: vast parks and gardens, big blockbuster sights, exceptional food and drink and, of course, the unmistakable and infectious thrum and buzz of the nation's capital. You might not be allowed to take the dog into its world-famous galleries and museums but bringing them along gives you an excuse to focus on some of London's lesser-visited highlights. Consider,

↑ View over Hyde Park. (Alexey Fedorenko/S)

for example, dog HQ at The Kennel Club (10 Clarges St, W1J 8AB ⌀ thekennelclub.org.uk ☉ 09.30–16.30 Mon–Fri by appointment only ☂), where a wood-panelled gallery space hosts changing exhibitions about man's best friend.

Of course, you don't necessarily need to go inside to enjoy many of the city's best sights. Simply pounding the streets and many parks of London offers a view of some of its finest attractions. In west London, you can see the regal royal residences on foot: head to Hyde Park and Kensington Gardens to peek at Kensington Palace, home of the Duke and Duchess of Cambridge, or enjoy a stroll around St James's Park and stop by the gates of Buckingham Palace to see if Her Majesty is in.

On the South Bank, beside the River Thames, the 5km walk from Westminster Bridge to Tower Bridge in the east gives you spectacular views of the Houses of Parliament, London Eye, National Theatre, Shakespeare's Globe Theatre and the skyscrapers of the City of London. At the end, you can take the lift to the glass-floored viewing deck on Tower Bridge to gaze over the city from above.

As you head further east, London becomes less polished but more colourful, in areas like Shoreditch, where you can stroll down Brick Lane with the dog – if you can, send a travel companion into Beigel Bake (159 Brick Ln, E1 6SB ⌀ beigelbake.co.uk ☉ 24hrs) to pick up one of their famous salt-beef bagels or sweet pastries – or, on Sundays, wander among the riotous colour of Columbia Flower Market (Columbia Rd, E2 7RG ⌀ columbiaroad.info ☉ 08.00–14.00 Sun). For shopping, head to Spitalfields Market

(56 Brushfield St, E1 6AA ⚭ spitalfields.co.uk ⊙ 08.00–23.00 daily), where you'll find street-food vendors packed in with clothing boutiques and craft stalls.

You'll need to travel even further east, though, and cross the river, to find the real highlight for dog owners: Greenwich Park (♥ SE10 8QY ⚭ royalparks.org.uk). With over 74ha of grassy parkland, deer pasture and woodland, this is a glorious place to let your dog run free (except in the deer park), have a picnic and see that world-famous meridian line (Royal Observatory, Blackheath Ave, SE10 8XJ). Nearby, don't miss the magnificent buildings around the Old Royal Naval College (♥ SE10 9LW ⚭ ornc.org), and head into Greenwich Market (♥ SE10 9HZ ⚭ greenwichmarket.london ⊙ 10.00–17.30 daily) for excellent shopping and eating opportunities.

London is huge, and while the transport networks are extensive and largely reliable, excessive time on trains and buses might not be good for your dog, so it's best to pick a base and stick to exploring the surrounding area. If you want to take in the entire city, you'll need a little more than a weekend away.

SOLARSHUTTLE HYDE PARK (Boat House, Serpentine Rd, W2 2UH ⚭ solarshuttle.co.uk ⊙ every 30mins from noon daily; adult/child £12/£5) In the middle of the vast Hyde Park, the Serpentine is a 16ha lake that fills with boaters in summer. You can't hire a boat with the dog, but you can take the exciting SolarShuttle, a solar-powered vessel that seats up to 40 people. Take the hour-long cruise between the Princess Diana Memorial Fountain and the Boat House to see the park's elegant weeping willows with a backdrop of urban tower blocks.

TOWER BRIDGE (Tower Bridge Rd, SE1 2UP ⚭ towerbridge.org.uk ⊙ 09.30–18.00 daily; adult/child £10.60/£5.30 including Engine Rooms 🌂) While you can admire Tower Bridge from street level, it's even better to head to the top for views over the road and river below. You'll take the lift up to the top floor, where you can walk between its two towers on a reinforced glass walkway that offers a vertiginous look at what's beneath. Be lucky enough to time it with a sporadic bridge lift and you'll get an extra special show. Once you've explored the bridge's heights, you can head down the road to the Engine Rooms, where a fascinating exhibit shows how its mechanisms were powered by steam until 1976.

BRUNEL MUSEUM (Railway Av, SE16 4LF ⚭ thebrunelmuseum.com ⊙ 11.00–17.00 Fri–Sun; adult/child £6/£4 🌂) A celebration of all things engineering, this museum, 100m from Rotherhithe Overground station, is dedicated to London's most inventive and technologically influential family: the Brunels, including, most notably, Isambard Kingdom Brunel, the civil engineer behind many 19th-century firsts from bridges to steamships. Set inside a Grade II-listed tunnel shaft, around halfway along the Thames between Tower Bridge and Greenwich, the museum charts his achievements and those of his father, Marc Brunel, both of whom worked on the tunnel in the 1840s.

↖ A leisurely way to explore London. (Sandor Szmutko/S) ↑ The Diana Fountain. (Dado Photod/S)
← Inside Tower Bridge. (cowardlion/S)

EMIRATES CABLE CAR (27 Western Gateway, E16 1FA ∅ tfl.gov.uk ☉ 07.00–21.00 Mon–Thu, 07.00–23.00 Fri, 08.00–23.00 Sat, 09.00–21.00 Sun; adult/child £4/£2 one way 🦮) Though it is technically a form of public transport, there's something novel about riding on this cable car, swooping high above the River Thames between the Royal Docks (near Royal Victoria DLR station) and Greenwich Peninsula (near North Greenwich Underground station). On the 10-minute 'flight', you'll enjoy views over the glassy towers of Canary Wharf to the west and see the planes taking off from London City Airport in the east. This a fun activity to pair with a visit to Greenwich Park.

LONDON WALKS (∅ walks.com ☉ multiple tours, departing various locations daily; adult/child £10/£5) Get insights into some of London's most intriguing areas, from Notting Hill and Portobello Road in the west to the heart of the City of London, on these guided tours. All bar three of their 20 walks are outdoors, so you can bring the dog along.

↑ Emirates Cable Car. (I Wei Huang/S)

LET'S GO

GETTING THERE

London welcomes direct trains from all over Britain into its many terminals, including Paddington (♥ W2 1HB), Euston (♥ NW1 2RT), King's Cross (♥ N1 9AL), Waterloo (♥ SE1 8SW) and Liverpool Street (♥ EC2M 7PY). Driving into London can be time consuming and tedious, with congestion on the M25 and in the city itself, and parking is expensive and difficult, so public transport is recommended.

GETTING AROUND

Dogs are allowed on Transport for London buses at the driver's discretion. They're permitted on the London Underground, but mustn't sit on the seats and should be carried on all escalators. If you are unable to carry your dog, you'll need to take the stairs or, if available, a lift. London's Thames Clipper service also allows dogs, and is an entertaining way to see the city from the river. Check ♂ tfl.co.uk for public transport timetables and disruption information. The vast majority of London's black cabs allow dogs inside.

EATING

✕ **Bluebird Café** 350 King's Rd, SW3 5UU ♂ bluebird-restaurant.co.uk ☉ 09.00–22.00 daily. Bold, creative design makes Bluebird one of the most striking places to eat in west London. The café and courtyard area are dog-friendly, serving sophisticated dishes including lobster spaghetti, salt-and-pepper cauliflower and Keralan monkfish curry. At weekends it's all about brunch, with English Nyetimber sparkling wine offered by the glass.

✕ **The Culpeper** 40 Commercial St, E1 6LP ♂ theculpeper.com ☉ noon–23.00 Mon–Thu, noon–midnight Fri–Sat, noon–21.00 Sun. Good

negronis, London beer on tap, a great wine list and inventive food wins out at this lovely east London pub. Down the road from Spitalfields Market, it's a cosy spot for hearty homemade pies or Sunday roasts and the rooftop garden is gorgeous in summer.

✕ **Love My Human Townhouse** 330 King's Rd, SW3 5UR ♂ lmhtownhouse.co.uk ☉ 08.30–18.00 Mon–Fri, 09.00–18.00 Sat, 10.00–17.00 Sun. It's not an exaggeration to say this south London café and deli is dog mad. So much so, in fact, that there's an entire menu just for your pet. They're considered the most important customer here, so they can sit up at the table with you, sip 'puppaccinos', and even gorge on full-blown meals like courgetti with beef meatballs or chicken breast with pumpkin purée. Mere humans can order good open sandwiches, brunches or afternoon teas.

✕ **Maggie Jones's** 6 Old Ct Pl, W8 4PL ♂ maggie-jones.co.uk ☉ noon–14.30 & 17.00–21.30 Mon–Fri, noon–21.00 Sat–Sun. Once a favourite haunt of Princess Margaret, this intimate, rustic restaurant is around the corner from Kensington Palace and Hyde Park. The Sunday roasts are excellent, while the main menu lists decadent comfort food like guinea fowl in white wine or pork belly with apple sauce. There's a reasonably priced set menu, too, offering three courses for under £30.

✕ **Mercato Metropolitano** 42 Newington Causeway, SE1 6DR ♂ mercatometropolitano. com ☉ 08.00–23.00 Mon–Fri, 11.00–midnight Sat, 11.00–22.00 Sun. Just a 10-minute bus ride or 30-minute walk from Waterloo Station, this is a food hall you could spend an entire day enjoying. Indulge in Argentine arepas, American barbecue, Italian gelato and pastries, fresh pastas or pizza, and pick up top-quality bottles from the cosy wine ▶

◀ bar tucked away from the noise and crowds at the back. There's plenty of indoor and outdoor seating and dogs always get a warm welcome.

✕ Ole & Steen 1 Sir Simon Milton Sq, SW1E 5DJ ⌂ oleandsteen.co.uk ⊙ 07.30–21.00 Mon–Fri, 08.00–20.00 Sat–Sun. This spacious Victoria-based outlet of the Danish bakery chain serves light breakfasts, lunches and good coffee. The baked goods are devilishly tempting and the cinnamon buns are famously good. Other equally dog-friendly locations include Covent Garden, Leicester Square and Bond Street.

✕ The Sail Loft 11 Victoria Pde, SE10 9FR ⌂ sailloftgreenwich.co.uk ⊙ noon–23.00 Mon–Sat, noon–21.00 Sun. Overlooking the Thames and the masts of the *Cutty Sark* in Greenwich, this Fuller's pub is a solid bet for decent beers and reliable food. The outdoor terrace is an ideal summer drinking spot.

✕ WatchHouse 37 Shad Thames, SE1 2NJ ⌂ watchhouse.com ⊙ 07.00–18.00 Mon–Fri, 08.00–18.00 Sat–Sun. Some of London's finest coffee is served in WatchHouse's Tower Bridge branch. They buy direct from the supplier and roast the beans to create flavourful, punchy brews. Good breakfasts are on offer in the mornings, then brunches like sweetcorn fritters and salmon with eggs until 4pm. Other locations include Somerset House, Bermondsey Street, Commercial Street and Maltby Street.

SLEEPING

🏠 The Clarendon Hotel Montpelier Row, Blackheath SE3 0RW ⌂ clarendonhotel.co.uk 🐾 2. Perfectly placed for walks in Greenwich Park and on Blackheath, this hotel has comfortable bedrooms, a lovely dog-friendly bar and tempting afternoon teas served in the gardens. And unlike most London hotels, it offers free on-site parking. *From £125/night B&B; dogs £7.50/night.*

🏠 Holmes Hotel 83 Chiltern St, W1U 6NF ⌂ holmeshotel.com 🐾 1. Tucked away around the corner from Baker Street, this effortlessly stylish hotel is a brilliant central London bolthole. Dogs get a bed, bowl and treats from Lily's Kitchen, and they can join you downstairs in the bar for cocktails or breakfast. You're just a short stroll from Regent's Park here, too. *From £250/night B&B; dogs £20/night.*

🏠 Kimpton Fitzroy 1–8 Russell Sq, WC1B 5BE ⌂ kimptonfitzroylondon.com. As handsome inside as it is out, this hotel on the edge of Russell Square Gardens is a brilliant central base – and it welcomes animals of almost any kind as long as they fit in the elevators. Rooms are monochrome and cool, some with good views over the gardens, but, most importantly, there's a menu designed for dogs with healthy, nutritious meals prepared by an actual chef. Think salmon with kale or chicken with pumpkin, served in ceramic dog bowls and delivered to your room. Breakfast is served in the dog-friendly Burr & Co café downstairs. *From £245/night B&B.*

🏠 St Ermin's Hotel 2 Caxton St, SW1H 0QW ⌂ sterminshotel.co.uk 🐾 1. Just around the corner from St James's Park tube station, this hotel has one of the finest lobbies in London –all ornate plasterwork and fabulous staircases. Rooms are traditional, with dark wood furniture and pelmet-topped beds. Breakfast is served in their dog-friendly restaurant, and light lunches or afternoon teas can be taken on the terrace overlooking the leafy entrance. There's even a Canine Concierge offering tips on what to see and do nearby. *From £212/night B&B.*

🏠 Vintry & Mercer 19–20 Garlick Hill, EC4V 2AU ⌂ vintryandmercer.co.uk 🐾 1. In the heart of the City of London, this hotel is great if you want to be in a quieter end of town at the weekend. Dogs get a bed and bowl in the room and can join you for breakfast in the café downstairs or on the fantastic outdoor roof terrace. Bedrooms are plush with rich fabrics and clever nods to the historic guilds of the area. *From £125/night B&B*.

OTHER PRACTICALITIES

Tourist information centre Opposite platform 8, Victoria train station, SW1V 1JU ☉ 08.30–18.00 daily ⊘ visitlondon.com. Also: St Paul's Churchyard, City of London EC4M 8BX ☉ 10.00–16.00 Fri & Sun; 2 Cutty Sark Gdns, Greenwich SE10 9LW ☉ 10.00–17.00 Fri–Sun.

Pet supplies Bow Wow London (50a Earlham St, WC2H 9LA ☉ 11.00–18.00 Mon–Sat, noon–17.00 Sun) is a posh Covent Garden designer shop selling accessories and treats. There's a Pets at Home in Camden (85 Camden Rd, NW1 9EX ⊘ petsathome.com ☉ 09.00–19.00 Mon–Sat, 10.00–16.00 Sun) for all the usual bits.

Veterinary practices In West London, Elizabeth Street Veterinary Clinic (55 Elizabeth St, SW1W 9PP ✆ 020 7730 9102) offers emergency care and standard appointments. To the east, try Medivet Southwark (79 Grange Rd, SE1 3BW ✆ 020 7232 2637).

↑ (Balazs Rezmanyi/S)

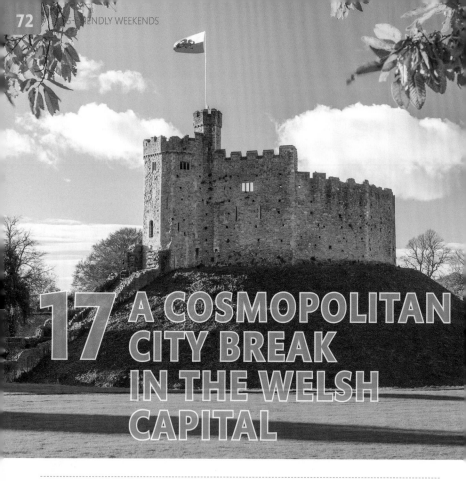

17 A COSMOPOLITAN CITY BREAK IN THE WELSH CAPITAL

WHERE	Cardiff, Wales
WHEN	Year-round
HIGHLIGHTS	Historic castles, river cruises and splendid shopping in a lively city.

As far as capital cities go, Cardiff is relatively young; while its port services grew dramatically during the industrial revolution, it has only held its title as Wales's principal urban centre since the 1950s. Today, its youthful glow is kept alive by a healthy population of students from the university who, during term-time, revel in its brilliant bars, while some relatively new and striking architecture – including the Millennium Centre, City Hall and the law courts – make it an attractive prospect for a contemporary metropolitan break.

That's not to say there's no history here, though. At its heart is a medieval castle and Gothic palace, enclosed by walls that date back nearly 2,000 years and are punctuated with intriguing animal sculptures. Meanwhile, down by the waterfront you'll find a 19th-century Norwegian church where Scandinavian seafarers would worship upon arriving at the port. It's these former docks that made Cardiff an international trade hub – today a modern development has transformed Cardiff Bay into a top destination for drinking, dining and walking.

↑ Cardiff Castle. (Billy Stock/S)

Thanks to its impressive shopping, Cardiff attracts many visitors to its pedestrianised high street. While dogs won't be welcome in most chain stores, the city's Victorian shopping arcades offer a warren of independent boutiques and shops where you can browse with your dog on a lead. Nip into the Castle Quarter Arcade (Castle St, CF10 1BU) to pick up local wines, gins and beers from the vast selection at Wally's Liquor Cellar (⊘ wallysliquorcellar.co.uk ⊙ 11.00–17.00 Mon–Sat, 11.00–16.00 Sun) or grab a drink at Coffee Barker (⊘ coffeebarker.com ⊙ 08.30–17.30 Mon–Sat, 10.00–17.00 Sun).

There are plenty of excellent walks to enjoy with your dog, from the waterfront at Cardiff Bay to the lawns and arboretums at Bute Park. Families are well catered for, too, with fun boat rides and a fascinating immersive museum just outside the city centre. If you find yourself with extra time, it's well worth the 25-minute drive – or 40-minute train journey – to Caerphilly, which is home to one of Wales' most impressive castles.

BUTE PARK (♀ CF10 3ER ⊘ bute-park.com ⊙ 07.30–19.15 daily 🐾) On the northern edge of Cardiff city centre, dissected by the snaking River Taff, Bute Park comprises a diverse 52ha of parkland, woodland and planting gardens created by the Bute family in the late 1800s and gifted to the public in 1947. This is the best place in the city for your dog to roam off lead, though beware of cyclists and runners on the footpaths. There are numerous trails to follow, including a tree tour, a wildlife trail and a story trail for kids – pick up maps at the park's visitor centre (35 North Rd, CF10 3DX) – and a few cafés where you can refuel with a hot drink. Try the Secret Garden (♀ CF10 3ER ⊙ 09.00–17.00 Wed–Mon) for great coffee and healthy food.

↑ Bute Park. (Leonid Andronov/S)

CARDIFF CASTLE (Castle St, CF10 3RB cardiffcastle.com 10.00–16.00 Mon–Thurs, 09.00–18.00 Fri–Sun; adult/child £14.50/£10) There are few cities in Britain today with such venerable monuments sitting so close to modern urban life, and yet Cardiff Castle doesn't feel any less ancient for it. While dogs aren't allowed inside the castle itself, you can admire it from the outside on the lawns of the public square – grab a coffee from one of the vendors and take in the historic view. If someone else can wait with the dog, and you do manage to step inside the walled compound, its Norman motte and keep will transport you back to the 11th century, while the spectacular Gothic palace will give you a taste of 19th-century grandeur created by art-architect William Burges.

PRINCESS KATHERINE WATER TAXI (♀ CF10 1BJ cardiffboat.com departures hourly 10.00–16.00 daily; adult/child £10/£6 round-trip) One of the best ways to reach Cardiff Bay is on the Cardiff Boat Tours water taxi, *Princess Katherine*, which cruises along the River Taff from the southern end of Bute Park. You might spot swans, cormorants, herons and even kingfishers on the 25-minute cruise, before arriving in the bay where you'll get brilliant views of the imposing Millennium Centre, the Norwegian Church and the striking red-brick Pierhead Building. An informative commentary offers insights along the way.

THE BAY TRAIL (♀ CF10 5BZ cardiffharbour.com) For a good long stroll with the dog, take the 10km trail around the entirety of Cardiff Bay. There's no official start or end as this is a circular walk, but if you take the water taxi (see above) you can hop off at Mermaid Quay and start the route from there. Walk eastward past the Pierhead Building and Norwegian Church – where Roald Dahl was baptised – and follow the water's edge. There's lots to see en route; don't miss the bronze *People Like Us* sculpture by John Clinch on Mermaid Quay, dedicated to those who lived and worked in the docks in the late 19th and early 20th centuries, and look out for the more-than 150-year-old Customs House on the southern section of the trail.

CARDIFF MARKET (5–7 St Mary St, CF10 1AU cardiffcouncilproperty.com 08.00–17.00 Mon–Sat) The city's Victorian covered market is a fantastic place to mooch, and vendors will welcome your dog with open arms. You can pick up fresh local cheeses and general groceries here, and browse everything from butchers to haberdashers, fishmongers and sweet stalls. A handful of cafés and takeaway restaurants will keep hungry shoppers happy.

ST FAGANS NATIONAL MUSEUM OF HISTORY (♀ CF5 6XB museum. wales 10.00–17.00 daily; free) For a glimpse into rural Welsh life over the

↑ Cardiff's dog-friendly central market. (JessicaGirvan/S) ← Looking out at Cardiff Bay from Mermaid's Quay. (Portia Jones)

centuries, head 10km west of the city centre (buses 17, 18, 64 and 320 leave from Cardiff Bridge) to St Fagans, the country's unrivalled history museum. Comprising more than 40 historic buildings, which have been painstakingly dismantled and rebuilt on the St Fagans Castle grounds, it's a fascinating ensemble: the oldest is St Teilo's Church, which dates back to the 12th century. There's a playground for kids, farm animals in paddocks throughout the 40ha grounds, and even a working bakery where fresh bread is made daily. Dogs are allowed throughout, except inside the historic buildings; water is available at the on-site café.

CAERPHILLY CASTLE (Castle St, Caerphilly CF83 1JD ⊘ cadw.gov.wales ⊙ daily 09.30–13.00 & 14.00–18.00; adult/child £8.40/£5 🏖) Eleven kilometres north of Cardiff – just a 20-minute drive or 25-minute train journey from the bay – lies the little town of Caerphilly, which is, rather surprisingly, home to the biggest castle in Wales. Beyond its sheer size, what's most impressive about this castle is that it was built in the space of just three years; in 1268, driven by fear of Llywelyn ap Gruffudd, the powerful Prince of Wales, the 7th Earl of Gloucester

LET'S GO

GETTING THERE

Cardiff is well connected by road and rail. Its central railway station (Central Square, CF10 1EP) has direct routes serving London, Bristol, Portsmouth and Cheltenham in England, as well as Holyhead, Penarth, Swansea and Barry Island within Wales. The city sits alongside the M4, making it easily accessible from the east and west.

EATING

✖ **The Botanist** 10 Church St, CF10 1BG ⊘ thebotanist.uk.com ⊙ noon–23.00 Mon–Fri, 09.00–01.00 Sat, 21.00–01.00 Sun. A plant-filled cocktail bar and restaurant serving burgers, sharing boards and Sunday roasts. The roof terrace is a good option on sunny days.

✖ **Brewhouse & Kitchen** Sophia Close, CF11 9HW ⊘ brewhousekitchen.com ⊙ 11.00–23.00 Mon–Thu, 11.00–midnight Fri–Sat, 11.00–22.30

Sun. Just over the river from Bute Park, this micro-brewery serves great rotisserie chicken with homemade BBQ sauce. There's a vast canopy-covered area at the back, kept toasty by patio heaters when it's chilly outside.

✖ **Coffi Co** Harbour Drive, CF10 4PA ⊘ coffico.uk ⊙ 08.00–20.00 daily. Set inside an old shipping container and serves the best hot chocolates in town (try the boozy version if you really need warming up) and 'puppaccinos' (whipped cream in a cup) for dogs.

✖ **Fabulous Welshcakes** Castle Arcade, CF10 1BW ☎ 029 2045 6593 ⊙ 10.00–17.30 Mon–Sat, 11.00–17.00 Sun. Nip in to pick up some small-batch handmade Welsh cakes – the best you'll ever try – at this take-away-only shop. They even do a dog-friendly version in the shape of a bone.

✖ **Hayes Island Snack Bar** St David's Centre, CF10 1AH ☎ 029 2039 4858 ⊙ 07.00–17.00 daily.

ordered its rushed construction at considerable cost. You can walk its bridges, lawns and inner halls, and dogs are allowed to join you in all ground-floor areas. Water for dogs is available at the entrance; watch out for the occasionally grumbly resident geese.

A Cardiff institution right in the city centre serving cheap and cheerful breakfast baps, burgers and fish and chips. It's here you'll find what are, quite simply, the best bacon sandwiches in the city; devour yours on the benches outside beneath the parasols.

SLEEPING

The Angel Hotel Castle St, CF10 1SZ angelhotelcardiffcity.co.uk. Dogs are warmly welcomed at this central Cardiff hotel, situated right by the castle. *From £60/night B&B; dogs £15/stay.*

Cardiff Caravan and Camping Park Pontcanna Fields, CF11 9XR cardiffcaravanpark. co.uk. While camping might not be your first port of call when considering a city break, this city-centre site makes a brilliant budget base. Directly next door to playing fields and Bute Park, it's got great off-lead walks on its doorstep. *From £30/pitch/night.*

New House Country Hotel Thornhill Rd, CF14 9UA petspyjamas.com 🐾 1. Located 8km from the city centre near Caerphilly, New House is a handsome estate with gorgeous grounds that are ideal for roaming with the dog. *From £92/night B&B.*

voco St David's Cardiff Havannah St, CF10 5SD ihg.com. A five-star hotel on the shores of Cardiff Bay, this stylish, colourful option is an excellent base. Ask for a bay-facing room for the best views of the handsome Pierhead Building, and enjoy a bit of pampering in the on-site spa. *From £110/night B&B; dogs from £30/night.*

OTHER PRACTICALITIES

Tourist information centre Cardiff Castle, CF10 3RB 029 2087 2167 10.00–16.00 Mon–Thu, 09.00–17.00 Fri–Sun.

Pet supplies and veterinary practice Pets at Home (Cardiff Bay Retail Park, CF11 0JR petsathome.com 09.00–20.00 Mon–Fri, 09.00–19.00 Sat, 10.30–16.30 Sun) has everything you need, plus a grooming parlour; Vets4Pets (029 2023 2957), on the same site, provides medical attention.

↑ Caerphilly Castle. (Billy Stock/S)

18 A RIVERSIDE ADVENTURE WITH LITERARY LEANINGS

WHERE	Pangbourne–Wallingford Thames Path, Berkshire/Oxfordshire
WHEN	Year-round
HIGHLIGHTS	Hike up ancient hill forts below soaring red kites, then settle into cosy old pubs or mess about on the river.

At nearly 300km, the Thames Path is one of the longest and most diverse walking trails in the UK, starting out at Kemble in Gloucestershire near the river's source, passing Oxford and wending its way to London before it ends at the Thames Barrier. One of the finest – and most dog-friendly – sections is on the Berkshire/Oxfordshire border, between the village of Pangbourne and the attractive market town of Wallingford. You could tackle sections of it by foot and use trains or buses to return to your base where necessary, but walk the entire 18km route and you'll skirt around the edge of the rolling hills of the Chilterns AONB, discovering lovely villages like Goring and Streatley which straddle the river and offer excellent places to stay or stop for lunch.

Herons, kingfishers and sometimes even otters can be spotted along this stretch – join GG Wildlife Experiences (⌀ ggwildlifeexperiences.co.uk; from £40) for an in-depth, private guided wildlife walk if you're that way inclined – and watch out for ever-present red kites circling in the skies. The bird of prey was reintroduced here in the 1990s and now has a thriving population, seen – and heard, with its shrill, unmistakable screech – across the Thames Valley and Chilterns.

This area also has a couple of high-profile literary connections. Not only did Kenneth Grahame live out his final days in Pangbourne, but Agatha Christie spent many years living and writing in Wallingford. She is buried at St Mary's Church (Church Rd, OX10 9PP) in Cholsey, around 13km from Pangbourne; see it on the circular, 8km Agatha Christie Trail (⌀ wallingfordtowncouncil.gov.uk), starting in Wallingford town centre, taking in Cholsey and returning along the river. Wallingford Museum (52 High St, OX10 0DB ⌀ wallingfordmuseum.org.uk ⊙ 14.00–17.00 Tues–Fri & Sun, 10.30–17.00 Sat; adult/child £5/free) isn't officially dog-friendly but may allow small, well-behaved pets to join you if it's quiet and you ask nicely; they organise dog-friendly walks around the town (from £10) for a taste of the area's rich history, which goes back as far as Saxon times. You can also walk among the remains of a near-1,000-year-old castle in the 20ha Castle Meadows (Cemetery Ln, OX10 8LG ⌀ earthtrust.org.uk), a 10-minute walk from the museum and set back from the Thames Path.

Wallingford is home to a delightful array of independent businesses and shops, many of which allow dogs – look out for the green 'Dogs Welcome' sticker in the window. Browse in the Wallingford Bookshop (10c St Martin's St, OX10 0AL ⌀ wallingfordbookshop.co.uk ⊙ 09.00–16.00 Mon–Sat) secure in the knowledge that your dog will get a good fuss on arrival, pop next door to the brilliant Grape Minds wine shop (10 St Martin's St, OX10 0AL ⌀ grapemindsdrinkalike.co.uk ⊙ 10.00–19.00 Mon–Sat, 10.00–15.30 Sun) to pick up a bottle of local plonk, or nip into Wildwood (21a St Mary's St, OX10 0EW ⌀ wildwoodwallingford.co.uk ⊙ 10.00–17.00 Mon–Sat) for upcycled and handmade furniture and homewares.

If the river walk is your main game and you're feeling active, the route can be done in a day, leaving you another day on your weekend to drive out to some of the fantastic nearby attractions. Or you could spread it across two days and get Walk The Thames (⌀ walkthethames.co.uk; from £15/bag) to ferry

← The village of Goring. (David Hughes/S)

your bags from one location to the next, giving you more time to explore the towns and villages along the route. If driving, you could choose a single base near the Thames Path and you'll be no more than a 25-minute drive from all the main attractions.

FORAGING & WILD COOKING (♥ RG8 7RY ⊘ secretadventures.org; around twice monthly in spring & summer; £50 🐾) Just a 10-minute drive north of Pangbourne lies the vast Greenmoor Wood, brimming with broadleaf woodland and low-growing shrubs. Secret Adventures' foraging and cooking courses (2hrs 30mins) will have you wandering through the trees, seeking out everything from bramble buds to purple deadnettle flowers. Your guide will introduce you to the edible species, help you gather a small feast of foliage to cook into a focaccia at their wood cabin, and make nettle hot chocolate and pesto around an open fire. Dogs can be off-lead if kept under control.

BASILDON PARK (♥ RG8 9NR ⊘ nationaltrust.org.uk ☉ 10.00–17.00 daily; adult/child £15/£7.50) Over 160ha of parkland surrounds the 18th-century mansion that Lord and Lady Iliffe bought as a ruin in the 1950s, which makes Basildon Park – just 2km along Shooters Hill from Pangbourne – a fantastic place to walk the dog. Dogs can't join you inside the house, so consider taking it in turns to visit, then enjoy the many footpaths at your disposal across the handsome estate; signposted routes range from 1km to 5km. There are water bowls outside the stables.

AV BOATS (Unit 3, Benson Waterfront, Benson OX10 6SJ ⊘ avboats.co.uk ☉ 09.00–18.00 daily; £25 for 2hrs) This marina in Benson, around 3km north of Wallingford along the Thames Path, provides equipment hire – sit-on-top kayaks, canoes, stand-up paddleboards – including buoyancy aids for you and the dog, and has an easy launch area next to the Waterfront Café. Paddle fast and you could reach the Wittenham Clumps within a couple of hours.

WITTENHAM CLUMPS (♥ OX14 4QZ ⊘ earthtrust.org.uk 🐕) These two small hills (around a 10-minute drive northwest of Wallingford) are an unmistakable sight in this little corner of south Oxfordshire. The two mounds, each topped with their own clump of beech trees, aren't just visually appealing and fun to climb, they're packed with fascinating history and exciting wildlife. Castle Hill is an Iron Age hill fort with a distinctive bank and ditch surrounding its centre, while Round Hill commands fantastic views north towards Dorchester and the River Thames. There are countless (unmarked) trails, some leading down to the river and others through a nature reserve where you will hear woodpeckers and – if you're lucky – spot great-crested newts. You'll often see friendly cattle grazing on the hills, so be sure to keep your dog under control.

↑ Benson Lock. (Neal Wailing/S) → Edible plants for sale, near Goring. (Baptiste Buisson/DT)

LET'S GO

GETTING THERE

Three train stations along the river – Pangbourne (Shooters Hill, RG8 7DY), Goring (Gatehampton Rd, RG8 0ES) and Cholsey (OX10 9LN) – all have excellent connections to London Paddington, Swindon and Cardiff, easy access to the Thames Path and regular trains between one another. Wallingford isn't on a train line but can be reached by the 136 bus from Cholsey (⏱ oxfordbus.co.uk; every 30mins). The region sits between the M40 and A34 and is well served by A-roads.

EATING

✕ **The Beetle & Wedge** Ferry Ln, Moulsford OX10 9JF ⏱ beetleandwedge.co.uk ⏱ 08.00–23.00 daily. Sitting prettily on the River Thames 10km north of Pangbourne, this hugely popular pub has the best beer garden for miles. Come for mussels cooked in garlic, Sunday roasts or superb brisket burgers. There's a pair of dog-friendly rooms in the next-door cottage from £125/night (dogs £10/night).

✕ **Five Little Pigs** 26 St Mary's St, Wallingford OX10 0ET ⏱ fivelittlepigs.co.uk ⏱ noon–23.30 Tue–Wed, 10.00–midnight Thu–Sat, 10.00–18.30 Sun. This stylish restaurant, funded by locals

with a Kickstarter campaign, is a huge part of the community in Wallingford. With local producers at its heart and a creative young team, it offers exceptional cocktails, moreish small plates and excellent hearty mains like steaks and lamb shanks. There's a suntrap garden for when the weather's good.

✕ **The Miller of Mansfield** High St, Goring RG8 9AW ⏱ millerofmansfield.com ⏱ noon–23.00 Weds–Sat, 08.00–18.00 Sun. In the centre of Goring, around halfway between Wallingford and Pangbourne, this pub serves superb steaks from a Josper grill, filling bar snacks including venison sausage rolls, and excellent local cheeses.

✕ **Ox Shed Café** 5 Ratcliffe Ct, Cholsey OX10 9QF ⏱ oxshed.co.uk ⏱ 08.30–17.00 daily. It's impossible not to be tempted by the ludicrous baked goods here – think Nutella cruffins (croissants-cum-muffins) and gooey brownies – but the breakfasts and lunches are equally as good. A short detour from the Thames Path, 3km south of Wallingford, it's a perfect pit stop.

✕ **Waterfront Café** A4074, Benson OX10 6SJ ⏱ waterfrontcafe.co.uk ⏱ 09.00–18.00 daily. Sandwiches, cakes, burgers and larger mains like fish and chips make up the hearty comfort food

↑ Panorama as viewed from Wittenham Clumps. (Konmac/S)

menu at this riverside café, just a 30-minute walk along the river from Wallingford.

SLEEPING

🏠 **The Elephant** Church Rd, Pangbourne RG8 7AR 🖊 elephanthotel.co.uk 🐾 **2**. Cosy hotel with decorative nods to the Indian subcontinent (including some huge wooden elephants), offering dog-friendly ground-floor rooms with direct access to a delightful communal lawn. Have dinner and breakfast in the BaBar with the dog or, if they're happy to be left in the room, don't miss the theatrical steak restaurant The Herd, where cuts are grilled to perfection on coals in the fireplace. *From £58/night B&B; dogs £20/night.*

🏠 **The Hayloft** Roke OX10 6JD 🖊 staycation-uk.com 🐾 **1**. A 10-minute drive north of Wallingford, this lovely, rustic barn conversion is a gorgeous base. Sleeping up to three people, it has one double and a single bed, plus a full kitchen and en suite. There are excellent countryside walks nearby. *From £120/night.*

🏠 **The Swan at Streatley** B4009, Streatley RG8 9HR 🖊 theswanatstreatley.com 🐾 **2**. The location of this riverside hotel, midway between Wallingford and Pangbourne, cannot be beaten; rooms overlook the River Thames with its weeping willows and moored narrowboats. Dogs aren't allowed into the Coppa Club restaurant, but breakfast can be served in your room and there's a dog-friendly bar for light lunches or a pre-dinner aperitif. *From £110/night B&B.*

🏠 **The Town Arms** 102 High St, Wallingford OX10 0BL 🖊 thetownarmswallingford.com. With their own handsome American bulldog, Goose, residing upstairs, the team at the Town Arms are dog mad – you and your pet will feel very welcome to hole up here for a night or two. Bedrooms are bright, contemporary and airy; though breakfast isn't included, you'll get a 50% discount if you eat downstairs in the pub in the morning. Don't miss dinner, either: the burgers are the best in town and there are creative vegan options. *From £90/night.*

OTHER PRACTICALITIES

Tourist information centre Town Hall, Market Pl, Wallingford OX10 0EG 🖊 wallingfordtowncouncil.gov.uk 🕑 09.30–15.30 Mon–Fri, 09.30–13.30 Sun.

Pet supplies Around 2km from Wallingford, Blakes Pet Food (Old Reading Rd, Crowmarsh Gifford OX10 8BW 🖊 blakespets.co.uk 🕑 09.00–17.00 Mon–Sat) has an extensive collection.

Veterinary practices Larkmead Vets (Ilges Ln, Cholsey OX10 9PA 📞 01491 651379) is a reliable local practice taking emergency calls 24/7.

19 A SPECTACULAR BEACH BREAK WITH WILDLIFE-WATCHING TRIPS

WHERE	The south Pembrokeshire coast, Wales
WHEN	May–Oct
HIGHLIGHTS	Coastal walks connect swathes of sandy beaches, while forbidding castles and stupendous seafood abound.

Tucked away in the southwest corner of Wales, well beyond the end of the M4, the Pembrokeshire coast might seem like a bit of a schlep. But make the journey here and you – and the dog – will be richly rewarded. The main attraction is the undulating coastal path, which dips in and out of sweeping sandy bays and around towering, dramatic headlands. Part of the 1,400km Welsh Coast Path, which hugs the country's coastline from north to south, Pembrokeshire's section has some of the finest sea views and, in summer, is littered with colourful wild flowers that give it an almost Mediterranean vibe when the weather's right.

The southern section of the National Park, between Tenby and Freshwater West, is great for holidays with the dog – you could easily fill a week here, but if you're short on time pick a handful of things to do and enjoy a slow weekend by the sea. A string of remote beaches – including Manorbier and Barafundle Bay – will tempt you to spend lazy days on the sand while the dog runs free, chasing waves and sniffing about the rock pools.

A smattering of seaside towns and villages make for compelling days out, or excellent weekend bases. Perhaps try Tenby, in the east, with its multicoloured townhouses and hilltop castle, or Manorbier, just a 10-minute drive to the west, where you can enjoy another castle and while away time in a tea room with Welsh cakes and a hot drink.

The sea itself here harbours a wealth of wildlife – and some of the best seafood you can eat. Dog-friendly boat trips out to remote islands like Skomer and Ramsey promise seal sightings and, between April and August, puffin-spotting. You might even glimpse a porpoise fin breaking through the slick surface on the edge of St Bride's Bay.

HEATHERTON WORLD OF ACTIVITIES (St Florence SA70 8RJ ⊘ heatherton.co.uk ☉ 10.00–18.00 daily; passes from £14.60) Just a 10-minute drive northwest of Tenby, Heatherton has plenty to entertain the family, including the dog: playgrounds, go-karts, zip lines and tree-top ropes courses, and even a dog agility course. Dogs can roam with you on the lead everywhere except the indoor facilities.

MANORBIER CASTLE (♥ SA70 7SY ⊘ manorbiercastle.co.uk ☉ 10.00–16.00 daily; adult/child £5.50/£4) Sitting on the grassy slopes that lead down to Manorbier Beach, around 15 minutes' drive west of Tenby, Manorbier Castle was formerly the baronial home of Odo de Barri, a Norman knight who helped conquer Pembrokeshire in 1093. It's an impressive medieval monument: the ruins you see today date largely from the 13th century, including the well-preserved round tower and gatehouse. You can explore everywhere with

← Taking the boat around Skomer. (LG)

your dog, including the 12th-century Hall Keep, which offers spectacular sea views. There's an excellent café serving hot drinks and cakes, and self-catering accommodation for groups of up to 12 (plus dogs) in a 19th-century house within the grounds.

PEMBROKE CASTLE (♀ SA71 4LA 𝒶 pembrokecastle.co.uk ⊘ 09.30–17.00 daily; adult/child £7/£6 ⛱) With origins dating back to 1093, Pembroke Castle, in the centre of Pembroke, a 15 minute-drive northwest of Manorbier, has a fascinating history. Like many of Wales' fortifications, it has withstood various sieges and battles, and it was also the birthplace of Henry VII, the first Tudor monarch. Visit the tower where he reportedly came into the world in 1457, and don't miss the gatehouse with its trio of portcullises or the late 12th-century keep with its unusual domed tower. Dogs are allowed everywhere except in the shop and café; bowls of water are provided at the entrance.

BARAFUNDLE BAY (♀ SA71 5LS 𝒶 nationaltrust.org.uk 🐕) A gloriously remote sweep of soft yellow sand a 15-minute drive south of Pembroke and 20 minutes west of Manorbier, Barafundle Bay has to be one of Pembrokeshire's finest beaches. It's part of the Stackpole Estate, which used to sprawl out around a now-demolished mansion, and is managed by the National Trust. Accessible only on foot (park at Stackpole Quay's National Trust car park), it rarely gets busy – even on a hot summer's day. It's sheltered by its surrounding cliffs, so is an ideal spot for a lazy picnic on the sand and, if you're brave enough, a swim in the surf. Dogs can be off-lead providing they're under control.

BOSHERSTON LILY PONDS (♀ SA71 5DH 𝒶 nationaltrust.org.uk) Like Barafundle, the Bosherston Lily Ponds, around 3km west along the coast path – or a 12-minute drive –from Barafundle Bay, are part of the Stackpole Estate. To enjoy a 1½km-long circular walk with midway access to the stunning sands of Broad Haven South Beach, bear left on the trail from the car park and you'll cross boardwalks over the three 'arms' of water that reach out from a large central pond. In June and July the ponds are packed with flowering lilies, and if you're lucky you might see otters sloping in and out of the waters. Take some time on Broad Haven (no restrictions for dogs) to admire the striking Church Rock out at sea before continuing lakeside to the car park.

FRESHWATER WEST BEACH (♀ SA71 5AH) A vast sweep of soft golden sand with good surf, Freshwater West is a popular, dog-friendly beach on the southwest coast of the national park, around 20 minutes' drive northwest from Bosherston. Keen-eyed Harry Potter fans might recognise it as where Dobby the house elf died in *Harry Potter and the Deathly Hallows Part 1*; people still lay stones at 'Dobby's grave' in the dunes here.

SKOMER ISLAND BOAT TRIPS (St Justinian's boat ramp, SA62 6PY ⌀ ramseyisland.co.uk; daily May–Jul; 2hrs; adults/under 4s £52/£5, book online) Just over 1km off the southwest coast of Pembrokeshire, on the fringes of St Bride's Bay, Skomer Island is a haven for wildlife. Its grassy clifftops are prime nesting places for puffins – between April and August, around 10,000 of the distinctive birds can be spotted on the island or in the water hunting for fish. There are seals on its lower rocky outcrops and Manx shearwater can be seen gliding gracefully just above the water's surface. Small and medium dogs can sit on your lap on the blustery *Voyages of Discovery* Skomer RHIB tours, but larger animals might

↑ Exploring Freshwater West Beach. (LG)

struggle to get comfortable, so these are best avoided if you've got a bigger dog. Tours depart from St Justinian's boat ramp, around an hour's drive north of Freshwater West or from Tenby; bring binoculars and waterproofs. Tours around Ramsey Island and other isles are also available throughout the year.

ROCKPOOLING, FORAGING & BUSHCRAFT (⊘blackrockoutdoorcompany. co.uk; rockpooling adult/child £25/£15, foraging £40/free, bushcraft £40/£15) Dog lover Dan Moar, an outdoor instructor for over ten years, runs fantastic family- and dog-friendly bespoke private tours along the Pembrokeshire coast. He can take you coastal foraging and cook a beachy feast by the sea, or show you the wonders of the rock pools around Manorbier, Pendine or St Davids. He also offers bushcraft courses.

LET'S GO

GETTING THERE

It's not straightforward to reach by public transport: there are train stations at Tenby (Station Rd, SA70 7LZ), Penally (A4139, SA70 7PS), Manorbier (Station Rd, SA70 7SN) and Pembroke (Station Rd, SA71 4AH), which can all be reached from Cardiff by changing at Carmarthen.

EATING

✖ **Beach Break Tearooms** Manorbier SA70 7TD ✆ 01834 871709 ⊙ 10.00–17.00 daily. This cosy little tea room-cum-gift shop is a brilliant spot for simple sandwiches, morning fry-ups and serious ice-cream sundaes.

✖ **Simply Seafood** Castle Sq, Tenby SA70 7BW ✆ 07828 046047 ⊙ 10.00–17.00 Tue–Sat. Seafood lovers won't want to miss a lobster roll from this tiny, rustic shack-like takeaway. Crab sandwiches and cups of cockles are also on offer, best eaten on the wall nearby overlooking the ocean from whence they came.

✖ **St Govan's Country Inn** Bosherston SA71 5DN ✆ 01646 661311 ⊙ noon–14.30 & 18.00–20.30 Mon–Fri, noon–20.30 Sat–Sun. A simple, homely place serving comfort food such as lasagne, mac and cheese, and burgers with plump homemade buns. There's a good selection of local beers on draught and the Sunday roasts are unbeatable. Dining reservations essential.

✖ **The Stackpole Inn** Stackpole SA71 5DF ⊘ stackpoleinn.co.uk ⊙ noon–20.00 Mon–Sat, noon–15.00 Sun. A great option if you've spent a morning or afternoon at Barafundle Bay, this fantastic little pub focuses on Pembrokeshire's excellent local produce and includes good vegetarian and vegan options. Dining reservations essential.

SLEEPING

🏠 **Castlemead Hotel** Manorbier SA70 7TA ⊘ castlemeadhotel.com 🐾 2. A hotel with resident dogs is always a good sign for dog owners;

↑ Tenby. (Lukasz Pajor/S)

the Castlemead has five of them roaming around. Pet-friendly rooms are in the Coach House, with private access, and the gardens are ideal for late-night loo duties. Dogs can dine with you inside, but you're encouraged to eat alfresco if the weather's right. *From £115/night B&B.*

⚓ Freshwater East Caravan & Motorhome Club Site Trewent Hill SA71 5LJ ⌀ caravanclub. co.uk. On the south coast of Pembrokeshire, this campsite (campervans, motorhomes, caravans and tents) is all of 5 minutes from sandy Freshwater East beach, a brilliant dog-friendly stretch. It has a walking area for your dog's late night or early morning toilet trips, and friendly staff on hand for recommendations. *From £6.60/night.*

🏠 The Stables Penally ⌀ petspyjamas.com 🐾 2. Just a short drive west of Tenby, this lovely little two-bedroom house sleeps three people and two dogs. There's an enclosed garden with patio, and inside is finished to a high standard. *From £465/week.*

🏠 Swallow Barn Saint Twynnells ⌀ petspyjamas.com 🐾 2. Tucked away down a quiet country lane a few kilometres inland from Bosherston Lily Ponds, this beautiful, modern property (sleeps four) and comes with an enclosed lawned garden with decking for alfresco dining, airy vaulted ceilings and a cosy wood burner for when the temperature drops. *From £635/week.*

OTHER PRACTICALITIES

Tourist information centre Commons Rd, Pembroke SA71 4EA ⌀ visitpembrokeshire.com 📞 01437 776499 🕐 10.00–13.00 & 14.00–17.00 Mon–Sat.

Pet supplies Burns (Moorfield Rd, Narberth SA67 7AB ⌀ burnspet.co.uk 🕐 9.00–17.00 Mon–Sat) is a packed store with plenty of food, treats and kit. There's also a branch of Pets at Home in Haverfordwest (Springfield Retail Park, SA61 2AT ⌀ petsathome.com 🕐 09.00–20.00 Mon–Fri, 09.00–19.00 Sat, 10.30–16.30 Sun).

Veterinary practices Tenby Vets (Lower Park Rd, SA70 8ES 📞 01834 842278) has 24-hour emergency service; further west is Medivet Pembroke (83–85 Main St, SA71 4DB 📞 01646 622943).

20 A RIVERSIDE ROMP ON THE ENGLISH-WELSH BORDER

WHERE	Wye Valley AONB & Forest of Dean, Monmouthshire, Gloucestershire & Herefordshire
WHEN	Mar–Oct
HIGHLIGHTS	Exploring the river by canoe before enjoying spectacular aerial views on foot.

The seductive twists and turns of the River Wye, which snakes its way north from the Severn Estuary near Chepstow, and the splendid, rugged scenery that surrounds it, have long inspired artists and writers – most famously, William Wordsworth. It was 'these steep woods and lofty cliffs' that gave rise to his poem, *Lines Written A Few Miles Above Tintern Abbey* in 1798, and still today, taking a walk along its banks – as the poet did many times as boy and man – it's easy to get lost in the beguiling beauty of it all.

While Tintern Abbey doesn't actually feature in Wordsworth's poem, it is an unmissable sight on the banks of the southern Wye. In the 18th century, Romantic writers and poets flocked to the ruined Cistercian abbey, which was founded in 1131 and left to decline in 1536, to picnic and pontificate, and today you can do the same, wandering among its awe-inspiring ruins with the dog by your side. Once you've explored, nip across the footbridge and take the 2½km trail to the Devil's Pulpit clifftop viewpoint for fine views from above. If you prefer to drive, head for Tidenham Chase Car Park (♥ GL15 6PT), around 15 minutes from Tintern on the other side of the river; from where there's a 1½km footpath to the viewpoint.

Around Tintern are a handful of lovely pubs, cafés and even a vineyard you can visit with the dog, but the real fun begins further north: for those seeking adventure, canoeing the Wye will be the highlight. Some 30km north of Tintern, the tiny hamlet of Kerne Bridge is an ideal place to get on the water and spend a few hours paddling down to Symonds Yat, where you can hop out and hike for 30 minutes up to the Symonds Yat Rock viewpoint (♥ GL16 7EL ⬙ forestryengland.uk) for that winding Wye view.

↑ The Wye Valley. (Matthew Dixon/S)

Around 7km further north, the lovely town of Ross-on-Wye is packed with good pubs and has peaceful riverside walks where the dog can roam off lead, while to the east of the river is the vast Forest of Dean, which cloaks the valley's hills in oak, chestnut and beech woodland. It's just a 35-minute drive between Tintern and Ross-on-Wye; base yourself almost anywhere along this stretch of river to be within a short distance of the main attractions.

TINTERN ABBEY (Tintern NP16 6SE ⌀ cadw.gov.wales ⊙ 10.00–17.00 daily; adult/child £5.90/£4.10) Once a masterpiece of Gothic architecture, this striking ruin by the southern River Wye is mesmerising. All soaring arches and dramatic lancet windows, at one time filled with stained glass that would have painted the nave in a multitude of colours, it's almost more impressive as a ruin than it would have been as a functional monastery. You can walk with your dog on a lead through the cloisters, monk's refectory, old infirmary and kitchens.

PARVA FARM VINEYARD (♀ NP16 6SQ ⌀ parvafarm.com ⊙ noon–17.00 Fri–Mon; adult/child £2.50/free) Just a 5-minute drive north of Tintern, this gorgeous vineyard is set beneath the rolling, forested hills of the southern Wye. You can take a self-guided tour of the vines before indulging in a tasting in the on-site farm shop: there are sweet Bacchus whites and light, dry reds, plus Welsh mead and cider to sample from the local orchards.

THE OLD STATION (Tintern Heights, Catbrook NP16 7NX ⌀ visitmonmouthshire.com ⊙ 09.00–17.00 daily) Trains haven't stopped at

this railway station for over 60 years, but there's still plenty to see at the handsome 19th-century stop, 5 minutes' drive east of Parva Farm. Four carriages feature exhibitions on the area's railway heritage plus activities for kids, who will also love the play area and zip wire. The old Signal Box has been turned into a delightful café, and there are picnic benches scattered across the lush lawns.

THE FOREST OF DEAN SCULPTURE TRAIL (Speech House Rd, Coleford GL16 7EL ⊘ forestofdean-sculpture.org.uk 🐾) Around a 25-minute drive north of Tintern on the eastern side of the Wye Valley, the Beechenhurst visitor centre for the Forest of Dean is the starting point for a thrilling sculpture trail that's has seen artworks hidden among the trees for over 35 years. Download the map online and follow the 7km trail through the ancient forest, detouring from the path to look at the 16 works in detail (allow 3 hours to see them all, or take the shortcut options for a 90-minute tour). *Cathedral*, by Kevin Atherton (1986), a striking piece of suspended stained glass, depicts the plant and animal life seen in the forest, while Sophie Ryder's *Searcher* (1988) is a life-size deer sculpture made from wire.

WYE ADVENTURES (Kerne Bridge Canoe Launch, HR9 5QT ⊘ wyeadventures. com ⊙ 09.00–17.00 daily; from £50/canoe) If messing about on the water sounds like fun, hire a launch from Wye Adventures at Kerne Bridge (a 15-minute drive north from the Beechenhurst visitor centre) for the leisurely 4-hour canoe down the Wye to their main base in Symonds Yat. You'll paddle around the base of leafy Coppett Hill and pass the entrance to the natural caverns at Coldwell Rocks, and see the famous 120m-high Yat Rock from below.

↑ Canoeing along the River Wye. (Clem Hencher-Stevens/S)

LET'S GO

GETTING THERE

The region is easily reached from the M4, M5 and M50. The closest train station is in Gloucester (Bruton Way, GL1 1DE), but public transport isn't hugely practical so it's best to have your own vehicle.

EATING

✖ **Saracens Head Inn** Symonds Yat East HR9 6JL 🐾 saracensheadinn.co.uk ⊙ noon–21.00 daily. Great sandwiches and baguettes at lunch, burgers, fish and chips and steak pies for dinner, and local Wye Valley ales on tap.

✖ **Woodsaw & Wheel** Wye Valley Centre, Tintern NP16 6SE 🐾 abbeymill.com ⊙ 10.30–17.30 daily. It's well worth stopping by the coffee house at this dog-friendly shopping complex for a pork and leek Welsh dragon pie or 'Gilpin's chowder', packed with salmon, prawns, haddock and cod. Don't miss a browse in the craft shop to pick up souvenirs made by local creatives.

SLEEPING

🏠 **Brambles** Hadnock Rd, Monmouth NP25 3PR 🐾 cottages.com 🐾 1. This three-bedroom self-catering option, sleeping up to six people on the edge of Monmouth, is a great base, with an enclosed garden, barbecue and outdoor hot tub. *From £135/night.*

🏠 **The Roost Luxury Glamping** Jubilee Rd, Mitcheldean GL17 0EE 🐾 theroostglamping.co.uk 🐾 2. Set within a small field on a hillside in the Forest of Dean, around 15 minutes southeast of Ross-on-Wye, these two gorgeous little glamping huts, with double beds, en suites and Japanese-style outdoor bathtubs for evening soaks, are a peaceful getaway. Wood burners inside keep it cosy, while outdoor fire pits are great for alfresco cooking after a day on the footpaths in the nearby forest. *From £175/night.*

🏠 **The Wild Hare** Main Rd, Tintern NP16 6SF 🐾 thewildharetintern.co.uk 🐾 1. A brilliant pub with stylish, contemporary rooms that loves dogs so much they've created a menu especially for them. *From £115/night B&B, dogs £10/night.*

OTHER PRACTICALITIES

Tourist information centre The Corn Exchange, High St, Ross-on-Wye HR9 5HL 🐾 visitherefordshire. co.uk ⊙ 09.00–13.00 Mon–Fri.

Pet supplies Creature Comforts (32 Gloucester Rd, Ross-on-Wye HR9 5LF 🐾 nrgpetsupplies. myshopify.com ⊙ 09.00–17.00 Mon–Sat) has toys, food and treats.

Veterinary practices Vinetree Vets (Walford Rd, Ross-on-Wye HR9 5RS ☎ 01989 564687) offers appointments and emergency care.

↑ Tintern Abbey. (Billy Stock/S)

21 A CHOCOLATE-BOX WEEKEND IN THE COUNTRYSIDE

WHERE	North Cotswolds: Worcestershire, Gloucestershire and Oxfordshire
WHEN	Year-round
HIGHLIGHTS	Classic Cotswolds scenery and grand Baroque palaces, with fabulous walks in between pretty stone villages.

There are areas of the Cotswolds that haven't changed for centuries. Walk out into the countryside here and you could find yourself alone, in the middle of verdant pasture, surrounded by drystone walls that were built hundreds of years ago and which still keep the grazing sheep within the boundary of the owner's land. Aside from tell-tale electricity poles and parked cars, some of the tiny towns and villages, built from local golden-hued limestone, that dot this otherwise emerald landscape are a picture of a bygone age. It's this – the sheer quaintness of it all – that makes the region such a beguiling destination.

The Cotswolds Area of Outstanding Natural beauty stretches from Chipping Campden, a good base in the north, right down to the city of Bath, encompassing the towns of Cheltenham, Stroud and Cirencester. But it's the northern half of the Cotswolds that makes the best terrain for dog-friendly breaks: in between its cutesy towns and villages and myriad walking routes lies a smattering of interesting attractions where the entire family is welcome.

Families with young children may want to stay in or near Burford, a handy base on the eastern edge of the region. The town is ideal for days out at the Cotswold Wildlife Park, where big cats and lofty

↑ The view from Dover's Hill, Chipping Campden. (Andrew Roland/S)

giraffes won't be fazed by the presence of a dog. Kids will also enjoy Cogges Manor Farm (Church Ln, Witney OX28 3LA ⌁ cogges.org.uk ⊙ 09.30–16.30 daily; adult/child £7.50/£5), 12km to the east in Witney — a medieval manor house and estate that was used as the location for Yew Tree Farm in the *Downton Abbey* series and hosts family-focused events from apple-picking days to seasonal trails. Some 6km northwest of Cogges, you can set young imaginations alight with a picnic at the romantic ruins of the 15th-century Minster Lovell Hall (⚐ OX29 0RR ⌁ english-heritage.org.uk ⊙ daylight hours; free), on the banks of the Windrush.

If regal history is your thing, base yourself in the east near the bustling town of Woodstock, home to quirky boutiques and the Blenheim Estate, where the magnificent Baroque palace is the focal point for any dog walk through its parkland. Or consider Chipping Campden, a 45 minute-drive northwest of Woodstock, beyond lovely villages like Charlbury and Kingham, where dog-friendly pubs and fancy farm shops such as Daylesford Organic make for delicious diversions. A vividly golden town, built of classic Cotswold oolite limestone, Chipping Campden charms with its thatched cottages and arched 17th-century market hall. In addition to the captivating Court Barn Museum, it also marks the start of the Cotswold Way (⌁ nationaltrails.co.uk), a 164km National Trail that wends its way south and finishes in Bath. You can take in part of the trail on circular walks around Chipping Campden or Broadway (both excellent bases for walkers), 6km to the west, where the brutally steep hill yields sweeping views of the Severn Vale and beyond to Wales. For a longer hike, take the Cotswold Way route between the two towns and return by bus, or make a day of it by hiking back a slightly different way.

↑ Broadway's High Street. (Caron Badkin/S)

COTSWOLD WILDLIFE PARK (Bradwell Grove, Burford OX18 4JP ⬧ cotswoldwildlifepark.co.uk ⊙ 10.00–16.00 daily; adult/child £17.50/£12) Watching a small herd of rhinoceros roaming on the lawns in front of a Gothic-Victorian manor house is a rather peculiar sight, and that's exactly what you'll see if you visit this small, family-owned and -run wildlife park just 3½km from Burford's High Street. This estate offers you a dog walk with a difference – and it's an ideal day out if you've got young children, as you can come face-to-face with giraffes, meet meerkats in the Walled Garden and watch big cats snoozing the day away. Dogs are allowed in most of the park except in enclosures where animals roam free, or indoor exhibitions like the reptile house – signs make it clear where they can and can't go.

BLENHEIM PALACE PARK (Woodstock OX20 1PP ⬧ blenheimpalace.com ⊙ 09.30–16.00 daily; adult/child £29.50/£4.80) It doesn't matter from which angle you view Blenheim Palace, the combination of its regal porticos and ornate belvederes is mesmerising. Set in the east of the AONB, around 25 minutes' drive from Burford, the 187-room house, home to the Duke of Marlborough, sits within 800ha of parkland where you're allowed to roam with the dog (on a lead) along public and private footpaths. You can walk across manicured lawns, over a pair of picturesque lakes and through tree-lined avenues, and enjoy fine views of the palace from the Grand Bridge and Column of Victory. The Shakespeare's Way long-distance footpath (⬧ shakespearesway.org) passes through Blenheim Park, so if you're not planning on taking turns to visit inside the palace, gain free entry

↑ Cotswold Wildlife Park. (Skowronek/S)

to the park by following the right of way through Woodstock town centre and into the West Woodstock Gate (♀ OX20 1TL).

COTSWOLD LAVENDER (Hill Barn Farm, Snowshill WR12 7JY ⊘ cotswoldlavender.co.uk ⊙ Jun–Aug 10.00–17.00 daily; adult/child £5/£2) Around 45 minutes north of Blenheim lies a patchwork of fields which, in summer, take on a bright purple hue thanks to the 200km of lavender beds set within them. The strong-scented plants love the limestone soil and have been farmed in this region since 1999. Now the family who run the farm has opened it up to the public for the peak months and encourage picnicking and dog walking throughout the pleasing purple rows. Pop into the shop to pick up some dried lavender or scented toiletries on your way out.

COURT BARN MUSEUM (Church St, Chipping Campden GL55 6JE ⊘ courtbarn.org.uk ⊙ 10.00–17.00 Tue–Sun; adult/child £5.50/free 👶) Sitting on the northern edge of Chipping Campden, around 10 minutes' drive from Cotswold Lavender, this tiny but fascinating museum explores the work of the Guild of Handicraft within the Cotswolds. It was to this town in 1902 that architect and designer Charles Robert Ashbee moved 50 guildsmen from their workshops in east London to help foster their creativity and lead healthier lifestyles. The museum displays some of Ashbee's own work, along with that of other guildsmen, and highlights local creatives making hand-crafted items, from hats to knives, today (check out the Robert Welch kitchenware studio, just around the corner on Lower High Street).

↑ Blenheim Palace. (Fulcanelli/S)

LET'S GO

GETTING THERE

The Cotswolds is dissected by a number of A-roads which make it relatively easy to reach and get around by car. Along its western edge is the M5 and to the east the M40, and running through the northern half of the AONB are the A40 and A44, connecting Oxford to Cheltenham and Evesham. Direct trains run from London and Great Malvern to Hanborough (♀ OX29 8FX), Charlbury (♀ OX7 3HH), Kingham (♀ OX7 6UP) and Moreton-in-Marsh (♀ GL56 0AA).

EATING

✖ **The Angel** 14 Witney St, Burford OX18 4SN ⌂ theangelatburford.co.uk ⊘ 08.30–23.00 daily. A characterful pub hidden down a lane just off Burford's High Street. Expect exposed brick fireplaces, chunky wooden ceiling beams and a pretty terraced garden at the back. They offer local ales on draught and excellent lunches – the salads are especially good.

✖ **Broadway Deli** 29 High St, Broadway WR12 7DP ⌂ broadwaydeli.co.uk ⊘ 08.00–17.00 Mon–Sat, 08.00–16.00 Sun. Pick up local cheese, fresh cakes and other Cotswolds produce in this vast dog-friendly deli – perfect for building a picnic before you tackle Broadway Hill.

✖ **The Bull Inn** Sheep St, Charlbury OX7 3RR ⌂ bullinn-charlbury.com ⊘ noon–22.00 Wed–Sun. Great little rustic pub in a charming village around 15 minutes' drive from Woodstock. The Sunday roasts are the highlight here, and the leafy patio at the back is great for post-walk pints on sunny days.

✖ **Daylesford Organic** Kingham, GL56 0YG ⌂ daylesford.com ⊘ 08.00–20.00 Mon–Sat, 10.00–16.00 Sun. This somewhat over-the-top farm shop on the Daylesford Organic estate is a great place to visit if you've got money to burn on lovely skincare products and local food and drink. Dogs can't go into the shop, but grab a table in or outside the Old Spot restaurant for breakfast or brunch and take it in turns to browse.

SLEEPING

⚐ **Caravan & Motorhome Club Burford Site** Bradwell Grove, Burford OX18 4JJ ⌂ caravanclub.co.uk. Located opposite the Cotswold Wildlife Park, this campsite is supremely dog-friendly, with its own dog-walk area and some rewarding

↑ Cotswold Lavender. (Raphael Comber Sales/S)

woodland walks nearby. Tents, campervans, caravans and motorhomes are welcome, and a fish-and-chip van stops by some nights during peak season. *From £15/night.*

🏠 **The Kingham Plough** The Green, Kingham OX29 0RN ⟶ thekinghamplough.co.uk 🐾 **1**. This excellent pub with rooms sits halfway between Chipping Campden and Woodstock in well-heeled Kingham and has lots of homely touches. Dog beds and bowls are provided, some guestrooms have roll-top bathtubs, and exceptional meals draw upon the brilliant local producers nearby. It's an easy 4½km walk to Daylesford Organic farm shop from here. *From £150/night B&B; dogs £10/stay.*

🏠 **The Lygon Arms** High St, Broadway WR12 7DU ⟶ lygonarmshotel.co.uk 🐾 **2**; see ad, inside-front cover. The staff at this historic coaching inn in Broadway love dogs. They've thought of everything, from designer beds your pet can snooze in beneath the table when you're dining in the courtyard, to a warm-water, dog-height, outdoor rainfall shower for fixing those muddy post-walk paws. Dinners are well worth sticking around for, and there's a spa and pool for a properly relaxing break. *From £190/ night B&B; dogs from £25/night.*

🏠 **Notgrove Holidays** Notgrove GL54 3BS ⟶ notgroveholidays.com 🐾 **2**. A privately owned estate midway between Broadway and Woodstock, Notgrove offers dog-friendly self-catering in safari tents and barn conversions. Best are the safari tents, which are insulated with cladding for autumn and winter breaks and have enclosed decking. Each one sleeps up to six people, has a patio heater for chillier evenings and a fully equipped kitchen. Walks around the site are spectacular, though be wary of your pet around the farm animals. Dogs can even join you on some activities such as foraging and falconry courses. *From £100/night, dogs £30/stay.*

OTHER PRACTICALITIES

Tourist information centre Russell Sq, Broadway WR12 7AP ⟶ broadway-cotswolds.co.uk ⟳ 10.00–17.00 Mon–Sat, 11.00–15.00 Sun.

Pet supplies The Cotswold Dog Boutique (8 Cotswold Ct, Broadway WR12 7AA ⟳ 09.00–17.30 Mon–Sat, 10.00–17.00 Sun ⟶ cotswolddogboutique.com) is tiny but packed with excellent treats, some food and essential accessories and toys.

Veterinary practices Medivet Woodstock (62 Hensington Rd, OX20 1JL ⟶ 01993 811355) and Abbey Green Vets (Church Cl, Broadway WR12 7AH ⟶ 01386 852421) both have 24-hour cover.

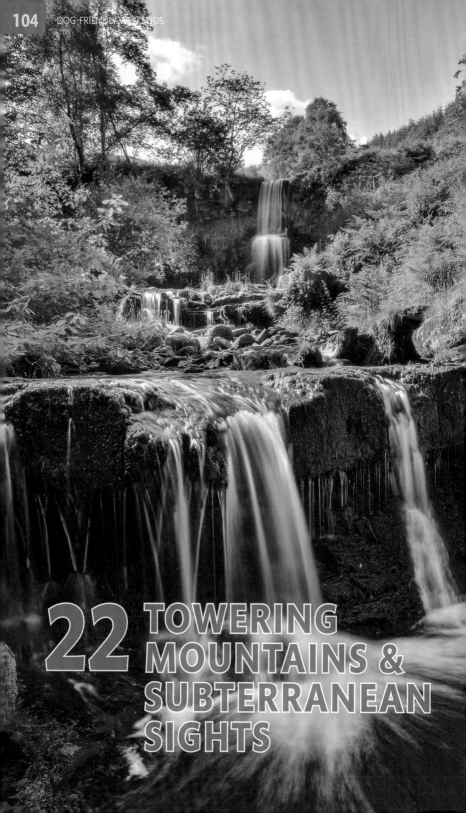

22 TOWERING MOUNTAINS & SUBTERRANEAN SIGHTS

WHERE	Brecon Beacons National Park, Wales
WHEN	May–Sep
HIGHLIGHTS	A hiker's playground with some of the finest scenery in Wales, plus a handful of lovely towns.

For walkers, the Brecon Beacons National Park is spectacular. Endless footpaths criss-cross its grassy hillsides and mossy moors, and easy-to-follow, well-used trails take you up to its highest peaks. Soaring mountains include central Pen y Fan, at more than 883m the region's loftiest, and various peaks in the Black Mountains, which make up the dramatic, undulating landscapes in the park's eastern end. If you'd rather stay closer to sea level, walks along the Brecon Canal or around the circumference of Llangorse Lake (♀ LD3 7TR) make much easier rambles.

The park is huge – it stretches from the little town of Llandeilo in the west, all the way to the English border in the east, a distance of around 72km – and you could easily spend a week or two exploring its mountains, waterfalls and pleasant little market towns. Brecon town, which sits centrally on the northern side of the park, makes a convenient base. Here, you've got easy access to many of the park's highlights, such as the National Showcaves Centre or the breathtaking Gospel Pass – the highest mountain road pass in Wales, which begins at lovely bookish Hay-on-Wye (30 minutes' drive northeast). Alternatively, southeast of Brecon, the town of Crickhowell, with its dog-friendly boutiques and old pubs, is a delightful place to stop overnight. Abergavenny is a convenient base, too, sitting at the confluence of the A40, A4042 and A465.

Note that dogs should be kept on leads around the Brecons' ubiquitous livestock.

DRAGONFLY CRUISES (Canal Rd, Brecon LD3 7EW ⊘ dragonfly-cruises. co.uk; noon & 15.00 daily; adult/child £8/£5 🐾) A cruise on the canal from Brecon town centre makes a great rainy-day activity. Hop on to the *Dragonfly* narrowboat and enjoy a scenic excursion (2hrs 20mins) along the Monmouthshire and Brecon Canal and across a 200-year-old aqueduct. Self-drive boats are also available for hire (from £30/hr).

SUGAR LOAF VINEYARDS (Pentre Ln, Abergavenny NP7 7LA ⊘ sugarloafvineyards.co.uk ⊙ 10.30–17.00 Wed–Sat, 11.00–17.00 Sun; free) Sugar Loaf Vineyards, a 30-minute drive southeast of Brecon, are spectacularly located at the base of Sugar Loaf Mountain. Take a self-guided tour of the estate before enjoying a tasting and sharing platter (around £32) at their restaurant and bottle shop, which also sells homemade dog treats.

DARK SKY WALES (Glan Tarrell, Libanus LD3 8ER ⊘ darkskywales trainingservices.co.uk; group tours usually daily, dependent on weather; £20) The Brecon Beacons was declared the world's fifth, and Wales's first, Dark Sky Reserve in 2012 thanks to its stunningly clear night-time skies. After dark, look up and on a good night you might see the Milky Way, major constellations or even a

← Waterfalls in the Brecon Beacons. (zen_light/S)

meteor shower if you get the timing right. The best way to see all this, of course, is with a professional astronomer – which is where Dark Sky Wales comes in. You'll meet at the Brecon Beacons Visitor Centre in Libanus, a 15-minute drive southwest of Brecon, and take a short walk up to the observatory, where you can train telescopes on the fascinating world of stars and planets above.

NATIONAL SHOWCAVES CENTRE (Abercraf, Swansea SA9 1GJ ⌀ showcaves.co.uk ⊙ 10.00–16.00 daily; adult/child £16.50/£13.50 ☂) You could spend an entire day at the National Showcaves Centre, 30 minutes' drive southwest of Brecon, where there's as much to see above ground as beneath it. Kids will love the dinosaur park and Iron Age village, but the main attractions are the three subterranean spaces – Dan yr Ogof, Bone Cave and, most impressive of all, Cathedral Cave (396m), which culminates in two 12m waterfalls.

CARREG CENNEN (Trapp, Llandeilo SA19 6UA ⌀ carregcennencastle.com ⊙ 09.30–17.00 daily; adult/child £5.50/£3.50) Sitting atop a dramatic rocky hill around an hour's drive southwest of Brecon, the ruins of Carreg Cennen are rather striking. Built by the Prince of Deheubarth in the 12th century, the castle was conquered and rebuilt by King Edward I in the late 1200s. Dogs are welcome on leads in all outdoor and ground-floor areas. Pair this with the National Showcaves (a 45-minute drive away) for a cracking full day out.

↑ The on-site dog walk at Brecon Caravan and Motorhome Club Site. (LG)

WILD TRAILS WALES (⌀ wildtrailswales.com; group experiences from £45) Nia Lloyd Knott is a joy to hike with and, as a fellow dog owner, she can ensure you and your dog stay safe on the mountains. Her Beacons Horseshoe Experience, starting around 30 minutes south of Brecon near Merthyr Tydfil on the southern edge of the park, is a brilliant all-day hike which takes in four of the main central peaks, but bespoke walks can also be requested.

LET'S GO

GETTING THERE

Brecon sits at the crossroads of the A40 and A470, making it easy to reach by road from cities like Cardiff and Hereford. The town itself has no train station and getting around the region without a car is a challenge, but if you need to travel by rail there are direct hourly connections to nearby Abergavenny from Cardiff; the hourly X43 bus from Abergavenny to Brecon (around 50mins) also stops in Crickhowell.

EATING

✖ **The Bank** 37 The Watton, Brecon LD3 7EG ⌀ 01874 623997 ⏲ 11.30–23.00 daily. This place offers decent pub food and a vast collection of craft beers and ale – and there's even a Dog Hall of Fame.

✖ **The Brecon Tap** 6 Bulwark, Brecon LD3 7LB ⌀ 01874 622353 ⏲ noon–23.00 Mon–Tue, 09.30–23.00 Wed–Sat, 09.30–20.00 Sun. A fantastic tap room serving hearty pies ideal for post-hike refuelling.

✖ **Skirrid Mountain Inn** Llanvihangel Crucorney, Abergavenny NP7 8DH ⌀ 01873 890258 ⏲ 17.30–23.00 Mon, 11.30–23.00 Tue–Sat, noon–17.00 Sun. A 10-minute drive north of Abergavenny town centre, the Skirrid is said to be one of Wales' oldest pubs, and has a fascinating history. Come for classic pub grub and ghostly tales.

SLEEPING

⌂ **The Bear Inn** Crickhowell NP8 1BW ⌀ bearhotel.co.uk. Gorgeous 15th-century pub in dog-friendly Crickhowell, a 25-minute drive southeast of Brecon. Dogs get a bowl of chicken on arrival. *From £104/night B&B.*

⚑ **Brecon Caravan & Motorhome Club Site** Brecon LD3 7SH ⌀ caravanclub.co.uk. A 30-minute walk from Brecon along the canal, this is a fantastic option for campers. A fenced-in on-site dog exercise area runs along a babbling brook where you can let dogs off the lead. *From £13.25/pitch.*

⌂ **Sugar Loaf Vineyards** Pentre Ln, Abergavenny NP7 7LA ⌀ sugarloafvineyards.co.uk 🐾 1. Lovely single-storey, one-bedroom cottages on the vineyard at the base of Sugar Loaf Mountain. *From £280 for three nights.*

OTHER PRACTICALITIES

Tourist information centre Glan Tarrell, Libanus LD3 8ER ⌀ breconbeacons.org ⏲ 09.30–17.00 daily. Ask about the walk up to the Iron Age hill fort for a good stroll from the car park.

Pet supplies Brecon Pet and Garden Centre (53 High St, LD3 7AP ⌀ 01874 625913 ⏲ 09.30–17.00 Mon–Sat) stocks treats and a small selection of toys and food.

Veterinary practices Honddu Veterinary Practice (26 Ffrwdgrech Industrial Estate, LD3 8LA ⌀ 01874 611811) is a reliable vet just outside Brecon.

23 ART & HISTORY BY THE BEACH

WHERE	Aldeburgh, Suffolk
WHEN	Oct–Apr
HIGHLIGHTS	Crisp wintry sunrises over vast beaches, plus marshland walks with wildlife aplenty.

Wintry seaside breaks don't get much better than in Aldeburgh, a quiet little town in the heart of the Suffolk Coast AONB. The seafront, with its multicoloured cottages and pebble beach, makes for bracing sunrise walks, while a host of old inns and pubs in its handsome centre will welcome you in from the cold to defrost with a pint of local ale or a piping hot cup of tea. You might just want to walk along the seafront or play fetch on the beach (dogs allowed Oct–Mar), but you could also opt for a fantastic 4km stroll from town along the coast path north towards neighbouring Thorpeness. It's on this route you'll see the famous **Aldeburgh Scallop**, an enormous steel shell sculpture by

↑ Sunset over fishing boats, Aldeburgh. (Helen Hotson/S)

Suffolk-born artist Maggi Hambling, dedicated to local musician and composer Benjamin Britten, which reflects the morning light in a mesmerising way.

It's easy to get into that pleasing, slow rhythm here – walk, eat, sleep, repeat – and if you're in need of a little deceleration this is the place. But there's plenty to do for a busier weekend. Around a 10-minute drive inland, you can wander along the boardwalks through wild, reedy Snape Marshes. The boardwalks form part of the 9½km **Sailors' Path** (Snape, Saxmundham IP17 1SW), a route taken by seafarers for centuries between Aldeburgh and Snape. Keep an eye out for otters, kingfishers and marsh harriers as you walk. At Snape, the Victorian **Snape Maltings** factory now houses galleries, independent boutiques and a renowned concert hall (dogs allowed in grounds only). Another 15 minutes south is **Sutton Hoo** (Tranmer House, Woodbridge IP12 3DJ ⌀ nationaltrust.org.uk ☉ winter 10.00–16.00 Sat–Sun; rest of year 10.00–17.00 daily; adult/child £14/£7), the site of the famous 1938 archaeological dig that uncovered the remains of a 27m-long ship and an Anglo Saxon burial site. You can't take the dog inside the buildings, but there are tie-up points if they're happy to be left outside for a short while and plenty of walks, including a sculpture trail, around the estate.

For spectacular sea views, drive north for 30 minutes from Aldeburgh to the thriving seaside town of Southwold and head out along the 190m-long **Southwold Pier** (N Parade, IP18 6BN ⌀ southwoldpier.co.uk ☉ 10.00–17.00 Sun–Thu, 10.00–20.00 Fri–Sat) where the dog can join you in the arcades and attractions, including the eccentric Under the Pier Show, which is packed with interactive machines invented by local engineer Tim Hunkin.

LET'S GO

Aldeburgh is remote so driving here is best; it sits just 10km from the A12.

Excellent cakes and coffee can be had at **Two Magpies Bakery** (183a High St, IP15 5AL ⌀ twomagpiesbakery.co.uk ☉ 08.00–17.00 daily) while classic pub dinners are best enjoyed in the Adnams-owned **Cross Keys** (Crabbe St, IP15 5BN ⌀ thecrosskeysaldeburgh.co.uk ☉ 11.00–21.00 Sun–Wed, 11.00–23.00 Thu–Sat). In Thorpeness, head to **The Kitchen @ Thorpeness** (Barn Hall, Remembrance Rd, IP16 4NW ⌀ thekitchenatgroup.co.uk ☉ 10.00–15.00 daily) for a hot drink and hearty English breakfast made with local produce.

A 10-minute walk along the coast from Aldeburgh, the Landmark Trust's self-catering **Martello Tower** (Woodbridge IP15 5NA ⌀ landmarktrust.org.uk; from £166/night) is the most interesting place to stay; **The White Lion** (Market Cross Pl, IP15 5BJ ⌀ whitelion.co.uk; £120/night, dogs £10/night) has lovely dog-friendly rooms, too.

Pick up treats and accessories at **Wag and Bone** (127b High St, IP15 5AR ⌀ wagandbone. dog ☉ 10.30–16.00 Mon–Sat, 11.00–15.30 Sun) and for medical assistance, call **Leiston Veterinary Clinic** (Eastlands Industrial Estate, IP16 4LL ☎ 01728 833566).

24 TIME TRAVEL WITH THE TUDORS

WHERE	Stratford-upon-Avon, Warwickshire
WHEN	May–Sep
HIGHLIGHTS	A wealth of attractions for fans of the Bard and gorgeous river rambles to boot.

Stratford-upon-Avon has been an important and wealthy town since medieval times, when it thrived as a trade hub for the Midlands. Take a stroll down **Chapel Street** to see architectural marvels from various centuries, including 16th-century timber-framed homes and red-brick Victorian banks. For a self-guided walking tour, start at the top of **Henley Street** and look out for the pavement plaques that divulge the history of buildings like the 17th-century **Town Hall** (23–24 High St, CV37 6AU) and the **Guild Chapel** (Chapel Lane, CV37 6EP), which is thought to date back to the 1200s.

Of course, Stratford is most famous as the home of the great British bard, William Shakespeare. You can't miss him: **Shakespeare's Birthplace** (Henley St, CV37 6QW ⚲ shakespeare.org.uk ☉ 10.00–16.00 daily; adult/child £24/£15.50) sits at the top of Henley Street, where you can start your self-guided walk. It's possible to explore the handsome grounds with the dog, but sadly dogs aren't

↑ Anne Hathaway's Cottage. (David Steele/S)

permitted into the fascinating exhibitions inside. Under the same ticket, you can visit the Bard's adulthood home which sits halfway down Chapel Street at **Shakespeare's New Place** – where the grounds feature specially commissioned sculptures and a clever knot garden – as well as the attractive timber-framed **Anne Hathaway's Cottage** (Cottage Ln, CV37 9HH), which also allows dogs in its pretty floral gardens.

For a more immersive look at the 15th and 16th centuries, head to **Tudor World** (40 Sheep St, CV37 6EE ⊘ tudorworld.com ⊙ 10.30–17.30 daily; adult/child £6.75/£3.50 🐾), a 5-minute walk east of Shakespeare's Birthplace, where actors in Tudor costume will transport you back to the 1500s. Kids love having a go in the stocks, and if you're (un)lucky you might just find yourself the subject of a witch trial.

With the River Avon running through Stratford's centre, scenic **walks** are always an option. For a serene 6km stroll from town, cross the river at Tramway Bridge (♀ CV37 6YS), 5 minutes' walk east of Tudor World, and follow the footpath south along the banks before crossing back over Stannells Bridge (♀ CV37 6BA) and heading north again. Alternatively, explore the river with **Avon Boating** (Swans Nest Boathouse, CV37 7LS ⊘ avon-boating.co.uk; adult/child £7/£5 🐾), which offers 30-minute guided cruises or your own vessel to hire.

LET'S GO

Just beyond the northern edge of the Cotswolds, Stratford-upon-Avon is well connected by the A46 and sits 10km east of Junction 15 on the M40. The train station (Brunel Way, CV37 6PL) has direct services to Kidderminster, Warwick, Banbury and Leamington Spa.

The **tourist information centre** is near the river (Bridge Foot, CV37 6GW ⊘ stratford.gov.uk ⊙ 09.00–17.00 Mon–Sat, 10.00–16.00 Sun).

For lovely lunches, coffee and cakes head to **No 37 Café** (37 Sheep St, CV37 6EE ✆ 01789 209956 📷 ⊙ 10.00–16.00 daily) or **Boston Tea Party** (St Gregory's Hall, Henley St, CV37 6QW ⊘ bostonteaparty.co.uk ⊙ 08.00–17.00 daily). Evening meals at the riverside **Dirty Duck** (Waterside, CV37 6BA ⊘ greeneking-pubs.co.uk ⊙ 11.00–23.00 daily) include nacho sharing platters, meatless burgers and mac and cheese.

The Arden Hotel (Waterside, CV37 6BA ⊘ petspyjamas.com 🐾 2; from £120/night) offers a stylish riverside stay; enjoy bar snacks or afternoon tea with your dog and clean their muddy paws at the outdoor washing station. Alternatively, the gorgeous timber-framed **Hathaway Hamlet** (Cottage Ln, CV37 9HH ⊘ petspyjamas.com; from £125/night), a couple of hundred metres from Anne Hathaway's home, is all wonky walls and thatched roofing with an enclosed front patio and a supremely cosy inglenook fireplace for quiet nights in.

Sniff & Bark (20 Chapel St, CV37 6EP ⊘ sniffandbark.co.uk ⊙ 10.00–17.30 Mon–Fri, 10.00–17.00 Sat, 10.30–16.30 Sun) has all the food and accessories you could need; **Riverside Vets** (2b Loxley Rd, CV37 7DP ✆ 01789 299455) will look after your animal in an emergency.

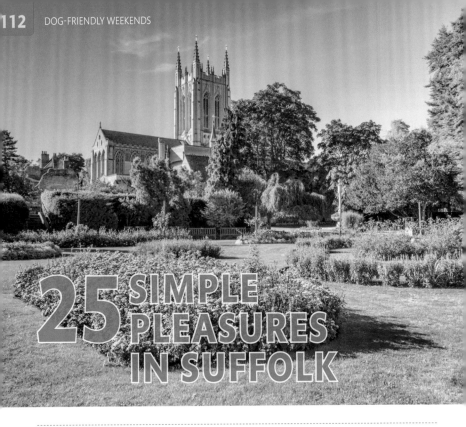

25 SIMPLE PLEASURES IN SUFFOLK

WHERE	Bury St Edmunds, Suffolk
WHEN	Year-round
HIGHLIGHTS	Delightful gardens and an independent shopping scene, plus interesting day trips to picturesque villages or a living museum.

B ury St Edmunds, a quiet but appealing little town in the heart of Suffolk, doesn't get many tourists, and it's all the better for it. From the 10th to the 16th centuries this was one of the most important pilgrimage sites in Europe, with devout visitors walking vast distances across Britain and the Continent to pay respects to England's original patron saint – St Edmund – in his gold and silver shrine. Today the most obvious place to begin any visit is at that famous pilgrimage site, the Abbey of St Edmund. Over a thousand years old, there's not much left of it today, but its crumbling ruins are set within the gorgeous 6ha **Abbey Gardens** (Angel Hill, IP33 1UZ ⚲ english-heritage.co.uk ⊙ 07.30–20.00 Mon–Sat, 09.00–20.00 Sun). Browse with the dog in the likes of **Javelin** (37–38 Abbeygate St, IP33 1LW ⚲ javelinonline.co.uk ⊙ 09.30–17.30 Mon–Sat, 10.00–16.00 Sun), great for unusual homewares and on-trend fashion, and **Luna House Boutique** (2 Butter Market, IP33 1DB ⬛ ⊙ 10.00–16.00 Mon–Sat, 11.00–15.00 Sun) for pre-loved and vintage pieces. You could also pick up a new pair of kicks at **Shoephoric** (49 Abbeygate St, IP33 1LB ⌂ shoephoric.co.uk ⊙ 09.30–17.00 Mon–Sat, 11.00–16.00 Sun).

Bury St Edmunds can also be used a lovely base for day trips out to rural museums and stately homes. Head east along the A14 for 20 minutes to Stowmarket to the **Museum of East Anglian Life** (Iliffe Way, IP14 1SL ⌂ eastanglianlife.org.uk ⊙ 10.00–16.00 Tue–Sun; adult/child £12/£10), where the dog can join you in exploring some 15 historic buildings throughout its 30ha, or take a trip to the National Trust's **Ickworth Estate** (The Rotunda, Horringer IP29 5QE ⌂ nationaltrust.org.uk ⊙ 09.00–17.00 daily; adult/child £10/£5), just a 10-minute drive west of Bury St Edmunds, where you can walk in 730ha of parkland around a spectacular Italianate palace.

A true time travel excursion can be had in **Lavenham**, a fantastically preserved medieval village with crooked timber houses and a creaking Guildhall (Market Pl, Market Ln, Lavenham CO10 9QZ ⌂ nationaltrust.org ⊙ 10.30–16.00 Weds–Sun; adult/child £8.50/£4.25) where dogs can join you in the gardens and at the tea room's outdoor seating area.

For off-lead walks, **Nowton Park** (Bury Rd, IP29 5LU ⌂ westsuffolk.gov.uk ⊙ 08.00–21.00 daily 🐾), a 5-minute drive (or half-hour walk) south from the town centre, has marked walking trails across its playing fields, through wild woodland and a beautiful arboretum. Finish off with a coffee at its dog-friendly **Grounds Café** (Bury Rd, IP29 5LU ⌂ groundscafe.co.uk ⊙ 09.30–17.00 Mon–Fri, 08.30–17.30 Sat, 09.00–17.30 Sun).

LET'S GO

Plenty of A-roads lead to Bury St Edmunds, making it simple to get to from Norwich, Cambridge and Ipswich. The railway station (Station Hill, IP32 6AE) has direct connections with Peterborough, Cambridge and Ipswich.

The town's dog-friendly restaurants, shops and cafés display stickers in their doorways or windows to show they'll welcome your pet, so it's easy to find places to eat and drink. Don't miss the excellent coffee, cakes and toasties at **Really Rather Good** (31a Abbeygate St, IP33 1LW ⌂ rrgood.co.uk ⊙ 09.30–16.00 Mon–Fri, 09.00–16.00 Sat–Sun) or the varied global comfort food at **Edmundo Lounge** (28 Cornhill, IP33 1DY ⌂ thelounges.co.uk ⊙ 09.00–23.00 daily).

The best place to stay in town is **The Angel Hotel** (3 Angel Hill, IP33 1LT ⌂ theangel.co.uk 🐾 2; from £75/night, dogs £15/night), which has spacious rooms and a dog-friendly dining area, and offers treats, bowls and toys for your pet on arrival.

Tourist information is inside The Apex (Charter Sq, IP33 3FD ⌂ visit-burystedmunds.co.uk ⊙ 10.00–17.00 Mon–Sat). **Bury St Edmunds Veterinary Centre** (Unit A, Eastgate St, IP33 1YQ ✆ 01284 630650) is best for medical queries; there's a **Pets Corner** (Rougham Rd, IP33 2RN ⌂ petscorner.co.uk ⊙ 09.00–17.00 Mon–Sat, 10.30–16.30 Sun) inside Dobbies Garden Centre just south of town.

26 A HILL-WALKING ADVENTURE WITH A TOUCH OF HISTORY

WHERE	Ludlow, Shropshire
WHEN	Year-round
HIGHLIGHTS	Undulating hills and towering ruins to climb, plus fantastic local produce to feast on.

The Shropshire Hills Area of Outstanding Natural Beauty is an 802km² landscape of gorgeously curved hills, some reaching as high as 540m, topped with woodland or cloaked in rich green grass for grazing cattle. This rural region, bordering Wales, with just a handful of towns and villages within its bucolic boundaries, is best explored from Ludlow – an enticing little town just south of the AONB.

Ludlow began life as a planned Norman settlement in the 11th century and its grid of lanes, alleyways and streets was later hemmed in by fortified walls. Today, the ruined castle and several medieval gates remain, as well as some truly charming architecture spanning the last 400 years – including The Feathers Hotel on Bull Ring, a marvellous 17th-century house with a magnificent, warped timber façade.

Spend at least a morning mooching around the town's independent shops and cafés – Eclectica (56 Mill St, SY8 1BB ⊘ eclecticaofludlow.co.uk ⊙ 10.00–17.00 Mon–Sat, 11.00–16.00 Sun) has striking

↑ The Shropshire Hills. (James Sedgemore/S)

jewellery and stylish scent diffusers, while Dugan's Patisserie (16 Tower St, SY8 1RL ⊘ dugans.co.uk ⊙ 09.00–15.00 Fri–Sat) sells tempting cakes and tarts to take away – and let yourself get distracted by the market stalls that set up each Monday, Wednesday, Friday and Saturday on Castle Square, where you can buy local honey, cheeses and gins – Ludlow is something of a foodie hotspot with plenty of talented local producers to fill your plate. A visit to Ludlow Castle is a must, and its spectacular hill views give a taster of what's to come: for keen walkers, branching out from Ludlow is where the real fun begins.

One lovely 4km stroll into the countryside heads west out of town, across Dinham Bridge and north on to the long-distance Shropshire Way (⊘ shropshireway.org.uk). The footpath crosses pasture and crop fields with arresting views back towards the castle before entering the manicured Ludlow Estate. You end up at the village of Bromfield, where you can finish with a pint in the Clive Arms or lunch at Ludlow Kitchen. The 435 bus will take you back into town if your legs are weary.

South of Ludlow town centre is Mortimer Forest (⊘ forestryengland.co.uk 🐾), reached either via a steep hill from Whitcliffe Common (♀ SY8 2HB) on the south side of the River Teme, or from one of three car parks – two on Killhorse Ln (♀ SY8 2HF) and one just off the B4361. Here, wide tracks cut through plantations of Douglas fir and larch trees perfect for off-lead walks; marked trails range from 1.6km to 15km long. You will also find spectacular walks further into the AONB at historic locations like the Iron Age hill fort of Bury Ditches or nature hotspots such as Carding Mill Valley.

LUDLOW CASTLE Castle Sq, SY8 1AY ⊘ ludlowcastle.com ⊙ 10.00–16.00 daily; adult/child £8/£3.50) Lording over the River Teme at the western end of Ludlow, this medieval castle is an arresting sight. In 1461 it became Crown property and was a royal dwelling for almost 230 years before being abandoned in

↑ Ludlow Castle. (travellight/S)

1689. Its grounds make an atmospheric spot for a picnic, and there are gorgeous views of the surrounding hills from the tower, which can be climbed with the dog for those brave enough to tackle the centuries-old stone spiral staircase.

LET'S GO

GETTING THERE

Ludlow, around 67km west of Birmingham, sits on the A49, which cuts through the centre of the Shropshire Hills all the way up to Shrewsbury to the north. The train station (Station Dr, SY8 1PY) has direct connections with Cardiff, Holyhead, Milford Haven and Carmarthen in Wales, and Manchester Piccadilly.

EATING

The Church Inn King St, Ludlow SY8 1AN thechurchinn.com noon–22.00 daily. Proper pub food from pies to mighty roast dinners served in a 14th-century inn, alongside local ales. The Ploughman's Platter includes a cracking local pork pie.

Ludlow Kitchen Bromfield SY8 2JR ludlowfarmshop.co.uk 08.00–16.00 daily. Food miles rarely get lower than at this lovely little café next door to the Clive Arms set within the Ludlow Estate. Expect seasonal produce made on this very land, such as pork sausages, bacon and eggs, and freshly baked cakes. There's even a locally roasted coffee to top it all off.

Postcard Café Church St, Clun SY7 8JW 01588 640474 10.00–17.00 Tue–Sun. Just a 10-minute drive from Bury Ditches, this is a charming stop for tea, cake or cold light lunches. While you're here, browse their vinyl collection or pick up greetings cards from local artists.

↑ Arty exploring the Ludlow Estate. (LG)

You can also stand inside the original Norman chapel and explore a warren of tiny rooms and corridors.

BURY DITCHES (Lydbury North SY7 8BD ⊘ forestryengland.uk 🐾) A 30-minute drive northwest of Ludlow takes you into the heart of the southern Shropshire Hills, and a short climb from the car park along a wooded footpath leads you up to this fantastically preserved Iron Age hill fort. It's thought a small community lived here in round, thatched huts from 500BC; today, you can see the remains of their fortifications in the distinctive ridges at the top of the mound and enjoy panoramic views of the forested Shropshire Hills. Various trails cross the hill fort and lead down into forest; there's no map and trails are unmarked, so it's best to use an OS map or similar.

CARDING MILL VALLEY AND THE LONG MYND (Church Stretton SY6 6JG ⊘ nationaltrust.org.uk) Just off the A49, 30 minutes north of Ludlow and a similar distance northeast of Bury Ditches, this 800ha National Trust-managed landscape of heather-clad hills and streams is utterly beautiful. Come to paddle or swim in the reservoir, walk on the many trails that criss-cross the undulating terrain, or simply enjoy a cuppa and a cake in the dog-friendly tea room. Livestock grazes here so it's best to keep the dog on a lead.

SLEEPING

🏠 **Clive Arms** Bromfield SY8 2JR ⊘ theclive.co.uk. Excellent dog-friendly rooms around a courtyard. Rates are room only, but guests get free tea and coffee when they eat breakfast in the next-door Ludlow Kitchen. The upscale hotel restaurant does a posh twist on ham hock with fried egg and chips for dinner and the dog's allowed in too. Don't miss a taste of the local Pinckneys Gin. *From £95/night.*

🏠 **The Feathers Hotel** 25 Bull Ring, Ludlow SY8 1AA ⊘ feathersatludlow.co.uk 🐾 2. It's small dogs only at this 17th-century hotel in Ludlow town centre, which might look ancient from the outside, but is all mod cons and contemporary décor in the bedrooms. You can drink and dine in the atmospheric bar – and the dog might even get a sausage for breakfast. *From £80/night B&B.*

🏠 **Steeple Mews Stays** Pepper Ln, Ludlow SY8 1PX ⊘ holidaycottages.co.uk 🐾 1. Three holiday homes in the heart of Ludlow, sleeping between four and six. Each has a garden or terrace and tasteful modern décor. *From £155/night.*

OTHER PRACTICALITIES

Tourist information centre Ludlow Assembly Rooms, 1 Mill St, SY8 1AZ ⊙ noon–17.00 Mon, 10.00–17.00 Tue–Sun.

Pet supplies C W A Cycles & Pet Supplies (12 Upper Galdeford, Ludlow SY8 1QD ⊘ 01584 875695 ⊙ 09.00–16.00 Mon–Sat) has food, treats, bones and accessories.

Veterinary practices Marches Veterinary Group (Coronation Ave, Ludlow SY8 1DN ⊘ 01584 877877) offers medical advice and 24-hour emergency care.

27 AN UNDERRATED FOODIE FEAST

WHERE	Rutland, East Midlands
WHEN	Year-round
HIGHLIGHTS	Splash around with watersports or visit regal stately homes, and indulge in the region's truly exceptional food and drink.

'**M**ultum in Parvo', or 'much in little', is the motto of England's smallest county, and it's right on point. Despite its small size – just 30km wide and 27km from north to south – Rutland, sitting between Leicester and Peterborough, is packed with great things to do for a long weekend. There's an enormous reservoir, Rutland Water, in the centre of the county, offering watersports, osprey spotting and walks around its perimeter, and a handful of stately homes, including Burghley House where you can walk the dog in the grounds of an opulent Elizabethan palace. Small market towns like Stamford, often ranked among the best places to live in Britain, and Oakham – a picturesque little town on the other side of the reservoir – are enjoyable diversions, with a few enticing attractions and shopping opportunities. Cavells (16 Mill St, Oakham LE15 6EA ⊘ cavells.co.uk ⊙ 09.00–17.30 Mon–Sat), for example, is a dog-friendly department store that could easily eat up a couple of hours of your time (not to mention a fair chunk of your cash).

Speaking of eating – that is the real highlight here. Dining – and drinking – in Rutland is a total treat, and the county prides itself on a smattering of award-winning restaurants; it was the only county in England without a McDonald's until November 2020, so it has long been a place of good taste. Follow

↑ Rutland Water. (Ash Oli/S)

the region's own 40km Food & Drink Trail (maps available from the Discover Rutland website, ⟨⟩ discover-rutland.co.uk) which skirts around the reservoir and dips in and out of rural villages, and you'll have yourself a delicious day out. The best way to hit the trail is by bike; on the northern side of the reservoir and right on the route, Whitwell-based Rutland Cycling (Whitwell Leisure Park, LE15 8BL ⟨⟩ rutlandcycling.com ⊙ 09.00–17.30 daily) hires out bikes, e-bikes and dog buggies.

Along the trail, don't miss Oakham's gravity-fed Grainstore Brewery, where they pair ales with pork scratchings and a homemade dipping relish (see page 122), or the nearby Hambleton Bakery (17 Gaol St, LE15 6AL ⟨⟩ hambletonbakery.co.uk ⊙ 08.00–17.00 Tue–Sat; take-away only, dogs wait outside) which won ITV's *Britain's Best Bakery* for its Rutland pippins (a sausage and Stilton pastry).

If cycling isn't your thing, you could taste your way around Rutland at one of the region's markets: Oakham Farmer's Market is held every third Saturday on Gaol St (♀ LE15 6AQ ⊙ 11.00–16.00), while Uppingham Market is every Friday (Market Pl, LE15 9QH ⊙ 08.00–16.00). Rutland Cakeaway (⟨⟩ rutlandcakeaway.co.uk ⊙ 17.00–20.30 Wed, 17.00–21.30 Fri–Sun) caters for lazy cravings and will deliver all manner of homemade cakes to your door (or hotel reception) – they'll even bake for the dog, too, if you ask in advance.

Should you need to walk off any extravagances, check out the countless footpaths that connect Rutland's towns and villages, and its lovely countryside walks – note, though, that lots of the cross-country routes will have stiles, so might not be suitable for larger dogs. A delightful 8km there-and-back from Oakham follows Oakham Canal (⟨⟩ meltonwaterways.org.uk), conveniently leading to the Garden Village Café (Rutland

Village, LE15 7QN ⏚ rutlandgardenvillage.co.uk ⊙ 09.00–16.00 Mon–Sat, 10.00–16.00 Sun) before you turn back. Alternatively, head to Barnsdale Wood (♥ LE15 8AB) on the shores of Rutland Water and walk to Whitwell (1½km each way) – it's particularly glorious in spring when the bluebells come out in force.

As it's a compact little county, you could base yourself almost anywhere in Rutland and be no more than a 40-minute drive from its furthest reaches, but the most sensible place to stop overnight is Oakham. Here, pretty roads like Dean Street and Mill Street are lined with old cottages and independent boutiques, and you've got easy access to a glut of the region's best food producers.

OAKHAM CASTLE (♥ LE15 6DR ⏚ oakhamcastle.org ⊙ 10.00–16.00 Mon & Wed–Sat 🌂) What remains of Oakham Castle, in Oakham town centre, doesn't look much like a castle at all, but it is one of the best-preserved pieces of Norman architecture in Britain. Sitting within the grounds where a Norman castle once stood, the Great Hall is a unique building with a rather unusual collection of more than 230 ceremonial horseshoes hanging on its walls. Its dramatic timber-vaulted ceiling is spectacular; look out, too, for the six well-preserved columns topped with sculptures of musicians. Pop in with the dog and you'll be able to see horseshoes donated to the county by royals and gentry throughout the ages; there's even one from Queen Elizabeth II, which looks somewhat like a toilet seat.

RUTLAND WATER (main car park, Sykes Ln, LE15 8QL ⏚ anglianwaterparks. co.uk ⊙ watersports 09.30–16.00 daily) Sitting right in the middle of Rutland, around 2km east of Oakham, this 1,250ha reservoir is often the centre of the action come summertime. Families flock to its beach (no dogs, sadly) and the water park gets busy with swimmers. For dog owners, it's all about getting out on the water, either on a sailing boat or canoe, rowboat, kayak or paddleboard (from £15, buoyancy aids included). A 36km walking trail follows the reservoir's shores, but it's best tackled in sections; the 9½km circular walk around the Hambleton Peninsula is ideal with the dog, and you can finish at the Finch's Arms (see page 122) for a drink or lunch in the bar. Due to the wildlife along the route, it's best to keep your dog on a lead, but they can run free at the Sykes Lane enclosed dog walking area next to the main car park (a 10-minute drive from Oakham).

BURGHLEY HOUSE (♥ PE9 3JY ⏚ burghley.co.uk ⊙ 07.00–18.00 daily) Just outside the lovely town of Stamford, a 25-minute drive east of Oakham, Burghley House is one of the country's most magnificent Elizabethan 'prodigy' houses. Built by William Cecil between 1555 and 1587, with parkland landscaped by Capability Brown 200 years later, the estate today is a stunning place to walk the dog. You can't go inside the house or the gardens, but access to the parkland is free and you'll get to walk right by the house's elegant domed façade. Deer roam the park, so dogs must be kept on leads.

↑ Oakham Castle. (Fotimageon/S) → Burghley House interior. (trebantos/S)

LET'S GO

GETTING THERE

Rutland is relatively easy to reach by road and rail. The A1 passes through its eastern side, while the A47, A606 and A6003 cut through the west. Oakham's centrally located train station (Station Rd, LE15 6RE) connects directly with Birmingham New Street.

EATING

✖ **The Admiral Hornblower** 64 High St, Oakham LE15 6AS ⌔ hornblowerhotel.co.uk ☺ 08.00–23.00 daily. A brilliant town-centre pub offering a higher quality of food than your average boozer: come here for fancy dinners or mammoth Sunday roasts.

✖ **Fika** 10D Mill St, Oakham LE15 6EA ⌔ fikacafe.co.uk ☺ 08.00–16.30 Mon–Fri, 09.00–16.30 Sat–Sun. Tucked down a little alleyway, this bright, airy café serves fantastic sandwiches, salads and cakes. Dogs are very welcome and will garner more fuss than their owners. There's a sister branch in Stamford (32 High St, PE9 2BB), with similar hours.

✖ **The Finch's Arms** Oakham Rd, Hambleton LE15 8TL ⌔ finchsarms.co.uk ☺ 11.00–23.00 Mon–Sat, 11.00–22.30 Sun. Ideally located on the Hambleton Peninsula, the bar here offers a welcome place to refuel with a post-walk pint or a grazing board. Main meals are more hearty and include expertly cooked Gressingham duck breast and Derbyshire steaks.

✖ **The Grainstore** Station Approach, Oakham LE15 6RA ⌔ grainstorebrewery.com ☺ noon–23.00 Mon–Fri, 09.00–23.00 Sat–Sun. You'll see Grainstore beers in pubs all over Rutland, but there's no better place to drink them than at their very own taproom. This place is famous for their enormous, utterly moreish burgers, too. Don't forget to pick up a few bottles and pork scratchings from their shop to take home.

✖ **The Kings Arms** 13 Top St, Wing LE15 8SE ⌔ thekingsarms-wing.co.uk ☺ 18.00–23.00 Tue–Thu, noon–23.00 Sat, noon–16.30 Sun. South of Rutland Water in the tiny village of Wing, this is by far the region's best pub. Owner and chef James Goss is deeply passionate about local produce and

↑ Sailing on Rutland Water (Nicola Pulham/S)

sources everything he cooks from farmers he knows. Expect to see slow-cooked beef shin, home-smoked trout and even grey squirrel (waste nothing is the motto here). Goss is also passionate about dogs – there's even a menu just for them; you could also consider the dog-friendly rooms in their Bakehouse building (from £80 room-only; dogs £10).

SLEEPING

🏠 **Hambleton Hall** Ketton Rd, Hambleton LE15 8TH ⌖ hambletonhall.com 🐾 2. Sitting on the Hambleton Peninsula, this is the place to stay if you're a real foodie: the hotel restaurant is home to England's longest-held Michelin star. Dogs can't sit with you in the dining room and shouldn't be left alone in bedrooms, but the hotel can offer dog sitting if you notify them in advance. They'll also provide special sheets if you want the dog to sleep in the bed with you. *From £210/night B&B; dogs £10/night.*

🏠 **Tom Cottage** Wing ⌖ petspyjamas.com 🐾 2. Stay just a stone's throw from The Kings Arms, the finest pub in Rutland, at this thatched cottage. It has a secure garden with a big lawn, a dining patio, and one room with its own claw-foot bathtub next to the bed. The cottage sleeps up to six people and has parking for up to two cars. *From £290/night.*

🏠 **The Wisteria** 4 Calmos St, Oakham LE15 6HW ⌖ wisteriahotel.co.uk. The most convenient hotel for exploring Oakham and one of the best-value in the region, the Wisteria has a dog-friendly bar area and supremely cosy bedrooms with double, king and super-king beds and plush carpets. *From £100/night B&B; dogs £20/stay.*

OTHER PRACTICALITIES

Tourist information centre Rutland Water Visitor Centre, Sykes Lane, Oakham LE15 8QL 🕙 10.00–17.00 daily.

Pet supplies Tails & Whiskers (38 High St, Oakham LE15 6AL ⌖ tailsnwhiskers.co.uk 🕙 09.00–17.00 daily) is a lovely little shop where you can pick up toys, essential accessories, treats and dog food.

Veterinary practices Rutland Veterinary Centre (Maresfield Rd, Oakham LE15 7WN ✆ 01572 770011) is the region's most reliable practice. It has an emergency line (✆ 01572 822399), as well as branches in Uppingham, Market Harborough and Priors Hall (see ⌖ rutlandvets.co.uk).

28 A COASTAL JAUNT WITH COUNTRYSIDE FUN

WHERE	Holkham & Wells, Norfolk
WHEN	Year-round
HIGHLIGHTS	Wild nature, big beaches and seaside fun, from seal spotting to crabbing, plus ample walking trails on a glorious country estate.

Norfolk is Britain's 'big sky country' and nowhere is that more apparent than on the sands of Holkham Beach (♀ NR23 1RG) on the north Norfolk coast. Walk through the pine forest that backs the beach and a vast golden landscape spreads out before you as you step on to the sand. This area is part of the hugely important Holkham National Nature Reserve, home to myriad seabirds, lugworms and cockles beneath the sand. It's a spectacular place to walk the dog (on the lead from April through August, to protect the ground-nesting little terns) – especially at sunrise.

Walk east along the beach and after around 45 minutes you'll come to Wells-next-the-Sea, a tiny but once important port and fishing village which in the 9th century saw the import and export of everything from grain and salt to wax and building materials. Today, it's a cheerful resort town with ample seaside activities: go crabbing on the quay (buckets and line available from most of the seafront shops), take a harbour boat tour with Wells Harbour Tours (West Quay, NR23 1AT ⊘ wellsharbourtours.com ⊙ multiple departures daily; adult/child £15/£10), or simply take up residence in one of the colourful huts that preside over the sand at this end of the beach (available to hire by the day from Pinewoods holiday park; see page 127).

↑ Beach huts, Wells. (LG)

Inland, south of the sweeping sands of this north-facing coastline, lies a flat agricultural landscape planted with rapeseed, sugar beets and malting barley – used by many local breweries to make their ales. This is all part of the Holkham Estate (Holkham Rd, NR23 1AB ⌖ holkham.co.uk ⊙ 09.00–17.00), the heart of which is a great stately home built in the Palladian style sitting within 1,200ha of parkland. Come here to walk the dog on its many trails – some up to 10km long – or hire bikes with a dog buggy attached (from £20 for 2 hrs). Dogs can go everywhere on the estate, including the tempting gift shop (pick up some Holkham-reared game dog biscuits), the Walled Garden, the exhibitions and the on-site café, meaning you can really make a day of it.

Other enjoyable excursions include Norfolk Lavender (Lynn Rd, Heacham PE31 7JE ⌖ norfolk-lavender. co.uk ⊙ 10.00–17.00 daily), just a 30-minute drive west from Holkham village, where you can walk among herb gardens and see a lavender oil distillery, or the ruined 13th-century Creake Abbey, southwest of the Holkham Estate (Burnham Rd, North Creake NR21 9LF ⌖ english-heritage.org.uk ⊙ 24hr). The gardens here are beautiful, and the neighbouring shopping complex has a farmers' market on the first Saturday of each month.

The most exciting excursion of all, though, is to Blakeney Point – a National Trust-run nature reserve of salt marshes, mudflats and sand dunes where a colony of grey seals rears around 3,000 pups each winter. For the safety and protection of the seals, you absolutely must not walk around Blakeney with the dog; instead, take one of the non-landing boat tours to see them from a safe and respectful distance.

HOLKHAM STORIES (Holkham Rd, Holkham Estate, NR23 1AB ⌖ holkham. co.uk ⊙ 10.00–16.00 daily; adult/child £5.50/£3.50 ☂) Get acquainted with the history of Holkham and its modern make-up with this engaging exhibition in

↑ Holkham Hall. (SS)

the estate's courtyard. There are historic photographs, displays on farming and food, interactive exhibits and a great table-top quiz that tests your knowledge of the local produce.

HOLKHAM WALLED GARDEN (Holkham Estate, Holkham Rd, NR23 1AB ♂ holkham.co.uk ⊙ 10.00–16.00 daily; adult/child £5.50/£3.50) One of Britain's largest walled gardens, this beautiful space comprises 2.4ha of decorative planting, vegetable patches, vines and glasshouses surrounded by a handsome red-brick wall on the Holkham Estate. In spring and summer, it's a riot of colour as the flowers bloom, and come autumn there's pumpkin carving and fig picking during the harvest season.

WELLS & WALSINGHAM LIGHT RAILWAY (Stiffkey Rd, Wells-next-the-Sea NR23 1QB ♂ wwlr.co.uk ⊙ multiple departures daily; adult/child returns £9.50/£7.50 🚂) Families will love this merry steam train experience, which bills itself as the world's smallest public railway. Connecting Wells-next-the-Sea, 2½km east of Holkham, and the lovely little village of Walsingham, 9km to the south, its steam engines chunter along the former Great Eastern Railway line, from which you might see deer, brown hares and birds of prey. The full return journey takes around an hour.

↑ Blakeney's seals basking on the sand. (Colin Seddon/S)

TEMPLE SEAL TRIPS (Morston Quay, Blakeney NR25 7BH ⌂ sealtrips.co.uk ☺ multiple departures daily; adult/child £20/£10) The safest way to see Blakeney's seals basking on the sand – up to 10,000 of them during the December breeding season – is to take one of these boat trips from Blakeney village, around 20 minutes' drive east from Holkham, round to the point. In summer, you'll spot common seals, who have their pups between June and August, while in winter grey seals come here to breed – December is an ideal time to see their gorgeous, fluffy white offspring. Seals can be curious and sometimes swim up to the boat, so keep dogs away from the edges to ensure safety for all.

LET'S GO

GETTING THERE

North Norfolk is relatively remote so be prepared for a long drive if you're coming from Cambridge or beyond – there are no motorways this far east and even a dual carriageway is hard to come by. The A148 and A1065 are the main roads that take you towards Holkham. It's not practical to come by train or bus.

EATING

✗ **Great Walsingham Barns Café** Great Walsingham NR22 6DR ⌂ walsinghamcafe.co.uk ☺ 09.00–16.00 Wed–Sun. Proper home-baked pies, quiches and scones, plus crowd-pleasers like burgers, served in a delightful little café just a short walk from Walsingham.

✗ **The Lookout** Lady Anne's Dr, Holkham NR23 1RG ⌂ holkham.co.uk ☺ 10.00–17.00 daily. Architecturally striking café behind the beach with excellent views over the marshes. The baked goods are sublime, and pre-made sandwiches and wraps are available.

✗ **Platten's** 12a The Quay, Wells-next-the-Sea NR23 1AH ⌂ plattensfishandchips.co.uk ☺ 11.30–22.00 daily. Classic fish-and-chip shop with a dog-friendly indoor seating area. Look out for the daily specials featuring the morning's catch.

SLEEPING

⌂ **Pinewoods** Beach Rd, Wells-next-the-Sea NR23 1DR ⌂ pinewoods.co.uk 🐾 **2**. Static caravans and lodges sleeping up to seven people on a picturesque holiday park right on Wells beach. *From £120/night.*

⌂ **The Victoria Inn** Park Rd, Holkham NR23 1RG ⌂ holkham.co.uk 🐾 **2**. An exceptional pub with very spacious, homely rooms just a 10-minute walk from Holkham Beach. Brilliant local beef, lamb and deer served in the dog-friendly restaurant. Guests receive a parking pass for local car parks and complimentary prosecco in the room. *From £200/night B&B, dogs £15/stay.*

OTHER PRACTICALITIES

Tourist information centre Holkham Hall, Holkham Rd, NR23 1AB ⌂ holkham.co.uk ☺ 10.00–17.00 daily.

Pet supplies Wells Pet Store (42 Staithe St, Wells-next-the-Sea NR23 1AF ☎ 01328 711161 ☺ 09.00–17.00 daily) sells all the essentials.

Veterinary practices Glaven Veterinary Practice (The Old Mill, Maryland, Wells-next-the-Sea NR23 1LY ☎ 01328 711022) offers medical advice and an emergency service.

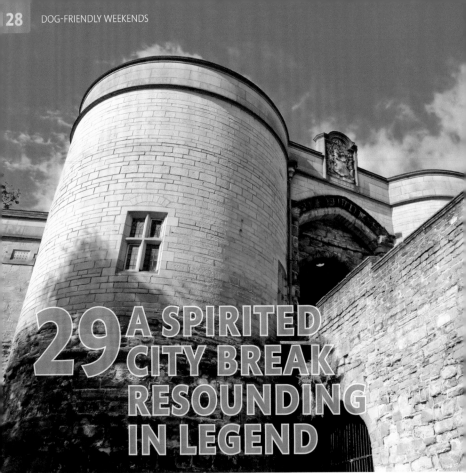

29 A SPIRITED CITY BREAK RESOUNDING IN LEGEND

WHERE	Nottingham, East Midlands
WHEN	Year-round
HIGHLIGHTS	Take lively city tours, hole up in cosy old pubs and discover the Robin Hood folklore that's characterised the city for centuries.

The Saxon town of Nottingham, once a great lace-making centre, has long been famed as the birthplace of fabled rebel Robin Hood. Today, the East Midlands city has plenty more strings to its bow, with great pubs, a thriving music scene and boutique-lined cobblestone streets in the creative Hockley and Lace Market areas – but the man in Lincoln Green tights is written into the city's DNA (and yes, there is still a sheriff in town).

Keen hikers can trek past the city's landmarks and famous forests along the 168km Robin Hood Way, which begins at the **Robin Hood statue** (Castle Rd, NG1 6AA) by **Nottingham Castle** (Lenton Rd, NG1 6EL ⊘ nottinghamcastle.org.uk ⊙ 10.00–16.00; adult/child £13/£8.50) – whose grounds are dog-friendly – and

↑ Nottingham Castle. (Jaime Pharr/S)

heads north to Sherwood Forest. A quicker way to take in Nottingham's history is with the outlaw himself, as charismatic Ezekial Bone dons his green tights to lead a **Robin Hood town tour** (Fletcher Gate, NG1 2GJ *ezekialbone.com*; adult/child £14.50/£8). Enjoy a whirlwind wander of the city's ancient sandstone caves and Old Market Square, and stop by England's oldest inn, **Ye Olde Trip to Jerusalem** (Brewhouse Yard, NG1 6AD *greeneking-pubs.co.uk* 11.00–23.00 daily). The legendary pub is built into the rocks Nottingham Castle sits upon, so it's only right to order a pint of local Castle Rock ale. It's also said to be haunted: the **Nottingham Ghost Walk** (Brewhouse Yd, NG1 6AD *thenottinghamghostwalk. co.uk*; adults/under 12s £7.50/free) starts here and is an entertaining, if spooky, way to see the city after dark.

For an excellent dog walk there's Nottingham's oldest public park, the **Arboretum** (Waverley St, NG7 4HF *nottinghamcity.gov.uk* 10.00–16.30 daily), widely believed to have been the inspiration for J M Barrie's Neverland. Head further afield, 5km west of the centre, to Elizabethan palace **Wollaton Hall** (NG8 2AE *wollatonhall.org.uk* 09.00–16.00 daily), which has plenty of roaming space and which fans of the Batman movie *The Dark Knight Rises* may recognise as Wayne Manor. A 30-minute drive beyond Nottingham lie both **Belvoir Castle** (Grantham NG32 1PE *belvoircastle.com* 10.00–16.00 daily; adult/child £12/£7), which stood in for Windsor Castle in TV's *The Crown*, and **Newstead Abbey** (Ravenshead NG15 8NA *newsteadabbey.org.uk* 10.00–16.00 daily; £6/car or £2/pedestrian), Lord Byron's former home. Dogs aren't allowed inside these historic mansions, but the gardens and grounds afford great views of the buildings. After Newstead Abbey, stop by **The Hutt** (Nottingham Rd, Ravenshead NG15 9HJ *chefandbrewer.com* 11.00–23.00 Mon–Sat, 11.00–22.30 Sun), a cosy and dog-friendly 15th-century country pub that delivers when it comes to quality British produce and Sunday roasts with all the trimmings.

LET'S GO

Nottingham train station (Carrington St, NG2 3AQ) has direct connections with London St Pancras, Skegness, Liverpool Lime Street, Leeds, Cardiff, Norwich and Birmingham New Street. The city lies 11km east of Junction 25 on the M1.

Beyond the city's excellent pubs, **Tuckwell & Co.ffee Bar** (26 Upper Parliament St, NG1 2AD *tuckwellandco.uk* 09.00–17.00 Tue–Sat) is a great stop for hot drinks and cakes. For the night, book into the central **Hart's Hotel & Kitchen** (Standard Hill, Park Row, NG1 6GN *hartsnottingham.co.uk* 2; from £190/night, dogs £10/night) which has dog-friendly garden rooms with direct access to the lawn.

Stock up on supplies at **Pets at Home** (Castle Marina Retail Park, NG7 1GX *petsathome.com* 09.00–19.00 Mon–Sat, 10.30–16.30 Sun). **Ambivet Wollaton** (11 Lambourne Dr, Wollaton, NG8 1GR 01159 829730) is a reliable vet with a 24-hour emergency line.

30 A MOUNTAIN ADVENTURE WITH MINING HERITAGE

WHERE	Snowdonia National Park, Wales
WHEN	May–Sep
HIGHLIGHTS	Scale Wales's highest peak, enjoy stunning forest walks and go glamping in the middle of an historic slate quarry.

These days, Snowdonia National Park is most famous for that towering peak – Mount Snowdon or, to give it its Welsh name, Yr Wyddfa, which juts some 1,066m into the sky at the northern end of the region. Wales's tallest mountain is supremely popular, and in summer you might just find yourself in a queue to get to the top. Thankfully, though, there are 13 other peaks in the national park that can be scaled with far fewer crowds and – arguably – more enchanting views, especially those that look on to Snowdon itself.

But the mountains are just one element of what makes Snowdonia such a thrilling destination. Deep underground in its northern stretches lies a warren of fascinating stories – this was the Welsh slate mining capital, home to the largest slate mine in the world. Today, the mining has ceased, but the remnants of

↑ Taking in Snowdonia's magnificent views. (Kath Watson/S)

the old mines still lie beneath the surface while in former industrial towns, like Blaenau Ffestiniog, great slag heaps tower above terraced miners' cottages – looming, constant memorials to the many men who lost their lives underground in the 18th and 19th centuries.

Today, the slate landscape within the national park and wider northwest Wales is a UNESCO World Heritage Site and a number of museums, immersive tours and adventure activities allow you – and in many cases, the dog too – to explore its history.

The south of Snowdonia is a little less lofty, with a handful of peaks around 914m and some lower woodland ideal for gentler walks with the dog. Out west, the park stretches towards the coastline where a handful of beaches at Barmouth and Porthmadog have year-round dog-friendly sections; at the latter, Black Rock Sands (📍 LL49 9YH) is a highlight as you can drive right on to the beach and set up camp for a day by the sea with views of the mountains behind.

Snowdonia National Park is so vast and varied it could fill an entire dog-friendly summer holiday, but if you've just got a weekend, base yourself in the north around Betws-y-Coed or the quaint riverside town of Beddgelert and you'll have the highlights on your doorstep.

NATIONAL SLATE MUSEUM (Llanberis LL55 4TY ⊘ museum.wales ⊙ 10.00–17.00 daily; free ☂) Located in Llanberis – a popular start point for hiking Mount Snowdon, around 30 minutes' drive west of Betws-y-Coed – and set within the old workshops of the now-closed Dinorwig Quarry, the National Slate Museum is a brilliant place to learn about slate mining and quarrying. See old photographs and equipment, step inside the Chief Engineer's house (someone will have to wait outside with the dog), and watch slate splitting demonstrations by a local craftsman who once worked within the quarries. There's also the Llanberis Lake Railway opposite (⊘ lake-railway.co.uk), which accepts dogs on board.

GELERT'S GRAVE WALK (Beddgelert LL55 4YA ⊘ nationaltrust.org.uk) Around 30 minutes south of Llanberis, the pretty village of Beddgelert is an idyllic little place, set on the confluence of two rivers – the Glaslyn and Colwyn – and surrounded by steep, rocky mountain slopes. It's here that the legend of Gelert, Prince Llywelyn's beloved dog, was born – a story that has a tragic end – and it's said that the dog is buried in a field just south of the village. A riverside footpath will lead you through a field of sheep towards his memorial, beneath a tree, and then to a ruined farm building where a bronze sculpture of Gelert stands guard. Keep going south along the River Glaslyn, then cross the bridge and return towards the village on the other side. The whole walk will take around 30 to 40 minutes.

FFESTINIOG RAILWAY (Harbour Station, Porthmadog LL49 9NF ⊘ festrail. co.uk ⊙ numerous departures daily; exclusive compartment for four £60, dogs £3 ☂) Snowdonia's railways were integral to slate mining in the 19th century. Before the arrival of steam, a network of rails was created in which carriages full of slate, powered by their weight and gravity, would travel down to Porthmadog before being unloaded and pulled back up empty by horses. Though now largely disused, the tracks have been kept alive by a group of passionate volunteers and a number of heritage and modern trains run along the routes. There are five different options from Porthmadog's Harbour Station (a 15-minute drive south from Beddgelert), including the Mountain Prince (3hrs), served by old steam trains, which takes you through Snowdonia's forests before opening out to spectacular mountain views. Other routes cover the tracks between Porthmadog and Beddgelert, Caernarfon, Tan-y-Bwlch and Dduallt.

COED Y BRENIN FOREST PARK (Dolgefeiliau, Ganllwyd LL40 2HZ ⊘ naturalresources.wales 🐾) Around 15km inland and a 30-minuite drive south from Porthmadog, Coed y Brenin Forest Park is a popular mountain-biking

↓ The Ffestiniog Railway leaving Porthmadog. (Jason Wells/S)

centre and also has plenty of lovely, well-marked walking trails – a favourite of which is the 7km Gain Waterfall Trail. Hiking over the steep Cefndeuddwr ridge and heading down into the valley where two rivers meet, you'll pass through mossy forest and pine woodland and see a pair of powerful waterfalls. Dogs can be off lead if under strict control, but do beware of mountain bikes crossing the trail – look out for signage. The visitor centre (☉ 09.00–1700 daily) has maps and a café that allows dogs.

LLECHWEDD SLATE & ZIP WORLD (Blaenau Ffestiniog LL41 3NB ⬦llechwedd.co.uk & ⬦zipworld.co.uk ☉09.00–17.00 daily; prices vary/attraction, dog day care from £12/dog 🐾) At one time the world's biggest slate mine, where hundreds of men worked in near-darkness for 12 hours a day, Llechwedd Slate is now an exciting attraction for the adventurous. Attractions include Deep Mine Tours, in which a guide will take you into the depths of the chambers where slate

LET'S GO

GETTING THERE

With an excellent network of A-roads, Snowdonia is relatively easy to reach and drive around. The A470 runs its length, connecting with the A55 in the north and A489 in the south. For trains, the best arrival points are Bangor (Station Rd, LL57 2DP) or Llandudno (Augusta St, LL30 2AF) – which have direct connections with Birmingham, Cardiff, Manchester and Chester – where you can get the Conwy Valley Line down to Betws-y-Coed or Blaenau Ffestiniog. Various public transport operators connect some towns within Snowdonia (check ⬦ traveline.cymru) but having your own vehicle is the best option.

EATING

🍴 **The Big Rock Cafe** Porthmadog LL49 9EU ☎ 01766 512098 ☉ 10.00–16.00 Mon & Thu–Sat. A quirky café inside an old church, serving brilliant, healthy build-your-own salad boxes. There are handmade sandwiches and fresh pastries, too.

🍴 **Hangin' Pizzeria** Betws-y-Coed LL24 0AE ⬦ hanginpizzeria.co.uk ☉ noon–20.30 daily. Really great pizzas with unusual toppings such as feta and Stilton or Welsh rarebit. They will even cook a sausage for the dog if you ask.

🍴 **Moel Siabod Cafe** Capel Curig LL24 0EL ⬦ moelsiabodcafe.co.uk ☉ 08.00–17.00 daily. A Snowdonia mountaineering institution, this casual café serves great fry ups, strong coffee and tempting cakes, plus packed lunches for day hikes.

🍴 **Peak Restaurant** Llanberis LL55 4SU ⬦ thepeakrestaurant.co.uk ☉ 18.00–20.00 Wed–Sat. A family-run restaurant serving excellent dishes such as poached haddock or Gressingham duck breast. Dogs are allowed at tables in the bar.

SLEEPING

🏠 **Llechwedd Glamping** Llechwedd LL41 3NB ⬦ llechwedd-glamping.com 🐾 3. Sitting on top of a hill overlooking a slate mine and quarry, these beautifully furnished, supremely cosy self-catering

was once blown out using gunpowder and regale you with stories of the men who worked here. Bounce Below is an underground trampoline park inside the slate caverns, and the Titan2 zip-line network will take you on an adrenaline-fuelled aerial tour of the quarry. While dogs can't join in with any of the activities, an on-site day-care facility means you can enjoy the attractions while they hang out with the Pet Stop team ($\mathscr{D}$ 07498 023993).

KNOWDONIA TOURS (∂ knowdonia.com; from £325 for a full-day tour for four) See a slightly different side of Snowdonia with local Christian Wynne, who will tailor a day tour of the region to suit your location and your tastes. His knowledge of the area is unparalleled, and he has a black book of fascinating local contacts, from artisans using ancient skills to make unique crafts, to the owners of the world's fastest RIB boat ride. He can guide you on the mountains or take you on a foodie tour of Snowdonia. He might even bring his own dogs along.

glamping tents (sleeping up to four people) are a fantastic base. *From £180/night B&B; dogs from £20/stay.*

🏠 **Palé Hall Hotel** Bala LL23 7PS ∂ relaischateaux.com 🐾 2. This grand old building, a luxurious former mine owner's summer house, is one of the few luxury hotels within Snowdonia. Set a little further away from the main attractions (it's around 45 minutes south of Betws-y-Coed) it's worth travelling to for its excellent restaurant and vast grounds ideal for dog walks. Dog gates provided if you prefer to leave them in the bathroom while you're at dinner. *From £245/night B&B; dogs from £25/night.*

🏠 **Plas Weunydd** Llechwedd LL41 3NB ∂ plasweunydd.co.uk 🐾 3. Stay overnight in the former mine owner's home, right at the entrance to Llechwedd Slate. Rooms are cosy, and those at the front of the house have great views over the mountains. *From £105/night B&B.*

🏠 **The Rocks at Plas Curig** Capel Curig LL24 0EL ∂ therockshostel.com. An exceptional hostel with mountain views from the outdoor firepit, this place is incredibly dog-friendly – thoughtful touches include metal rings for tying your dog up when taking off your boots outside or by the table when you're eating dinner. There's a huge shared kitchen; private, family and dorm rooms available. *Doubles from £60/night; dogs from £5/night.*

🏠 **The Royal Goat** Beddgelert LL55 4YE ∂ royalgoathotel.com 🐾 2. A very homely hotel in the centre of pretty Beddgelert, with a great bar where you can dine with the dog. *From £130/night B&B; dogs from £10/night.*

OTHER PRACTICALITIES

Tourist information centre Snowdonia National Park Information Centre, Betws-y-Coed LL24 0AH $\mathscr{D}$ 01690 710426 ⊙ 09.00–12.30 & 13.30–16.30 daily.

Pet supplies Canine & Co (Betws-y-Coed LL24 0AH ∂ theultimatedogshop.co.uk ⊙ 10.00–16.30 daily) stocks treats, food, toys, leads and harnesses, plus a range of cosy knitted jumpers.

Veterinary practices Vets4Pets (Menai Retail Park, Bangor LL57 4SJ $\mathscr{D}$ 01248 353175) is inside Bangor's Pets at Home and has 24-hour emergency cover.

31 A CITY BREAK STEEPED IN HISTORY

WHERE	Lincoln, East Midlands
WHEN	Year-round
HIGHLIGHTS	A Gothic cathedral and 11th-century castle in the heart of the city, plus a fun independent shopping scene and plenty of cosy pubs.

An historic city atop the aptly named Steep Hill, Lincoln has both style and substance, and – with its compact little centre – is perfect for exploring on foot with the dog. The cobblestone Cathedral Quarter is where you'll find the most enticing activities. The imposing Gothic cathedral welcomes dogs on its fascinating tours while, nearby, William the Conqueror's castle, with its history spanning almost 1,000 years, occasionally allows dogs inside for walks along its walls and tours of its Victorian prison.

Lincoln's strong independent shopping scene is a welcome distraction, too, and most of the boutiques along Bailgate and Steep Hill will let you browse with the dog by your side. Stock up on locally made beers, gins and even salad dressings at A Little Bit Of Lincolnshire (30 Steep Hill, LN2 1LU ⌖ lincolnshire. shop ⊙ 10.00–16.00 Mon–Sat), or browse the unique gifts and trinkets at Follie (83 Bailgate, LN1 3AR ⌖ follie.co.uk ⊙ Tue–Sat 10am–5pm). Quaint little cafés and coffee shops with nooks and crannies for whiling away wet afternoons will tempt you inside for cakes or homemade lunches; at dinner time, a fair

↑ Lincoln Cathedral. (Alastair Wallace/S)

few excellent old-timey pubs make for a cosy pint and a pie. With so many businesses welcoming dogs, this has got to be one of the most dog-friendly cities in Britain.

Just beyond the centre, venture to the bottom of Steep Hill and you'll find a modern shopping complex and the Brayford Pool, where dog-friendly boat trips or walks along the Foss Dyke offer another view of the city. Strike out a little further and you can take the dog to the towering monument at the International Bomber Command Centre, which sits next to a vast common perfect for a game of fetch.

Finally, outside the city limits lies a bucolic landscape ripe for long walks. Visit Doddington Hall and Gardens for on-lead strolls in an Elizabethan estate, or Hartsholme Country Park, where you could hike for days among its 80ha of grass and woodland.

LINCOLN CATHEDRAL (Minster Yard, LN2 1PY ⊘ lincolncathedral. com ⊙ 09.00–16.00 Mon–Sat, 11.30–16.00 Sun; adult/child £8/£4.80 ☂) This magnificent church was described by John Ruskin as 'out and out the most precious piece of architecture in the British Isles' and it's easy to see why. It's the façade that gets you first: the vast edifice of intricate 12th-century carving is, frankly, breathtaking, and its three 80m-high towers give the cathedral a somewhat intimidating dominance over the surrounding houses; this was once the tallest building in the world. Construction began in 1072 and it was consecrated 20 years later, but its varying architectural features tell a tale of tumultuous history including devastating fire, earthquake and ever-changing monarchs. Inside, the ornate carvings, cavernous vaulted ceilings and beautiful stained-glass windows make it a triumph and, unlike the UK's more famous cathedrals and abbeys, dogs are allowed inside – they can even join you on the floor tours included in the entry fee. Alternatively, attend a service (we recommend Evensong for peak atmosphere) and you won't pay a thing – though you will miss out on all that fascinating history imparted by the knowledgeable volunteers.

LINCOLN CASTLE (Castle Hill, LN1 3AA ⊘ lincolncastle.com ⊙ daily, dogs allowed on select days – see website; adult/child £14/£7.50, wall walk extra £10/£5.50) A Norman fortification with 1,000 years of history, sitting just across from the cathedral, Lincoln Castle opens its gates to dogs on a few days each year – usually in summer. They're allowed to roam the medieval castle walls where you'll get the best views of the city and a new perspective on the cathedral, and visit the cells of the Victorian prison which has an eerie chapel, too. Dogs are also allowed inside the Magna Carta exhibition, though not in the actual vault where the historic document is kept.

BRAYFORD BELLE BOAT TRIPS (Brayford Wharf North, LN1 1YX ⊘ lincolnboattrips.co.uk ⊙ summer daily & bank hol weekends, no booking necessary; adult/child £7/£4 ☂) A pretty little red-and-white vessel, with inside

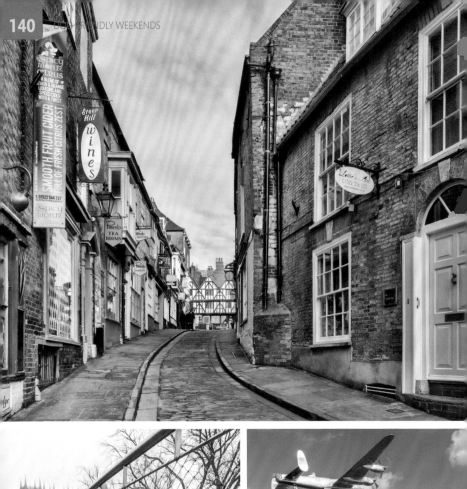

and outdoor seating, the *Brayford Belle* offers guided tours of the Fossdyke Canal that connects the Witham and Trent rivers. Live commentary from the skipper provides insight into Lincoln's past and present, and into the wildlife that lives on the water. Trips leave from Brayford Wharf North, a 1km walk southwest of the Cathedral Quarter.

INTERNATIONAL BOMBER COMMAND CENTRE (Canwick Ave, LN4 2HQ ⊘ internationalbcc.co.uk ⊙ 09.30–17.00 Tue–Sun; exhibition adult/child £9/£5.50, grounds & memorial free) Around 3km south of Lincoln city centre, a striking 31m-high rusty-red spike sits on top of a grassy hill with views back to that ever-present cathedral. As high as the wingspan of a Lancaster bomber, this is a memorial to the more than 57,000 people who gave their lives to supporting the RAF Bomber Command during World War II, and each and every name is etched on to a labyrinth of weathering steel walls surrounding the central column. It's a peaceful place and dogs are welcome at the monument, its gardens and inside the visitor centre, but they'll have to wait in the car if you want to look at the excellent immersive exhibition upstairs.

HARTSHOLME COUNTRY PARK (Skellingthorpe Rd, LN6 0EY ⊘ lincoln. gov.uk 🐾) Some 8km southwest of the city centre – a 20-minute bus ride on the 6 or S6 from Lincoln Central train station – more than 80ha of grassland, woods, lakes and landscaped Victorian gardens makes Hartsholme ideal for long walks. A play area will keep the kids happy and RSPB members run regular free guided walks for keen birders; herons, kingfishers and occasionally spotted woodpeckers can be seen. Dogs are allowed off-lead, but you will need to be respectful of the wildlife.

DODDINGTON HALL & GARDENS (Main St, Doddington LN6 4RU ⊘ doddingtonhall.com ⊙ daily; grounds free) Eleven kilometres west of the city centre, the grounds of regal Elizabethan manor Doddington Hall are a glorious setting for a dog walk. Be it spring bulbs or autumn colours, there's always something to catch your eye here, especially with the elegant red-brick house with its domes in the distance. Walks range from 20-minute strolls to 90-minute circular hikes around the entire estate (lead only); download a leaflet from their website. Dogs aren't allowed in the planted gardens, farm shop, tea room or main café, but you can grab refreshments together at the coffee shop within the bike store next door (water bowls provided), and they're welcome in the Country Clothing and Doddington at Home shops, too. The hall also has its own pet-friendly holiday cottage that sleeps ten; an option if you're planning a big weekend away.

↑ Steep Hill. (travellight/S) ← Milo walking the city walls. (LG) ↖ International Bomber Command Centre. (Jason Wells/S) ↙ Hartsholme Country Park. (Zazuneezan Abu Sarim/S)

LET'S GO

GETTING THERE

Lincoln is a fairly well-connected city, surrounded by a network of A-roads from urban centres including Nottingham, Leicester and Sheffield, and offering access from the M1. The train station (19 St Mary's St, LN5 7EW) lies south of the centre and River Witham, with direct connections to London St Pancras and King's Cross, as well as Sheffield, Peterborough, Doncaster and Grimsby. If you're coming by train, prepare for a bit of a hike up Steep Hill to get to the Cathedral Quarter.

EATING

Angel Coffee House Free School Ln, LN2 1EY ✆ 01522 567297 ⏲ 09.00–18.00 Mon–Fri, 09.00–17.00 Sat, 10.00–16.00 Sun. Bright and airy café in the newer part of town serving good coffee and pastries. They have indoor and outdoor seating.

The Duke William 44 Bailgate, LN1 3AP ⬡ dukewilliamlincoln.com ⏲ 08.00–23.00 Mon–Sat, 08.00–22.00 Sun. Excellent dishes such as bourbon-glazed rib-eye and vegan shepherd's pie are served here in a cosy – often busy – bar area.

Pimento 27 Steep Hill, LN2 1LU ⬡ pimentosteephill.com ⏲ 10.00–16.00 Wed–Sun. Lovely little vegetarian café with sofas, the ideal spot for a long, leisurely cooked breakfast. The teacakes are divine, too.

Sanctuary in the Bail 82 Bailgate, LN1 3AR ⬡ sanctuarycafelincoln.co.uk ⏲ 10.00–17.00 daily. A gift-shop-cum-café serving simple lunches from homemade soups to jacket potatoes. The tightly packed tables make it better for small dogs.

Wig & Mitre 32 Steep Hill, LN2 1LU ⬡ wigandmitre.com ⏲ 10.00–22.00 Tue–Fri, 09.00–23.00 Sat, 09.00–21.00 Sun. Traditional English pub with great ales on draught and a spacious bar area for dining with dogs. Don't miss the Lincolnshire sausages.

SLEEPING

Belfry Lodge Thorpe Park Lodges, Middle Ln, LN6 9AJ ⬡ sykescottages.co.uk 🐾 1. A pretty little wood cabin in a holiday park, Belfry Lodge is around 10km southwest of Lincoln. It sleeps four and has its own hot tub and underfloor heating. *From £857/week.*

Field View Escape Potterhanworth Booths LN4 2AU ⬡ caninecottages.co.uk 🐾 1. Just 10km southeast of the city centre and with easy access to the Lincolnshire Wolds, this lovely rural self-catering bolthole (sleeping four) even has an outdoor hot tub for post-walk soaks. *From £490/week.*

Tower Hotel 38 Westgate, LN1 3BD ⬡ towerhotellincoln.co.uk 🐾 2. Next to the castle, this is a charming boutique property with airy rooms, a suntrap garden and a restaurant and bar serving brilliant food. Dogs are welcome in the bar for meals; head next door to Wickham Gardens for essential toilet trips. *From £105/night B&B; dogs from £15/stay.*

White Hart Hotel Bailgate, LN1 3AR ⬡ whitehartlincoln.co.uk 🐾 2. Right in the historic quarter of Lincoln, the White Hart Hotel is a comfy hideaway from the bustle of town. With large rooms, there's plenty of space for the dog bed and pets are allowed to join you for all meals in the bar area next to the lobby. Some rooms have views of the cathedral. Dog biscuits are offered on arrival; the lawns around the cathedral are your best bet for your pet's late-night loo trips. *From £95/night B&B; dogs from £10/stay.*

OTHER PRACTICALITIES

Tourist information centre 9 Castle Hill, LN1 3AA ✆ 01522 545458 ⊙ 10.00–17.00 Mon– Sat, 10.30–16.00 Sun.

Pet supplies Wilkinson's (Waterside S, LN5 7EU ⊙ 09.00–17.00 Mon–Sat, 10.30–16.30 Sun) stocks some pet food and treats, and Pets at Home (⊘ petsathome.com) has two big stores (both 10.00–20.00 Mon–Sat, 10.00–16.00 Sun): Tritton Rd (♀ LN6 7AD) is closest to town, or there's the Carlton Centre to the north (♀ LN2 4UX).

Veterinary practices Lincvet (✆ 01522 534841; emergency ✆ 01522 262582) has three branches around the city (43 Friars Ln, LN2 5AL; Birchwood Neighbourhood Shopping Centre, LN6 0QQ; 270 Wragby Rd, LN2 4PX). The Tritton Road Pets at Home (see left) also has an in-house veterinary practice (✆ 01522 542781).

↑ Doddington Hall Estate. (Fotimageon/S)

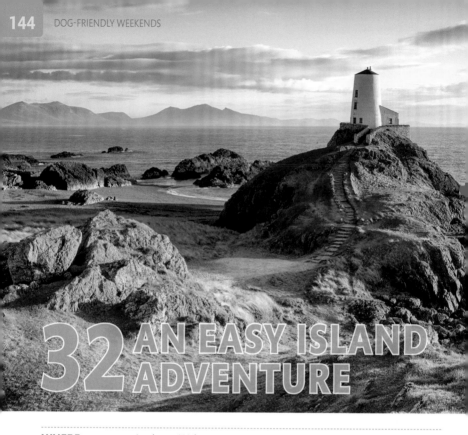

32 AN EASY ISLAND ADVENTURE

WHERE	Anglesey, Wales
WHEN	May–Sep
HIGHLIGHTS	Dreamy sandy beaches, fine fortresses and glorious seafood.

Hands down, Anglesey – a flattish island perched on the cusp of the northwest Welsh coastline, measuring just 45km by 33km – has some of the best views in Wales. Not that it's got particularly dramatic scenery of its own, but from its fringes you can gaze back to the mainland to see some of the country's finest natural terrain.

Standing on the sands of Llanddwyn Beach, for example, you'll get glorious views of the stunning Llŷn Peninsula to the south. From the lawns of the Plas Newydd country estate, look eastwards and on a clear day the mighty mountains of Snowdonia puncture blue skies. And on the western tip of Anglesey you can head out across Holyhead Island to see South Stack lighthouse – one of the greatest sunset-watching spots in Britain.

There's plenty to love about Anglesey itself, too. Its main town, Beaumaris, in the east, is a charming little place to spend a day or two pottering in shops and watching boats go by from the pier; around 35km to the west, Rhosneigr is a well-heeled base for beach breaks and brilliant seafood, including some piquant oysters pulled right from the Menai Strait. You could spend a week on the island enjoying its dog-friendly beaches and great walking territory, but it's perfectly possible to cherry-pick a handful of sights to see over a weekend.

↑ Anglesey. (Helen Hotson/S)

BEAUMARIS CASTLE (Castle St, LL58 8AP ⬡cadw.gov.wales ⊙ 10.00–17.00 daily; adult/child £6.90/£4.85) Less a castle ruin and more an unfinished fortress, Beaumaris Castle was supposed to be the most spectacular in Wales. That was Edward I's plan, anyway, until Scotland began to cause trouble up north and cash started to dry up. Today, you can explore its incomplete remains; dogs are allowed around the grounds and on all ground-floor spaces.

PUFFIN ISLAND BOAT TRIPS (Beaumaris Pier, LL58 8BS ⬡seacoastsafaris. co.uk ⊙09.30–15.00 daily; adult/child £16/£12) Despite its name, Puffin Island, at the northeastern end of the Menai Strait, just beyond Penmon Point (around 7km northeast of Beaumaris), doesn't have many puffins at all. It once hosted thousands, but stowaway rats decimated the population after a shipwreck in the 1800s. There's still plenty to see, though, including Atlantic grey seals, cormorants and green-tinged shags. With a jovial commentary from its skippers, Seacoast Safaris cruises make a great afternoon out, with dogs of all sizes welcome on board; boats depart from just beyond their ticket office on Beaumaris Pier.

PLAS NEWYDD (Ffordd Brynsiencyn, Llanfairpwllgwyngyll LL61 6DQ ⬡nationaltrust.org.uk ⊙ 10.30–17.00 daily; adult/child £10/£5) One of the best and most charming places to see red squirrels on Anglesey, the Plas Newydd estate offers wildlife spotting, dog walking and a little culture all in one place. The property, once the seat of the marquesses of Anglesey, was built in the late

↑ Beaumaris Castle. (LG)

18th century by James Wyatt in his typical Neoclassical style and sits a 20-minute drive south of Beaumaris on the Menai Strait. Walk through its 69ha of gardens and woodland, passing majestic, 100-year-old Monterey cypresses and aromatic eucalyptus trees, and through wild-flower meadows in summer. Dogs are allowed in the on-site café, too.

LET'S GO

GETTING THERE

Anglesey might be an island but, connected to the mainland by two bridges accessed via the A55 and A487, it's relatively easy to reach. Direct trains connect Cardiff to the stations at Holyhead (London Rd, LL65 2NE) and Bangor (Station Rd, LL57 2DP) on the mainland. From London you'll need to change at Crewe or Warrington Bank Quay. The hourly 58 bus runs from Bangor station to Beaumaris, and the 25 bus travels from Holyhead to Rhosneigr (both trips approx. 35 mins). Driving is the best way to get around the island.

EATING

✕ **The Oyster Catcher** Maelog Lake, Rhosneigr LL64 5JP ⬀ oystercatcheranglesey.co.uk ⏱ 10.00–22.00 Mon–Sat, noon–20.00 Sun.

With its large terrace overlooking the dunes, this huge, upmarket restaurant has the best views in Anglesey. Order local crab, Menai Strait oysters or surf and turf, and wash it down with Welsh gin or beer. There's a take-out shack downstairs.

✕ **Red Boat Ice Cream Parlour** 34 Castle St, Beaumaris LL58 8BB ⬀ redboatgelato.co.uk ⏱ 10.00–19.00 daily. Superbly creamy and moreish, flavours here range from classic vanilla and salted caramel to bara brith.

✕ **The Ship Inn** Red Wharf Bay LL75 8RJ ⬀ shipinnredwharfbay.co.uk ⏱ noon–20.00 daily. On Anglesey's north coast, a 20-minute drive north of Beaumaris, the Ship Inn has a prime location on the bay. Spend time on the dog-friendly beach outside, then relax on the pub's outdoor benches with a pint of local ale and a seafood chowder.

↑ Llydan Beach. (Mark Andrew Photography/S)

NEWBOROUGH WARREN NATURE RESERVE & FOREST

(Newborough Warren Car Park, LL61 6SG ⌂ naturalresources.wales 🐾) On a sunny day you could be forgiven for imagining you were hiking in the Mediterranean while exploring Newborough Warren, thanks to its forest of lanky Corsican pines and the soft-sand beach with tall dunes worthy of any Spanish costa. On the southern tip of Anglesey, around 20 minutes' drive from Plas Newydd, this is wonderful walking territory – especially as dogs with good recall are safe off-lead – and the beach is dog-friendly year-round. Park at the main Newborough Warren car park or leave your vehicle 4km north at Malltraeth car park (◉ LL62 5AU) from where you can enjoy an hour-long stroll through woodland down to the beach.

LLYDAN BEACH (◉ LL64 5JP 🐾) Most of Anglesey's beaches are dog-friendly year-round but this one, on the west side of the island, 30 minutes by car from Newborough, is particularly good – not least because the exceptional Oyster Catcher restaurant (see page 146) sits behind its dunes. South of Rhosneigr and a touch smaller than the town's northern beach, Llydan is usually a little quieter and thus perfect for games of fetch or paddles with the dog. Enjoyable walks among the dunes offer brilliant views along the coast.

SLEEPING

🏠 **The Bulkeley Hotel** 19 Castle St, Beaumaris LL58 8AW ⌂ bulkeleyhotel.co.uk. An unmissable hotel on Beaumaris seafront, opposite the pier, this vast Georgian property is a great base. Dogs are allowed in all rooms except the four-poster suites, and there's a dog-friendly dining area for meals. *From £80/night B&B; dogs from £15.*

🏕 **Penrhos Caravan and Motorhome Club Site** Benllech LL78 7JH ⌂ caravanclub.co.uk. With pitches for tents and travellers with wheels, this site in northeast Anglesey (a 20-minute drive from Beaumaris) is very dog-friendly: there are hooks for tying up dogs outside the facilities blocks and reception, water bowls throughout, and an enclosed field where they can run off-lead. *From £16.50/night.*

🏠 **Sandy Mount House** High St, Rhosneigr LL64 5UX ⌂ sandymounthouse.co.uk 🐾 2. In the heart of Rhosneigr and channelling some serious Hamptons beach house vibes, this is Anglesey's swishest place to stay. Rooms are bright and airy, the food in the restaurant is excellent, and dogs can join you for all meals in the bar area. *From £105/night B&B; dogs from £15/night each.*

OTHER PRACTICALITIES

Tourist information centre Town Hall, Beaumaris LL58 8AP ⌂ visitanglesey.co.uk ◷ 10.00–16.00 daily.

Pet supplies Pip's Pet Supplies (Benllech ◉ LL74 8TE & Menai Bridge, 6 Bridge St, LL59 5DW ⌂ pipspetsupplies.co.uk ◷ both 09.00–16.00 Mon–Sat) sells treats and food.

Veterinary practices Bodrwnsiwn Vets (Menai Bridge, LL59 5RW ✆ 01248 716617) takes appointments and has an emergency line (✆ 01407 720800).

33 AN ADVENTURE ON - & IN - THE ROCKS

WHERE   The southern Peak District, Derbyshire
WHEN   May–Sep
HIGHLIGHTS   Delving deep into cavernous rocks before heading up high to easy-to-reach viewpoints.

Sandwiched between Manchester and Sheffield and formed over 350 million years ago, the Peak District's distinctive landscape of craggy cliffs, boulder-strewn heathland, precipitous ridges and rolling dales was designated the UK's first national park in 1951. Don't be fooled by the name: there are no real peaks here, so you won't be climbing mountains, but there's still plenty to entertain the avid walker with riverside footpaths and well-trodden trails that lead to panoramic views of an endless, rich green landscape.

Beneath the grassy grazing fields fractured by drystone walls and the heather-clad moors, which sing with colour in late summer and autumn, lies a bed of rocks that have been instrumental in the region's

↑ Winnats Pass. (christographerowens/S)

history. In the southeast section of the national park, known as the Derbyshire Dales, you'll find the gritstone outcrops that proved so essential in the 18th- and 19th-century milling industry – the coarse stone was used to create millstones for grinding flour, and now hundreds of these spherical structures are scattered around the region. They even make up the national park authority's logo.

Further north, around the tiny village of Castleton, tucked beneath the dramatic winding Winnats Pass and 517m-high Mam Tor, it's Blue John that has made the region a small fortune. A mineral, not a man, Blue John is a semi-precious stone run through with yellow and blue or purple bands. Particularly popular in the 19th century, when it was used to create jewellery and ornamental objects, Blue John was mined by eagle-eyed craftsmen; today a network of caves beneath the rippling landscape make for a fascinating trip underground to see it in situ. The village's gift shops (all of which let you browse with the dog) are packed with items made from this rare, brindled stone.

Castleton makes an excellent base, with plenty of distractions nearby for a weekend break with the dog. Bases in the Derbyshire Dales include the likes of Matlock and Bakewell – where it's almost impossible to leave without trying one of the famous iced jam and almond tarts. This area is full of kid-friendly attractions, adventure aplenty – from subterranean explorations or elevated adventures on the likes of Froggatt Edge or Curbar Gap – plus a few pleasing little towns and villages for an afternoon of pottering.

There's another crop of family-friendly attractions slightly further south, just beyond the park's southeastern edge. Here, the Crich Tramway Village promises fun rides on old-world transport, while the Heights of Abraham cable car means the entire family can make it to the top of the hill that overlooks River Derwent. An engaging mining museum just five minutes south by car is another excellent diversion, too.

TREAK CLIFF CAVERN (Buxton Rd, Castleton S33 8WP ⌂ bluejohnstone. com ⊙ 10.00–17.00 daily; adult/child £13/£7.50 ☂) Peak District Blue John has been mined here, in the hills above Castleton, since the 18th century, and the tradition continues today, albeit on a smaller scale. You can explore the mine, now in the hands of the Turner family, on excellent self-guided audio tours: as well as the famous Blue John stone itself, you'll see jagged stalactite formations and you might even spot a rare orb-weaver spider.

SPEEDWELL CAVERN (Winnats Pass, Castleton S33 8WA ⌂ speedwellcavern. co.uk ⊙ 10.00–16.15 daily; adult/child £16/£9 ☂) At the foot of the winding Winnats lies a network of underground rivers and caverns. Descend the 106 steps into the Speedwell Cavern and board the guided boat tour and you'll cruise through cathedral-like caves and narrow tunnels, all created by a brave team of 18th-century miners 200m below ground. The highlight is the Bottomless Pit, a seemingly endless underground lake which sits in a vast, echoing chamber. It's not suitable for dogs larger than a Labrador, or anyone afraid of small spaces and the dark. Nearby, sister attraction Peak Cavern is also dog-friendly and hosts concerts throughout the year.

FROGGATT EDGE (Haywood car park, Grindleford S32 2HX) You don't have to be a hill walker to enjoy views over the Derbyshire Dales. Around 20 minutes southeast of Castleton you can park at the National Trust's Haywood car park and take the footpath that leads to the Froggatt Edge escarpment, which looms 125m above a lush green valley below. After a very short but steep dip down to a small stream and up the other side, there's a pleasant 10km there-and-back trail to Curbar Gap, with spectacular views of the villages and winding river below. Keep the dog on a lead – there's a mighty drop over the edge of the cliff.

CHATSWORTH (♀ DE45 1PP ⌂ chatsworth.org ⊙ 10.30–17.00 daily; gardens adult/child £14/£7.50; house & garden adult/child £26/£15) Perhaps one of the most famous stately homes in Britain, Chatsworth, around 10km south of Froggatt Edge, has been used as a filming location in the likes of *Peaky Blinders*, *Pride*

and Prejudice and the 1998 film *The Duchess*. The estate has been passed down through the Cavendish family for 16 generations – the house is pure opulence, but you'll have to leave the dog with a travel companion if you want to head inside. You can take in the elegant Baroque façade, however, while promenading in the gardens – wander down the tree-lined avenues, check out the 300-year-old Cascade water feature, and don't miss the maze. There's dog-friendly seating in the Carriage House Café, dogs are allowed in the gift shop, and water bowls are provided outside the toilet block. Bear in mind that cattle graze throughout the estate, so be sure to keep your pet on a short lead.

For gorgeous views from afar, walk or drive 3km south – park in Calton Lees car park (♥ DE4 2NX) – and wander around the Deer Park to soak up romantic views over this behemoth of a house and its gardens.

HEIGHTS OF ABRAHAM (Matlock Bath DE4 3NT ⊘ heightsofabraham. com ☉ 10.00–17.00 daily; adult/child £21/£14) Just south of the national park, around 20 minutes south of Chatsworth, the Heights of Abraham cable car is ideal for those with older dogs who can't walk so far or families with young children. Providing a means of scaling the 336m-high Masson Hill and offering sweeping views over the Derwent Valley, the cable car is just the beginning of the attraction here, though – there are also caves to descend into, fossil exhibitions, and towers to climb. Dogs can't enter the caves, but one of you can take your pet for a stroll on the 'Waggy Tails Trail' and you'll all end up at the cavern exit around the same time.

PEAK DISTRICT MINING MUSEUM (Matlock Bath DE4 3NR ⊘ peakdistrictleadminingmuseum.co.uk ☉ 11.00–16.00 daily; adult/child £10/£6 👕) Mining was big business in the Peak District and this museum, 1km south of the Heights of Abraham, is a brilliant place to learn more. Take a guided tour of the 1920s-era Temple Mine (dogs are welcome, providing it's not overly busy), go panning for gold minerals, and see thousands of examples of precious and semi-precious stones in the museum.

CRICH TRAMWAY VILLAGE (Crich DE4 5DP ⊘ tramway.co.uk ☉ 10.00– 16.30 Mon–Fri, 10.00–17.30 Sat–Sun; adult/child £19/£16.50 👕) For a proper blast from the past, just a 15-minute drive southeast of the mining museum, hop on the vintage trams that trundle along the tracks at Crich's open-air museum. Your ticket price includes unlimited journeys on the trams, plus access to woodland walks, lead mining displays and a period-style village with buildings rescued from across Derbyshire, including the old Red Lion Pub and a vintage sweet shop. Dogs can join you everywhere except inside the café and play area.

↑ The Heights of Abraham. (loocmill/S) ← Crich Tramway Village. (Rodney Hutchinson/S)

LET'S GO

GETTING THERE

Sandwiched between the M1 and the M6, the Peak District is easy to reach from north and south, and a network of A-roads makes it simple to get around. Generally, having your own vehicle is best but car-free trips are possible around Castleton with the Hope Valley Explorer service (⌖ peakdistrict.gov); take a train to Edale (Mary's Ln, S33 7ZN), which has direct connections to Sheffield and Manchester, and then hop on a Hope Valley Explorer bus for the 20-minute drive to the village.

EATING

✕ **The Devonshire Arms** Beeley DE4 2NZ ⌖ devonshirehotels.co.uk ⏲ 08.00–22.00 Mon–Sat, noon–21.00 Sun. With its creative starters and beautifully executed mains – the lamb is a highlight – this pub, on the Chatsworth Estate, around 3km south of the house, is worth seeking out for an evening meal. Request a table by the fire for cosy winter nights. Don't want to leave? There are dog-friendly rooms, too (£149/night, dogs £10/night).

✕ **The Grouse Inn** Longshaw S11 7TZ ⌖ thegrouseinn-froggatt.co.uk ⏲ noon–14.30 & 18.00–21.00 Mon–Fri, noon–21.00 Sat, noon–20.00 Sun. A simple pub near Froggatt Edge, serving comfort food including steak pies and battered scampi. Sit outside when the weather's good for views over rolling pasture.

✕ **Ye Olde Cheshire Cheese Inn** How Ln, Castleton S33 8WJ ⌖ cheshirecheeseinn.co.uk ⏲ 09.00–18.00 daily. Peak Ales on draught and enormous portions make this the best pub for filling up in Castleton. There's a good beer garden for sunny days.

↑ Mam Tor. (Pajor Pawel/S)

SLEEPING

Caravan & Motorhome Club Castleton Castleton Rd, Castleton S33 8WB caravanclub.co.uk. With its own dog walk on site and plenty of places to tie your pet up outside the facilities blocks, this is the most dog-friendly caravan site (campervans and motorhomes welcome; no tent pitches) in the Castleton area. Help yourself to mint, basil and more from the communal herb garden. *From £15/night*.

Landal Darwin Forest Matlock DE4 5PL darwinforest.co.uk **2**. Ideal for a self-catering family break, this holiday park has enough excellent facilities to keep you busy for a week at least. Dog-friendly accommodation is in smart lodges amid a pine forest, sleeping up to eight people and some with hot tubs. There's catering on site, mini golf and excellent woodland walks, and the spa is welcome after a day's walking. *From £110/night; dogs from £30/stay*.

Monsal Head Hotel & Stable Bar Monsal Trail, Bakewell DE45 1NL monsalhead.com **2**. Right by the limestone peak of Monsal Head, around 5km northwest of Bakewell, with views over the trail, this simple pub with rooms is a homely place to stay, and has the most atmospheric old bar in the area, with a sloping flagstone floor and stables converted to seating booths. *From £140/night B&B; dogs £10/night*.

OTHER PRACTICALITIES

Tourist information centre Bridge St, DE45 1DS peakdistrict.gov.uk 09.30–17.00 daily.

Pet supplies Barks & Co (1 Portland Sq, Bakewell DE45 1HA barksandco.co.uk 10.00–16.00 daily) sells accessories, treats and some food, including a homemade 'Barkwell Tart'.

Veterinary practices Bakewell Veterinary Clinic (Mill St, DE45 1DX 01629 812744) is a reliable practice with an out-of-hours service.

34 A CITY BREAK WITH INDUSTRIAL HERITAGE & FANTASTIC FOOD

WHERE	Liverpool, Merseyside
WHEN	Year-round
HIGHLIGHTS	Paddleboarding trips and city skyline cruises will entertain by day, while fabulous food and fancy wine bars make for great nights out.

This dynamic northern city, sitting on the banks of the River Mersey just before it empties out into the Irish Sea, has a rich social and industrial history, and a musical heritage that has woven its way into the fabric of modern culture. For dog owners, many of the key sights – including the Beatles Story and Tate Liverpool – are, unfortunately, off-limits, though Dave Callender (liverpoolanimalminding.co.uk) can entertain dogs for a day if need be – but you can still experience Liverpool's cheeky charm with the dog by your side.

Start at **Pier Head** (L3 1DP), where Liverpool's architectural wonders meet the banks of the Mersey, with the gargantuan granite **Royal Liver Building** at its centre and the much-photographed **Beatles statue** nearby. From here, you can take a guided **Mersey Ferries Explorer Cruise** (L3 1DP merseyferries.co.uk;

↑ Statue of The Beatles on the banks of the Mersey. (cowardlion/S)

adult/child £11/£7 🌂) around the waterfront, or stroll 500m south towards the **Royal Albert Dock** to see the handsome 19th-century red-brick warehouses that changed industry in Liverpool forever – the development of these buildings, and the hydraulic cranes that came with them, made this one of the most important cities in Britain.

Alternatively, explore the Royal Albert Dock area on a paddle board with **Liverpool SUP Co** (⊘ liverpoolsupco.co.uk; from £25), who provide buoyancy aids for you and the dog. Back on land, head 1km east into the **Baltic Triangle**, the former industrial area that's now an alternative hub for artisans, breweries and independent shops and bars. **The Baltic Market** (107 Stanhope St, L8 5RE ⊘ balticmarket.co.uk) food court is the culinary highlight, though best avoided by dog-owners on busy weekend evenings. Around 500m north, **Sugar and Dice Boardgame Café** (33 Cornhill, L1 8DP ⊘ sugaranddice.co.uk ⊘ 14.00–22.00 Mon & Wed–Fri, noon–22.00 Sat, 13.00–19.00 Sun) invites you to while away an afternoon with more than 100 games.

A 15-minute walk northeast of the Baltic Market is the **Georgian Quarter** – the best neighbourhood for a dog-friendly night out. Make a beeline for its leafy squares, lined with elegant townhouses, to find posh wine bars like **Bunch** (50 Berry St, L1 4JQ ⊘ bunchwinebar.co.uk ⊘ 08.00–22.00 Thu–Sat, 15.00–22.00 Sun) or to dine in some of the city's top restaurants.

Your second day in Liverpool could easily be spent touring more food and drink hotspots, like **Duke Street Market** (46 Duke St, L1 5AS ⊘ dukestreetmarket. com ⊘ noon–22.00 Wed–Sun), but a trip to **Crosby Beach** (♀ L22 8QA 🐾), 11km north, shouldn't be missed; dogs can run off-lead year-round amid Antony Gormley's eerie *Another Place* statues embedded in the sand.

LET'S GO

Liverpool Lime Street (Lime St, L1 1JD) has excellent rail connections to Manchester, London and Newcastle, and the city is well served by the M6, M62 and M58.

The Pen Factory (13 Hope St, L1 9BQ ⊘ penfactory.co.uk ⊘ 11.00–23.00 Wed–Sat, 10.30–18.00 Sun), serves standout small plates like tempura kale and cured trout, while **Chapters of Us** (44 Simpson St, L1 0AX ⊘ chaptersofus.co.uk ⊘ 09.00–18.00 Mon–Wed, 10.00–22.00 Thu–Sat) offers sharing boards for just £1 when ordered with a beer or wine.

The top stay is **Hope Street Hotel** (40 Hope St, L1 9DA ⊘ hopestreethotel.co.uk 🐾 2; from £105/night, dogs £15/night) in the Georgian Quarter; dogs are welcome in the restaurant. A good option midweek (avoiding the rowdy weekend crowds), **Aloft** (1 N John St, L2 5QW ⊘ marriott.com 🐾 1; from £79/night) has spacious modern rooms. Liverpool has a **Pets at Home** (Edge Ln, L13 1EW ⊘ petsathome.com ⊘ 09.00–19.00 Mon–Sat, 11.00–17.00 Sun); **Vets4Pets** (8 Broad Green Rd, L13 5SG ☎ 01512 520000) offers medical advice.

35 A SLOW ESCAPE TO A YORKSHIRE MARKET TOWN

WHERE	Beverley, East Yorkshire
WHEN	Year-round
HIGHLIGHTS	Great pubs, a fantastic Saturday market and brilliant local-led walking tours.

Beverley had its heyday in the Georgian period when it was a fashionable little market town on the outskirts of Hull. Today, the 18th- and 19th-century architecture prevails, as does its chic reputation – Beverley remains a smart market town with inviting shopping arcades and plentiful pubs. Add a huge, famous minster and a busy **Saturday market** (📍 HU17 8EA ⊙ 09.00–16.00) and you've got a pleasing weekend break.

First port of call is the majestic **Beverley Minster** (38 Highgate, HU17 0DN ⌂ beverleyminster.org.uk ⊙ 10.00–16.00 Mon–Sat, noon–16.00 Sun; free), at the

↑ Beverley. (Daniel J. Rao/S)

southern end of town. While dogs aren't allowed inside, it's an arresting building when viewed from the gardens around Minster Yard; take it in turns to head indoors if you're keen to see it in all its vaulted glory.

From here, you could wander aimlessly through the town centre and across its Market Square, admiring the timber-framed buildings and the medieval gate on North Bar Within, but a much better way to explore is on a walking tour with passionate local expert **Paul Schofield** (⌂ tourhull.com; from £50). He'll take you back to when St John of Beverley founded a monastery here, walking you through the town's history and peppering it with unusual and entertaining stories.

Beverley has so many fantastic pubs that you couldn't visit them all in a single weekend. The **White Horse Inn** (22 Hengate, HU17 8BN ☎ 01482 861973 ⊙ 11.00–23.00 Mon–Sat, noon–22.30 Sun) is one of the most enticing, with cosy nooks next to roaring fires and a vast selection of Samuel Smith's ales on draught. The **Chequers Micropub** (15 Swabys Yard, HU17 9BZ (☎ 0796 422 7906 ⊙ 14.00–22.00 daily) offers beers from the most exciting breweries from East Yorkshire and beyond, while the Sunday roast at the **Dog & Duck** (33 Ladygate, HU17 8BH ☎ 01482 862419 ⊙ 11.00–16.00 Mon–Thu, 11.00–23.00 Fri–Sat, noon–23.00 Sun) is legendary across town. Any one of these pubs makes an enjoyable stop-off after a long walk on the **Beverley Westwood** (Walkington Rd, HU17 8RQ), a vast green space just 500m west of the centre.

If you're here in spring or summer, be sure to take a day trip to **Bempton Cliffs** (♥ YO15 1JF ⌂ rspb.org.uk ⊙ dawn–dusk daily; adult/child £6/£3), an hour's drive from Beverley, where half a million seabirds nest between April and July, including puffins, guillemots and gannets. Alternatively, you could spend a day in **Hull** – just 15 minutes away by train or a 20-minute drive – where yet more historic pubs and a pretty old town awaits.

LET'S GO

Beverley is easily reached via the A1035 or the A164. The train station (Station Sq, HU17 0AS) offers good connections from Hull, Scarborough, Sheffield and York.

For a great dinner, don't miss the steaks and pizzas at **The King's Head** (38 Market Pl, HU17 9AH ⌂ kingsheadpubbeverley.com ⊙ 11.30–23.00 Mon–Thu, 11.30–midnight Fri–Sat, noon–22.30 Sun). **The Windmill Inn** (53 Lairgate, HU17 8ET ⌂ thewindmillinn.co.uk; from £40/night) is a lovely B&B with an Indian street-food restaurant; for self-catering, **Dragonfly Cottage** (Keldgate, HU17 8HY ⌂ petspyjamas.com 🐾 2; from £200/night) sleeps four and has a delightful, enclosed patio garden.

The Beverley Pet Shop (Unit C, Mill Lane Business Park, HU17 9DH ⊙ 09.00–17.00 Mon–Sat, 10.00–14.00 Sun) sells supplies while **Vets4Pets** (112 Flemingate, HU17 0NY ☎ 01482 870483) provides medical help.

36 ART MEETS NATURE IN THE YORKSHIRE DALES

WHERE	Nidderdale AONB, North Yorkshire
WHEN	Mar–Sep
HIGHLIGHTS	Classic Dales scenery meets unusual sculptures, both natural and manmade.

Following the winding River Nidd, the Nidderdale Area of Outstanding Natural Beauty is one of the Yorkshire Dales' most spectacular landscapes. On the eastern edge of the national park, it encompasses everything you'd want from a Dales adventure – fantastic walking routes, including the 85km-long Nidderdale Way, undulating hills peppered with grazing sheep and drystone walls, and a smattering of pretty towns and villages to stop in for tea, cake or evenings in cosy old pubs.

But it has a few surprises up its sleeve, too. The spectacular Himalayan Sculpture Garden offers artistic inspiration amid beautiful woodland plantings, while the National Trust's Brimham Rocks is a truly otherworldly landscape of bizarre geological formations – a different kind of sculpture, created by mother nature. Add a UNESCO World Heritage Site at Fountains Abbey, delightful market towns like Pateley Bridge in the centre of the AONB, and Ripon, just east of it – where gift shops and boutiques will welcome you and your pet, and cafés and restaurants will feed you both well – and there's a spectacular weekend to be had. Pateley Bridge makes a central base, but even from the edges of the AONB you're rarely more than a 45-minute drive from the highlights.

BRIMHAM ROCKS (Brimham Moor Rd, Summerbridge HG3 4DW ⌀nationaltrust.org.uk) Around 100 million years before the time of the dinosaurs,

↑ The Yorkshire Dales National Park. (Coatesy/S)

the landscape where Brimham Rocks stand now – a 10-minute drive east of Pateley Bridge – was part of an enormous river. Carved by water and wind over the next 320 million years, the geological formations you see today – a collection of what look like manmade cairns, sculpted by nature – are really rather ethereal, especially early in the morning when you might just find yourself alone among them. There are a number of trails from the car park and occasional guided walks (check website).

FOUNTAINS ABBEY (Fountains, Ripon HG4 3DY ⌀ nationaltrust.org.uk ⊙ 10.00–18.30 daily; adult/child £17/£8.50) One of the first places in the UK to be awarded UNESCO World Heritage status, Fountains Abbey and its Studley Royal Water Garden has been recognised as a 'masterpiece of human creative genius'. It's the landscape that surrounds the huge 10th-century Cistercian abbey ruin, just 15 minutes' drive east of Brimham Rocks, that has garnered such accolades, thanks to the curving waterways, perfectly manicured lawns and glassy lakes, all designed in the 18th century. Come to promenade around its pretty temples and walk through the Studley Royal Park, where red, fallow and sika deer roam wild.

HIMALAYAN GARDEN & SCULPTURE PARK (Hutts Lane, Grewelthorpe HG4 3DA ⌀ himalayangarden.com ⊙ 10.00–16.00 Tue–Sun; adult/child £10/£5) Outside the market town of Masham in the north of the AONB, around 25

minutes north of Fountains Abbey, this brilliant sculpture garden is a hidden highlight. Countless trails cross vast lawns, pass flourishing rhododendron gardens and cut through 18ha of woodland – all of it made even more intriguing by the myriad sculptures placed here by the garden's owner. Don't miss a moment of contemplation at the Balinese Pagoda, and look out for Rebecca Newnham's stunning *Magnolia* sculpture. There's a lovely tea room for cakes and sandwiches.

HOW STEAN GORGE (Lofthouse HG3 5SF ⊘ howstean.co.uk ⊙ 09.00–17.00 daily; adult/child £7/£5) For a dog walk with a little adrenaline, head to How Stean Gorge – around 35 minutes' drive southwest of the Himalayan Garden, and 20 minutes north of Pateley Bridge – where you can take a self-guided descent into a limestone ravine. Entering in magical style through an antique wardrobe, you'll get down to the water's edge to see trout swimming in a tributary of the Nidd. Follow the trail past sculptures and tunnels, then exit through the spooky Tom Taylor's Cave. Surfaces are very slippery when wet, so this is for sure-footed people and agile dogs only. Allow around an hour to complete the trail.

↑ Fountains Abbey. (Emily Marie Wilson/S)

LET'S GO

GETTING THERE

The A1(M) runs along the eastern edge of Nidderdale AONB, offering easy access from north or south, and a network of good A- and B-roads will get you into the heart of Nidderdale from there. Public transport isn't prolific, so driving is best; Harrogate has the nearest train station (Station Parade, HG1 1TE), with connections to major cities like London, Leeds and York.

EATING

The Blue Lion Inn East Witton DL8 4SN bluelion.co.uk noon–13.45 & 18.30–21.00 Mon–Sat, noon–16.30 & 18.30–21.00 Sun. Easily one of the best pubs on the fringes of the AONB, this inn offers locally sourced meat and game, fantastic Sunday roasts and a vast wine list. Rooms are available (see opposite).

Messy Buns Unit 1, Duck Hill, Ripon HG4 1BL 07584 414642 09.00–16.00 Mon–Sat, 10.30–14.30 Sun. It's all about cake here, with fresh bakes daily. Stop in for tea and something sweet after shopping around the cathedral and on Duck Hill.

The Pancake House 1 High St, Pateley Bridge HG3 5AP 01423 313435 09.00–17.00 Thu–Tue. Pancakes, crêpes and galettes sweet and savoury, plus excellent home-cooked, hearty lunches and all-day breakfasts. Don't forget to purchase a homemade sweet treat for the dog.

The White Bear Gun Bank, Wellgarth, Masham HG4 4EN whitebearmasham.co.uk noon–15.00 & 18.00–20.30 Mon–Fri, noon–20.30 Sat, noon–19.00 Sun. A brilliant pub serving sandwiches and soups for lunch and dinners featuring sea bass or slow-roasted pork belly. It's owned by Masham's Theakston Brewery – thus the great beers.

SLEEPING

The Blue Lion Inn East Witton DL8 4SN bluelion.co.uk. This excellent pub on the northern edge of Nidderdale offers dog-friendly rooms. *From £105 B&B; dogs from £15/night.*

Cuckoo Cottage Pateley Bridge petspyjamas.com 2. A handsome 200-year-old cottage on the southern edge of town, ideally situated for walks on the Showground. Three bedrooms sleep six and there's an enclosed courtyard. *From £520/week.*

The Devonshire Arms Hotel & Spa Bolton Bridge BD23 6AJ thedevonshirearms.co.uk. This four-star hotel, on the southern edge of the AONB, has individually styled rooms and an excellent dog-friendly restaurant. *From £230/night B&B; dogs from £10/night.*

Riverdale Rural Holidays West Tanfield HG4 5JG riverdaleruralholidays.com. On the northern edge of the AONB, lodges and luxury safari tents make up the bulk of the accommodation here, but it's the riverside shepherd's huts that steal the show. Each sleeps two and has an enclosed garden with lawn, decking, fire pit and twin bathtub. The owners really love dogs; bring an entire pack if you wish. *From £250/night.*

OTHER PRACTICALITIES

Tourist information centre Station Sq, King St, Pateley Bridge HG3 5AT nidderdaleplus.org.uk 10.00–16.00 Mon–Fri, 10.00–13.00 Sat.

Pet supplies Pets Corner (30 North St, Ripon HG4 1HJ petscorner.co.uk 09.00–18.00 Mon–Sat, 10.30–16.30 Sun) sells food, treats and accessories.

Veterinary practices Bishopton Vets (Bridgegate House, Pateley Bridge HG3 5HN 01423 712080) has a 24-hour emergency line (01765 602396).

37 HIKING & HERITAGE IN A NATIONAL PARK

WHERE	North York Moors, Yorkshire
WHEN	Mar–Oct
HIGHLIGHTS	Walk among ruined abbeys, ride a heritage steam railway and don't miss a hike across the vast heather moorlands.

I t is by no means the largest nor the most dramatic of the UK's national parks, but the North York Moors wins the prize for some of the most diverse landscapes in Britain. Its undulating hills and deep valleys are covered with wild-flower meadows that sing with colour in summer, and its pine, birch and hazel woodlands date back as far as the 1600s. It has one of the greatest expanses of heather moorland in England and Wales, covering a third of the 1,500km² national park, and on its eastern edge is an almost 60km-long coastline where cliffs reach heights of 200m and nesting seabirds come to reproduce in summer.

There are endless walks to be enjoyed here, from coastal romps to moorland hikes – download maps and instructions from the national park website (⊘ northyorkmoors.org.uk) – but by far the most romantic way to see the scenery of the North York Moors is by steam train. The North Yorkshire Moors Railway is a fantastic heritage line, running between Pickering on the southern edge of the park over the moors to the coastal town of Whitby on its northern coastline. Take the morning train and you can spend a pleasing

↑ The North York Moors National Park. (matrobinsonphoto/S)

day scoffing fish and chips by the harbour, exploring the spectacular clifftop ruins of Whitby Abbey, or perusing the gift shops selling the local jet stone and regional produce. The Little Bottle Shop (90 Church St, YO22 4BH ⌂ moorandtide.co.uk ⊙ 10.00–17.00 daily) and The Green Dragon (4 Grape Ln, YO22 4BA ⌂ thegreendragonwhitby.co.uk ⊙ 11.00–18.00 Mon–Thu, 11.00–21.00 Fri–Sun) have the best selection of local drinks and will fuss over the dog while you browse.

In the southern reaches of the park, conveniently spread along the A170, a handful of lovely towns, villages and intriguing attractions could fill up at least a day of your time. Head to Helmsley for good lunch options and brewery tours at the Helmsley Brewing Company (18 Bridge St, YO62 5DX ⌂ helmsleybrewingco.co.uk; £8 ☂), or explore Helmsley Castle (Castlegate, YO62 5AB ⌂ english-heritage. org.uk ⊙ 10.00–17.00 daily; adult/child £7.90/£4.70). Around 4½km northwest, you can visit the ruins of an 11th-century abbey at Rievaulx, or wend your way further into the park to learn about the region's history at the captivating Ryedale Folk Museum – a brilliant option for families just a short drive from town.

There's so much to do in the North York Moors, you could probably fill an entire month with exploration, but to make the most of a weekend visit it's best to choose a sensible base and pick a few of the most appealing sights. Base yourself on the coast at Runswick Bay, just 15 minutes from Whitby, to spend a weekend exploring by the seaside – perhaps hopping on the railway to see what lies inland – or stay further south within the park around Pickering or Helmsley for easy access to some of its historic highlights.

RIEVAULX ABBEY (Rievaulx Bank, Rievaulx YO62 5LB ⌂ english-heritage.org. uk ⊙ 10.00–17.00 daily; adult/child £10/£6) One of hundreds of ruined abbeys in the north of England, this former Cistercian monastery, a mere 10-minute drive northwest of Helmsley, was among the most powerful in the country during its 12th-century heyday. After being abandoned in 1538 it drew poets and artists

↑ Rievaulx Abbey. (LG)

to its tranquil location, and it's still as serene today. Walk the dog around the evocative site – don't miss a stroll down the vast, dramatic nave – then head into the museum to peruse the archaeological finds from its various excavations. Dogs are allowed throughout, including in the café and gift shop.

RYEDALE FOLK MUSEUM (Hutton-le-Hole YO62 6UA *∂*ryedalefolkmuseum. co.uk ☉ 10.00–17.00 daily; adult/child £8.75/£7) This brilliant little museum, set across 2½ha in the southern section of the park, a 20-minute drive east of Helmsley, is made up of 20 heritage buildings which have been painstakingly deconstructed at their original locations and reconstructed, brick by brick, here. See a 1950s village shop complete with vintage sweets, a number of quaint thatched cottages and 15th-century crofts with original-style furnishings, and, at the far end, a mock Iron Age roundhouse complete with ancient equipment. Dogs are permitted everywhere, including inside all the buildings.

NORTH YORKSHIRE MOORS RAILWAY (28 Park St, Pickering YO18 7AJ *∂* nymr.co.uk ☉ multiple departures daily 09.00–17.00; adult/child £40/£20 🏖) Built in the 1830s in a bid to boost Whitby's prospects after the whaling and shipbuilding industries waned, this railway now offers a pleasingly slow and scenic journey through the North York Moors. The most popular route is from Pickering, taking in Goathland Station, which doubled as Hogsmeade in the *Harry Potter* films, and passing through the pretty village of Grosmont in the Esk Valley before ending up in Whitby. Take the first train of the day and the last train back to enjoy a a few hours of exploring in Whitby.

↑ North Yorkshire Moors Railway. (Milosz Maslanka/S)

DALBY FOREST (Visitor Centre, Dalby Forest Dr, Pickering YO18 7LT 🖰 forestryengland.uk) Just north of Pickering, inside the national park's boundaries, Dalby Forest is a fantastic place for long and varied walks with the dog. There are 13 hiking trails, ranging from easy lakeside strolls to 6km woodland hikes: the excellent Adderstone Rigg Trail features interesting rock formations along the way, with a 2.4km option and a longer, 4.1km route, while the 5.7km Dalby Beck Yellow Trail offers views over Dalby Dale. Maps are available at the visitor centre (⊘ 10.00–16.00 daily). Dogs must be kept on the lead or under tight control due to the presence of cyclists and picnickers.

WHITBY ABBEY (♥ YO22 4JT 🖰 english-heritage.org.uk ⊘ 10.00–17.00 daily; adult/child £10/£6) One of Britain's most dramatic ruined monasteries, Whitby Abbey sits on high, blustery cliffs overlooking the town – around 30 minutes' drive from Dalby – and the sea beyond. The Gothic abbey was built in the 13th century but was, as so many were, suppressed in the 1500s during Henry VIII's dissolution of the monasteries. Today you can explore its ruins with an excellent free audio guide before heading into the museum (dogs allowed), which charts the site's history through the ages.

ROBIN HOOD'S BAY (♥ YO22 4QN 🐾) The delightful coastal village of Robin Hood's Bay, 15 minutes down the coast from Whitby, is all cobblestone streets and winding alleyways, leading down towards a vast sandy beach (only exposed at low tide) where dogs are allowed all year round. Come here for seaside games of fetch or afternoons spent building sandcastles on the shore.

↑ Robin Hood's Bay. (Ion Mes/S)

LET'S GO

GETTING THERE

Northeast of York, the North York Moors are well served by a network of A-roads that connect to the city and the A1(M), including the A64, A170 and the A171. Railway stations at Malton (Railway St, YO17 9RD) and Scarborough (Westborough, YO11 1TN) have direct connections to York and Manchester, but with sparse public transport throughout the park, driving is always best.

EATING

✕ **Cornercopia Cafe** 6 Castlegate, Helmsley YO62 5AB ☎ 07976 098073 ☉ 10.00–16.45 Wed–Sat, 10.00–16.00 Sun. Simple sandwiches, salads and cakes in a cosy little café just around the corner from Helmsley Castle. Order a pot of dog-friendly ice cream to keep your pet busy while you eat.

✕ **The Forge Tea Rooms** Hutton-le-Hole YO62 6UA ☎ 01751 417444 ☉ 09.30–17.00 daily. This cute little café next to Ryedale Folk Museum

↑ Arty at Pickering station. (LG)

is a great stop for cream teas, paninis and freshly baked cakes.

✕ **The Fox & Rabbit Inn** Lockton YO18 7NQ ⌖ foxandrabbit.co.uk ☉ noon–23.00 Mon–Sat, noon–22.30 Sun. Less than a 10-minute drive north of Pickering, this lovely pub sits right by Dalby Forest (follow the footpath behind the pub and head down the steep hill). Excellent pies and even better ales on tap are the highlight.

✕ **Rusty Shears** 3 Silver St, Whitby YO21 3BU ◼ Rustyshearswhitby ☉ 10.00–21.00 Thu–Sat, 10.00–17.00 Sun–Tue. Fantastic little café with a leafy courtyard, not far from the train station. Order fruit loaf with Wensleydale and a local porter for a solid afternoon pick-me-up or come for their varied lunch or evening menus, which always have great vegetarian/vegan options.

✕ **Sanders Yard Bistro** Church St, Whitby YO22 4BH ⌖ sandersyardbistro.co.uk ☉ 09.00–20.00 Fri–Sat, 09.00–17.00 Sun–Thu. A brilliant little bistro with a courtyard on the abbey side of town. Excellent salads, bottomless brunches and incredibly tempting cakes.

SLEEPING

⌂ **The Feathers** Market Pl, Helmsley YO62 5BH ⌖ feathershotelhelmsley.co.uk 🐾 2. Helmsley's best hotel welcomes dogs in all rooms bar four, and they're allowed to dine with you in the restaurant or bar. It's exceedingly cosy inside, with stone fireplaces, wood-panelled walls and soft tartan carpets ideal for snoozy hounds. *From £140/ night B&B; dogs from £10/night.*

⌂ **Forest Holidays** Cropton YO18 8ES ⌖ forestholidays.co.uk 🐾 4. Hide away in Dalby Forest in your very own log cabin at this holiday park. Cabins are cleverly designed to maximise space; they have enclosed decking and some have hot tubs, too. The on-site restaurant allows dogs inside. *From £230/night; dogs from £15/night.*

🏠 **Fox & Rabbit Holiday Cottages** Lockton YO18 7NQ 🐾 foxandrabbitcottages.co.uk 🐾 1. A trio of beautifully furnished self-catering cottages sleeping two each. There's an enclosed courtyard for the dog, and a fresh Victoria sponge on arrival; owner Adrian will go out of his way to make your stay special. You might even see him and his two Labradors in the pub next door. *From £240/night for three nights; dogs from £10/stay.*

🏠 **Runswick Bay Cottages** Runswick Bay TS13 5HU 🐾 runswickbaycottages.co.uk 🐾 2; see ad below. Set within the historic fishing village of Runswick Bay, 20 minutes north of Whitby, is this collection of lovely cottages run by Helen Massey, who grew up right here in the bay and is a font of local area knowledge. Seven of the options

(sleeping between two and eight people) are pet-friendly. *From £325 for three nights.*

OTHER PRACTICALITIES

Tourist information centre Sutton Bank National Park Centre, YO7 2EH 🐾 northyorkmoors. org.uk ☉ 10.00–17.00 daily.

Pet supplies The Pet Store (45 Market Pl, Pickering YO18 7AE 🐾 pickeringpetstore.co.uk ☉ 09.00–17.00 Mon–Sat) has food, treats, toys and more; on the coast, The Whitby Pet Shop (15 Station Sq, YO21 1DU ☉ 09.00–17.00 Mon–Sat) sells treats, some food and a few accessories.

Veterinary practices Ryedale Vets has a number of practices, including one in Pickering (133 Eastgate, YO18 7DW 🐾 01751 472204) and another in Helmsley (Station Rd, YO62 5BZ 🐾 01439 771166); call either of them for out-of-hours emergencies.

38 A LAKESIDE ADVENTURE FOR ALL AGES

WHERE	Ullswater, the Lake District
WHEN	Mar–Sep
HIGHLIGHTS	Walk and cruise on the spectacular Ullswater Way, and find a surprisingly engaging pencil museum further afield.

The Lake District is prime dog country — long walks up and around the region's 214 fells, innumerable cosy pubs with fireplaces for hunkering down on rainy days, and 16 lakes to choose from for canoeing trips or impromptu swims. Of course, you can't possibly take in all the Lakes have to offer in a single weekend — the national park sprawls across 2,362km² between the M6 and the Cumbria coastline — but luckily Ullswater and its surrounding towns and villages makes a fine base for dog owners.

The second-largest lake in the region, Ullswater spans almost 15km from north to south and is flanked by the peaks of Helvellyn and High Street. It's encircled by the 32km-long Ullswater Way (⌂ ullswater.com), so the walking is fantastic and, best of all, there are activities accessible for all abilities and ages. Use Ullswater Steamers to skip certain sections if you prefer shortish walks relatively close to the shore, or take the higher 6km trail from Howtown on the southern side of the lake for a more challenging hike up to the Cockpit Stone Circle on Askham Moor, where you'll get brilliant panoramic views of the surrounding peaks from the 5,000-year-old remains.

Ullswater is top-and-tailed by two villages: Pooley Bridge in the north and Glenridding to the south. Both are welcome pit stops on the Ullswater Way, the former with tea rooms, pubs and dog-friendly gift shops — don't miss the extensive local gin collection at Chestnut House (Finkle St, CA10 2NW ⌂ chestnuthouseonline.co.uk ◷ 08.00–22.00 daily) — and the latter home to one of the best hotels on the lake.

↑ The view over Derwent Water from Keswick. (Valery Egorov/S)

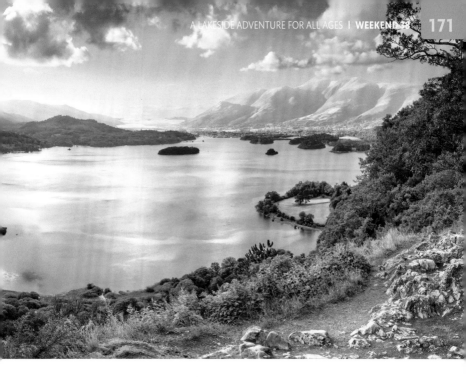

Keswick, some 20km west of Ullswater on the shores of Derwent Water, has a handful of engaging attractions that'll keep the whole family entertained on rainy days – try the Pencil Museum and the Puzzling Place house of illusions (♀ CA12 5DZ ♂ puzzlingplace.co.uk ⊘ 11.00–17.30 daily; adult/child £4.50/£4 ☂) – plus more dog-friendly stores for local souvenirs.

ULLSWATER STEAMERS (Glenridding CA11 0US ♂ ullswater-steamers. co.uk ⊘ regular departures 09.00–17.00 daily; round trip adult/child £12/£8, dogs £1 ☂) Originally a fleet of steamships that ferried passengers, produce and mail across Ullswater, these 'steamers' may now be powered by diesel but are no less enjoyable for it. Boats run between Glenridding and Pooley Bridge, stopping at Howtown along the way: you can take a cruise around the whole lake and enjoy the insightful commentary, or use them as a means of transport, taking in sections of the Ullswater Way on foot. The indoor deck keeps you dry on rainy days.

AIRA FORCE WATERFALL (♀ CA11 0JS ♂ nationaltrust.org.uk) The spectacular landscape that inspired Wordsworth's poem *The Somnambulist*, Aira Force, 5km north of Glenridding, is a lovely location for a hour-long stroll with the dog. Take the woodland trails past towering fir, spruce and pine trees towards Aira Beck, a nearly 20m-high waterfall which, after a good bout of rain, thunders over a steep, rocky drop. For a longer walk, tackle the circular 7km hike up to the 481m summit of Gowbarrow Fell for brilliant views over Ullswater (3hrs; see the website).

LOWTHER CASTLE (♥ CA10 2HH ⌀ lowthercastle.org ⊙ 10.00–17.00 daily; adult/child £12/£9) Most of Britain's ruined castles come with tales of bloody battles or deadly destruction by royals or rival families, but this 19th-century behemoth, sitting 30 minutes northeast of Glenridding and just 15 minutes from Pooley Bridge, has a more intriguing tale. Built in 1806 by the 1st Earl of Lonsdale, William Lowther, the castle was carefully deconstructed just over 150 years later due to the family's financial difficulties, in part thanks to the wayward extravagance of high-society socialite, Hugh Lowther. Today, the roofless, windowless ruin is an arresting sight, and you can walk between its walls and gaze up to the sky from where a grand staircase once stood. The wider estate offers 52ha of gardens and a 12km circular walk that joins up with the Ullswater Way. Dogs are allowed inside the exhibition space and in the café.

DERWENT PENCIL MUSEUM (Main St, Keswick CA12 5NG 🅵 pencilmuseum ⊙ 09.30–16.00 daily; adult/child £4.95/£3.95 👣) Around a 25-minute drive west of either Glenridding or Pooley Bridge, this small but compelling museum charts the history of graphite mining in the region and delves into how the popular Derwent pencils are made. See historic machinery and the world's longest pencil and learn how the pencil factory here helped create secret tools for MI6 spies. You'll get a quiz to fill out on arrival and a prize if you get all the questions right.

↑ Derwent Pencil Museum. (Aybige Mert/S) → Lowther Castle. (condruzmf/S)

LET'S GO

GETTING THERE

Ullswater is one of the easiest lakes to reach, sitting around 10km southwest of Penrith on the M6/A66. Penrith train station (Ullswater Rd, CA11 7JQ) has connections to London Euston, Manchester, Preston and Glasgow; buses run between the station, Pooley Bridge and Glenridding every couple of hours.

EATING

🍴 **Fellpack** 34 Lake Rd, Keswick CA12 5DQ 🖉 fellpack.co.uk 🕐 17.00–22.00 Tue–Sat. Come here for slightly unusual food in a trendy setting: classics, from curries to chilli, served with a modern twist.

🍴 **Granny Dowbekins Tearoom** Pooley Bridge CA10 2NP 🖉 grannydowbekins.co.uk 🕐 09.00–17.00 daily. The best place for refuelling in Pooley Bridge, this tea room serves mammoth portions of great, home-cooked food. The ploughman's is a highlight, and don't miss the dessert of the day.

🍴 **Helvellyn Country Kitchen** Glenridding CA11 0PA 🖉 helvellynkitchen.co.uk 🕐 09.00–17.00 Tue–Sun. Huge, hearty fry-ups, sandwiches served with chunky chips, and enormous scones with jam and clotted cream – this is the home of comfort food.

SLEEPING

🏠 **Another Place** Watermillock CA11 0LP 🖉 another.place 🐾 2. Exceptional spa hotel on the shores of Ullswater, with a dog-friendly restaurant and watersports facilities. *From £200/night B&B; dogs £15/night for one, £5/night for a second.*

🏠 **Inn on the Lake** Glenridding CA11 0PE 🖉 petspyjamas.com 🐾 2. This lovely lakeside property, conveniently located next to the Ullswater Steamers jetty, offers 6ha of grounds and dog-friendly dining in the Orangery and Rambler's Bar. *From £250/night B&B.*

🏕 **The Quiet Site** 📍 CA11 0LS 🖉 thequietsite. co.uk. The coolest campsite in the Lakes, this carbon-neutral holiday park, perched below Little Mell Fell, 5km southwest of Pooley Bridge, has tent pitches, glamping pods, gingerbread houses and hobbit homes. There's a wild-flower meadow where dogs can be let off the lead, a dogs-only shower room, and treats and poo bags to buy in the on-site shop. Great pizzas from their café in the evenings, too. *Glamping from £40/night; tent pitches £20/night.*

OTHER PRACTICALITIES

Tourist information centre 12 Main St, Keswick CA12 5JR 🖉 lakedistrict.gov.uk 🕐 09.30–17.30 daily.

Pet supplies Podgy Paws (4–6 Tithebarn St, Keswick CA12 5ED 🖉 podgypaws.co.uk 🕐 09.00–17.30 Mon–Sat, 10.00–17.00 Sun) sells a superb range of accessories, treats and food.

Veterinary practices Millcroft Vets (Southey Hill, Keswick CA12 5NR 📞 017687 72590) has a 24-hour emergency line (📞 01900 826666).

39 AN ADVENTURE THROUGH ROMAN BRITAIN

WHERE	Corbridge & Northumberland National Park, Northumberland
WHEN	Mar–Oct
HIGHLIGHTS	Roman ruins to roam across and a vast national park that has few crowds but mega scenery.

Some 30km west of Newcastle, the pretty little town of Corbridge is an appealing place to while away a day or two; with a healthy population of resident dogs, it's delightfully welcoming for you and your pet. Independent boutiques line the central streets – many of which will let you browse with your dog by your side – and a smattering of great pubs and cafés offer enticing places to rest your feet and fill your belly.

Beyond the town's leisurely appeal, though, lies an enthralling history. A few short kilometres from the centre you'll find Corbridge's original Roman settlement – a vast complex of fascinating ruins that will transport you back to the most northerly town in Britannia. It's just one of many ancient Roman forts that dot the landscape in Northumberland, the region that is most famously home to the empire's greatest frontier: Hadrian's Wall.

Stretching 117km from east to west, the UNESCO-listed wall is now a crumbling ruin, best explored up on the Whin Sill, a 300-million-year-old rock formation created by fresh magma spilling out on to the land after movement in the Earth's tectonic plates. Set within Northumberland National Park – a beguiling landscape covering more than 1,000km^2 of rolling hills – the Hadrian's Wall area is brilliant dog-walking territory that comes with its own history lesson and simply must not be missed.

Around 6km west of Corbridge you'll find another attractive market town – Hexham – which could make an alternative base, especially if you want to indulge in locally brewed beers and homemade pies at its Tuesday market (Market Pl, NE46 1XQ).

CORBRIDGE ROMAN TOWN (♀ NE45 5NT ♂ english-heritage.org.uk ⊙ 10.00–17.00 daily; adult/child £9/£5.40) The Romans settled in Corbridge around AD85, but it wasn't until AD160 that the town became the bustling hub you can see the remains of today. Situated 1km north of new Corbridge and just a few kilometres from Hadrian's Wall, this was an important support base, supplying the wall's various fortresses with food and ammunition, and had become a fully fledged civilian town by the third century. Stand on the paved stones of the old main road and you can really imagine its high street, buzzing with shoppers haggling at stalls amid the colonnades. Dogs on a lead are allowed to explore the site with you and are even welcomed inside the museum, where you can examine some of the best Roman stonework in Britain.

HEXHAM OLD GAOL MUSEUM (Hall Gate, Hexham NE46 1XD ♂ museumsnorthumberland.org.uk ⊙ 10.00–16.00 daily; adults/under 16s £5/free 🐾) Around 6km from Corbridge, Hexham's 14th-century prison is positively modern compared to many sights in Northumberland, but it's still

← Arty exploring Hadrian's Wall near Sycamore Gap. (LG)

the oldest of its kind in England. Making an ideal activity for soggy days, there's an interesting exhibition here detailing medieval crime and punishment – kids will love taking a turn in the stocks.

CHESTERS ROMAN FORT (Chollerford NE46 4EU ⌂ english-heritage.org. uk ⊙ 10.00–17.00 daily; adult/child £9/£5.40) Chesters is the most complete Roman cavalry fort in Britain, with a bath house and steam room dating back to AD124. Set beside the North Tyne River on the fringe of the national park, just a 15-minute drive north of Corbridge, it's a tranquil spot to learn about this era in history. Dogs are allowed in the outside areas only – you'll have to tag-team to visit the museum and sit outside to dine at the lovely on-site tea room.

HOUSESTEADS (Haydon Bridge NE47 6NN ⌂ english-heritage.org.uk ⊙ 10.00–17.00 daily; adult/child £9/£5.40) Another of the area's impressive Roman forts, this time within the boundaries of the national park, just 10 minutes west of Chesters, Housesteads offers impressive views of Hadrian's Wall to the west. One of 16 permanent bases along the wall, this fortress once housed 800 Roman soldiers and today you can walk among its ruins where the military headquarters and hospital still stand.

SYCAMORE GAP (Steel Rigg car park, NE47 7AN ⌂ nationaltrust.org.uk 🐾) Around 5km west of Housesteads lies one of the most photographed trees in Britain: a handsome sycamore that sits within a perfect dip in the precipitous

LET'S GO

GETTING THERE

Corbridge and the National Park are best explored by car, as the vast majority of the region's sights are fairly remote. If you're not too worried about getting around, though, you could arrive at Corbridge train station (Station Rd, NE45 5AY), just 40 minutes along the line from Newcastle; Hexham railway station (Station Rd, NE46 1ET) is the next stop along – from here the AD122 bus (⌂ hadrianswallcountry.co.uk) connects to Housesteads and Chesters Roman forts. Road-wise, Corbridge sits just off the A69 and A68, so is easily reached from all directions.

EATING

✖ **Cafe No 6** 6 Market Pl, Corbridge NE45 5AW ☎ 01434 634356 ⊙ 09.00–16.30 Mon–Sat, 11.30–16.30 Sun. A lovely little café in the heart of town serving cakes, afternoon teas, soups and sandwiches.

✖ **The Small World Café** Tribune House, Hexham NE46 3PB ⌂ thesmallworldcafe.com ⊙ 09.00–15.30 Mon–Sat. A brilliant café and gift shop, selling local gins and chocolates, and serving fantastic cakes and hot sandwiches.

✖ **The Wheatsheaf** St Helen's St, Corbridge NE45 5HE ⌂ thewheatsheafcorbridge.co.uk

Whin Sill escarpment. There are two options to visit: park at Steel Rigg Car Park and walk 1½km eastward along the Pennine Way and Hadrian's Wall, or take the National Trust's 8km trail from Housesteads Roman fort; allow around three hours.

↑ Sycamore Gap. (Droneworksnortheast/S)

⊘ noon–14.30 & 17.00–21.00 Mon–Sat, noon–17.00 Sun. The best place in Corbridge for pub classics and Sunday roasts. Bag a seat by the fireplace for cosy lunches or evening meals.

SLEEPING

🏠 **The Angel Inn** Main St, Corbridge NE45 5LA ⊘ theangelofcorbridge.com. A relaxed pub with rooms and a dog-friendly dining area in the lounge, the Angel is a central base for exploring Corbridge town and beyond. *From £100/night; dogs £20/night.*

🏠 **Twice Brewed Inn** Bardon Mill, Hexham NE47 7AN ⊘ twicebrewedinn.co.uk. Within the national park, this fantastically friendly inn is a rural hideaway with its own brewhouse. The staff love dogs and you're allowed to dine with them in the bar. *From £130/night; dogs £5/night.*

OTHER PRACTICALITIES

Tourist information centre Hill St, Corbridge NE45 5AD ⊘ visitnorthumberland.com ⊘ 11.00–16.00 Wed, Fri & Sat.

Pet supplies There's a Pets at Home in Hexham (Tyne Valley Retail Park, NE46 1EZ ⊘ petsathome.com ⊘ 09.00–20.00 Mon–Fri, 09.00–19.00 Sat, 10.00–16.00 Sun).

Veterinary practices Westway Veterinary Group has a branch on St Helen's St in Corbridge (📍 NE45 5BE ✆ 01434 632033).

40 A BIRDWATCHING ADVENTURE IN THE FOREST

WHERE	Galloway Forest Park, Scotland
WHEN	May–Sep
HIGHLIGHTS	Spectacular red kites, glorious walking trails and dark skies to boot.

S itting in Scotland's southwest corner, the 775km² Galloway Forest Park has a quiet, understated beauty: hills clad with tall, skinny pines, roadsides bristling with ferns and wild flowers, and occasional lochs and rivers to break up the greenery. It may not have the peaks of the Cairngorms or the striking scenery of the Highlands, but there's still plenty to inspire – you just have to look up.

This is red kite country. Formerly extinct in Scotland, the birds of prey, with their 1½m wingspan, were reintroduced here in 2001 and today can be seen circling high above the trees all over the park. The best place to spot them is along the **Galloway Kite Trail at Loch Ken**: a 64km driving route that starts at Laurieston village in the southeast corner of the park and heads north on the A762 before crossing the Water of Ken and turning south to follow alongside Loch Ken on the A719. Stops along the way include the **Bellymack Farm feeding station** (♀ DG7 2PJ ∅ bellymackhillfarm.co.uk ☉ noon–16.00 daily, feeding time 14.00; adult/child £5/free) where you'll watch the birds up close as they dive down to feast on meat laid out by the landowners, and the **Secret Cages** (♀ DG7 2NG), where you can see the original fake nests built for the reintroduction programme.

Along with a couple of spectacular **driving routes** (10km & 16km; pick up a guide at any visitor centre), ample marked **walking trails** cut their way through the park. Some of the best start at the visitor centres: **Kirroughtree** (♀ DG8 7BE ☉ 10.00–17.00 daily) in the south of the park, or **Clatteringshaws** (♀ DG7 3SQ ☉ 10.00–17.00 daily) and **Glentrool** (♀ DG8 6SZ ☉ 10.30–16.30 daily) in the

centre. Around 6km from Glentrool, **Bruce's Stone** (📍DG8 6SU) – a monument to the quick but brutal battle between Robert the Bruce and invading English soldiers that helped Scotland secure independence in 1314 – offers brilliant views over Loch Trool.

Galloway was Scotland's first **Dark Sky Reserve**; at night, clear skies dance with the light of more than 7,000 visible stars and planets. Pack a thermos and head to one of the visitor centres for a spot of stargazing to round off a perfect day.

Note that the park is a major mountain-biking hub, with trails at Kirroughtree and Glentrool, so beware of speeding wheels crossing your path as you walk the trails.

LET'S GO

The only way to get to Galloway Forest Park, which lies 35km west of Dumfries and around 70km south of Glasgow, is by car, along the A75 from the east or the A76 from the north.

There's little in the way of accommodation or eating inside the park; the best lunches are at the visitor centre cafés, all of which welcome dogs. The only pub inside the park is the cracking **House o' Hill** (Bargrennan DG8 6RN ⬡ houseohill.co.uk ◔ noon–23.00 Thu–Sat, noon–20.00 Sun), on its western fringes, which serves mussels by the bucket, pints of prawns and great veg and vegan options, including smoked tofu.

For accommodation, head 10km north of Loch Ken to **Glenhoul Brae Holiday House** (📍DG7 3UB ⬡ gallowayholidayhouse.com; £750/week), a lovely four-bedroom house with spectacular views. **Galloway Activity Centre** (📍DG7 3NQ ⬡ lochken.co.uk; from £45/night) on Loch Ken offers glamping in yurts, bothies and safari tents.

In Newton Stewart, on the southwest edge of the park, **Galloway Petfoods** (35 Victoria St, DG8 6NL ⬡ gallowaypetfoods.co.uk ◔ 09.00–17.00 Mon–Sat) sells provisions, while **Academy Vets** (Queen St, DG8 6JL ☎ 01671 404951) handles medical concerns.

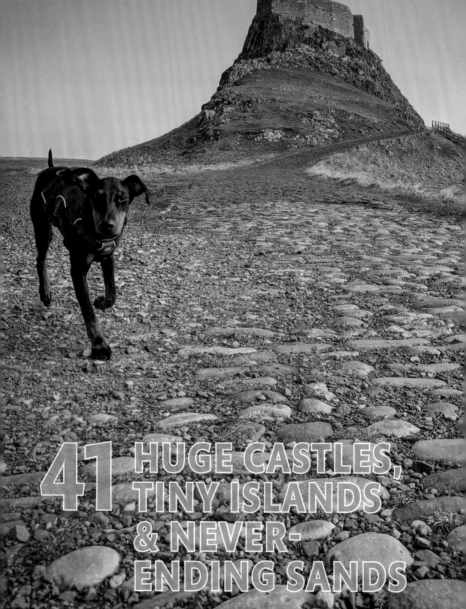

41 HUGE CASTLES, TINY ISLANDS & NEVER-ENDING SANDS

WHERE	Northern Northumberland
WHEN	Mar–Sep
HIGHLIGHTS	A majestic seafront fortress, beaches that go on forever and spectacular island walks.

No matter from which angle you approach Bamburgh, its imposing castle really makes an impact. Arriving from the village of Seahouses to the south, you round the corner with the grassy dunes on your right and fields to your left, and it just appears from around the bend, regal and red, its crenellations and keeps lording over the sea beyond. There is no other word for it: it is simply magnificent.

The castle may dominate this tiny village on the Northumberland coast, but it's not the only thing worth travelling here for. The beach that sits below Bamburgh's fortress is an expansive swathe of soft yellow sand where dogs are allowed to run about and play in the surf year-round. Head north from the castle and climb the sand dunes for spectacular views over Budle Bay, or head south and after 5km you'll find yourself in Seahouses, where boats bob in the harbour and fish and chips at Neptune Fish Restaurant is a lunchtime essential (3 Seafield Rd, NE68 7SJ ⌀ neptunefishandchips.co.uk ⏱ 11.30–20.00 daily). Cruises leave Seahouses Harbour for the Farne Islands, a remote collection of 20 or so rocky isles where seals, guillemots and puffins occupy the craggy cliffs and beaches.

Bamburgh Castle isn't the only fortress on this stretch of coastline, either. Starting at Boulmer, in the south, the 63km Northumberland Coastal Route (follow the brown road signs) wends its way along B-roads between the likes of Warkworth, Alnwick and the dramatic seaside ruins of Dunstanburgh Castle. The route ends north of Bamburgh at Holy Island, an outcrop only accessible during low tide, which makes another great base for this stretch of coast. On Holy Island you will find the arresting Lindisfarne Castle, which rises high above the ocean on top of a conical mound, and Lindisfarne Priory, a ruined church that was once home to the most important saint of the Middle Ages: St Cuthbert. Eleven years after his death in AD687, the cult of St Cuthbert was born and the island has been an important pilgrimage site ever since – today it's the final point on the St Cuthbert's Way hiking route (⌀ stcuthbertsway.info), which follows the old pilgrimage route from Melrose, 100km away in the Scottish Borders. Don't miss a taste of Lindisfarne mead, which was first produced on the island in the 7th century, at St Aidan's Winery (♥ TD15 2RX ☎ 01289 389230 ⏱ 10.30–15.00 daily).

While the coast could fill an entire weekend, you can find less blustery escapades just a 25-minute drive inland at the 6,000ha Ford and Etal estate (⌀ ford-and-etal.co.uk). Attractions here include a dog-friendly farm and heavy horse stables (⌀ hayfarmheavies.co.uk), and Etal Castle, starting point for a footpath south along the river towards the village of Ford; around halfway along the route, you could stop at the Heatherslaw Railway and ride back to Etal on the miniature train, or walk the full 5km towards Ford to visit the handsome Lady Waterford Hall (♥ TD15 2QG ⌀ ford-and-etal.co.uk ⏱ 11.00–17.00 daily; free ☂) and its fabulous Victorian murals.

BAMBURGH CASTLE (♥ NE69 7DF ⌀ bamburghcastle.com ⏱ 10.00–17.00 daily; adult/child £12.50/£6.15) This magnificent fortress, right on Bamburgh Beach, has worn many faces over the centuries. Its first incarnations were created

by Anglo Saxon kings in the 6th century, and a Norman keep was added by William Rufus, William the Conqueror's son, in 1095. It was a royal home for many years, but was later decimated – the first castle to be destroyed by guns in England – during the Wars of the Roses. After passing into private hands it was used as a hospital and pharmacy in the 18th century and then a coastguard station. To this day, it's still owned by the Armstrong family who bought the castle in 1894. Dogs aren't allowed inside the castle itself, but they can roam the grounds with you on a lead, enjoy views over the cannons to the sea and enter the excellent Armstrong & Aviation Museum.

FARNE ISLANDS TOURS (Seahouses harbour, NE68 7RN ⌀ farneislandstours. co.uk ⊙ Eight departures daily 09.00–15.00; adult/child £20/£15; book in advance) Just short of 2km offshore from Seahouses, the Farne Islands are a haven for wildlife. Over 100,000 seabirds can be seen here during spring and summer, including penguin-like guillemots, kittiwakes and puffins, and grey seals loll about on the beaches. Come in autumn and you'll see hundreds of fluffy white pups among the chaos, while during winter the boats have been known to pass migrating humpback whales. Cruises depart from Seahouses, 5km south of Bamburgh, and last around 2 hours; knowledgeable guides are on hand to offer insight about the islands and the wildlife. Some cruises land on Inner Farne (fees apply); the skippers will usually look after the dog if you want to disembark to meet the puffins up close.

PILGRIM'S WAY TO HOLY ISLAND WALK (Lindisfarne Causeway TD15 2PB ⌀ footstepsnorthumberland.co.uk; adults £17.50/£10, under 11s £10) You can drive on to Holy Island (25 minutes north of Bamburgh), but the absolute best way to visit is by walking along the Pilgrim's Way with local guide and history nut, Patrick Norris. On his 5-hour (12km) walk, you'll wander over the causeway at low tide (go barefoot for the full pilgrim experience), past hundreds of grey seals on the banks in summer, and on to the island where you'll end at Lindisfarne Castle. Private walks of the area can also be arranged. All dogs should be kept on the lead from April through June, when ground-nesting birds are present, and long-haired dogs should be kept on the lead in July and August as piri-piri burrs can damage their coats.

ETAL CASTLE (Etal TD12 4TN ⌀ english-heritage.org.uk ⊙ 10.00–17.00 daily; adult/child £5.90/£3.50) This small castle, a 30-minute drive west of Bamburgh, was built in the 16th century as a defence against Scottish raiders and is now an intriguing ruin with two intact towers. While there's not a huge amount to see or do on the site itself – aside from perhaps a picnic among the ruins or a quick mooch in the museum (dogs allowed) – it makes the ideal starting point for

↑ Bamburgh Castle. (Sara Winter/S) ← Puffins can be seen across the spring and summer on the Farne Islands. (Florian Sessler/S)

↑ Pilgrim's Way. (Gail Johnson/S)

walks through the Ford and Etal Estate. One of the best walks from here is up on to Etal Moor: it winds along the River Till, zig-zags up and over rolling hills and eventually to the 146m-high peak of Rhodes Hill. Download directions from ⊘ ford-and-etal.co.uk.

HEATHERSLAW RAILWAY (Ford Forge, Heatherslaw TD12 4TJ ⊘ heatherslawlightrailway.co.uk ⊙ departures every 75 mins 09.00–17.00 daily; adult/child £8.50/£4.50 return ⛱) Running along the banks of the River Till starting around 1km south of Etal Castle, this miniature light railway offers a more sedate way of seeing the scenery around Ford and Etal than walking. It's a 25-minute ride from Heatherslaw station up to Etal. Head across the bridge over the River Till, next to the Heatherslaw train station, for ice creams, coffee or tea at the dog-friendly Boes Café.

LET'S GO

GETTING THERE

Right up in the northeast corner of England, not far from the Scottish border, Bamburgh and its surrounding towns and villages are easily reached on the A1, which runs all the way down to Newcastle and up to Berwick-upon-Tweed. Bamburgh's nearest train station, a 15-minute drive south at Chathill (📍 NE67 5DE), has sporadic connections to Newcastle, but the local public transport network isn't great.

EATING

✕ **Bamburgh Castle Inn** Seahouses NE68 7SQ ⊘ inncollectiongroup.com ⊙ 07.30–21.00 daily. With the most sought-after dining tables in Seahouses, this pub with rooms overlooks the harbour and has a fantastic beer garden with sea views. Expect classics like fish and chips, scampi and great burgers.

✕ **The Black Bull Inn** Etal TD12 4TL ⊘ theblackbulletal.co.uk ⊙ noon–14.00 & 18.00–21.00 Mon–Sat, noon–18.00 Sun. The only thatched pub in Northumberland, inland in tiny Etal village, this old-timey boozer does excellent Sunday roasts and hearty dinners such as sausage and mash (with a vegan option) or slow-cooked lamb shank. Enjoy a taste of the Cheviot Brewery beers on tap.

✕ **The Cheviot Tap** Slainsfield TD12 4TP ⊘ cheviotbrewery.co.uk ⊙ noon–22.00 Fri–Sun, food 17.00–20.00 Fri & Sat, drinks only noon–20.00 Sun. The taproom at the Cheviot Brewery is a lovely covered outdoor space serving their own ales plus other northeastern beers, and great wood-fired pizzas on Fridays and Saturdays.

✕ **The Pantry** 1 Doctor's Ln, Bamburgh NE69 7BB ⊘ 01668 214455 ⊙ 09.00–17.00 daily. Pick up take-away sandwiches, teas, coffees and cakes, plus supplies from local producers for picnics or self-catering meals.

✕ **Pilgrims Coffee House & Roastery** Holy Island TD15 2SJ ⊘ pilgrimscoffee.co.uk ⊙ varies with tides but generally 09.00–17.30 daily. Serving up their own roasted coffee along with cakes, salt beef sandwiches and great salads, this trendy outdoor coffee shop is a gem on Holy Island.

✖ The Potted Lobster 3 Lucker Rd, Bamburgh NE69 7BS ⌀ thepottedlobster.co.uk ⊙ noon– 21.00 daily. Really excellent local seafood including mussels, Lindisfarne oysters and crab with a selection of brilliant wines.

SLEEPING

🏠 Bamburgh Castle Inn Seahouses NE68 7SQ ⌀ inncollectiongroup.com 🐾 2. Unassuming from the outside, but homely and comfortable inside, this pub has cosy rooms, some with sea views and private gardens for the dogs. Eat breakfast in the garden overlooking the harbour for the best experience. *From £125/night B&B; dogs from £10/night.*

🏠 Cheviot Glamping Slainsfield TD12 4TP ⌀ cheviotbrewery.co.uk 🐾 2. Sitting among the hills of the Ford and Etal Estate and on the site of the Cheviot Brewery, these luxurious glamping pods and bell tents are a wonderful place to wake up in the morning. *From £99/night; dogs from £10/stay.*

🏠 Manor House Hotel Holy Island TD15 2RX ⌀ manorhouseholyisland.com. A fine hotel right in the centre of Holy Island, overlooking the ruined priory. Dog-friendly rooms are at the rear; dogs are

allowed to join you for breakfast in the restaurant and for dinner in the bar. *From £120/night B&B; dogs from £10/night.*

🏠 Windley Cottage Church St, Bamburgh NE69 7BN ⌀ crabtreeandcrabtree.com 🐾 2. A stunning two-bedroom self-catering option (sleeping four) with décor so trendy you'll want to nick everything – even the coat hangers. An enclosed garden at the back (across an access lane) is great for games of morning fetch with the dog. *From £600 for three nights.*

OTHER PRACTICALITIES

Tourist information centre Seafield Car park, Seahouses NE68 7SW ⌀ 01670 625593 ⊙ 09.30–16.00 daily.

Pet supplies The Pet Shop (17 Main St, Seahouses NE68 7RE ⌀ 01665 720487 ⊙ 10.00–noon & 14.00–16.00 Thu–Tue) is a reliable option for toys, treats and more.

Veterinary practices Alnorthumbria Veterinary Group (29 Ryecroft Way, NE71 ⌀ 01668 281323) in Wooler (a 25-minute drive inland from Bamburgh) has vets on call for emergencies as well as standard appointments.

↑ Etal Castle. (Maya K. Photography/S)

42 SLOW TRAVEL ON THE SCOTTISH BORDERS

WHERE	Tweed Valley, Scotland
WHEN	May–Oct
HIGHLIGHTS	An idyllic winding river connecting ruined abbeys, spectacular country houses and a vast forest perfect for long walks.

Flowing more than 150km from west to east, the River Tweed cuts through the beautifully rural Scottish Borders, taking in attractive market towns, vast country estates and wild woodland along its way. The finest section, perhaps, is the 50km stretch that links Peebles and Dryburgh, with a handful of lovely towns and villages all conveniently connected by the A72.

It's along this section of the Tweed Valley that you'll find the magnificent home of Sir Walter Scott, Abbotsford, and the bucolic landscape that inspired so much of his writing – best viewed from the benches at Scott's View.

Base yourself in the delightful town of Peebles for pretty riverside walks taking in its three bridges, and an afternoon's stroll through Kailzie Gardens (♥ EH45 9HT ⊘ kailziegardenscom ⊙ 10.00–17.00 daily; adult/child £6.50/free). Stay overnight in popular Melrose, 38km to the east, on the other hand, and you'll have a pair of atmospheric ruined abbeys on your doorstep, and a smattering of excellent pubs and cafés in which to enjoy the region's best local produce.

A trip to the Tweed Valley isn't a high-octane affair – unless you want to take in the mountain biking trails at Glentress Forest – but instead it's the perfect place to slow down and take in some of Scotland's most serene lowland scenery.

↑ Splashing about in the River Tweed. (Jennie Routley/S)

GLENTRESS FOREST (Glentress Peel Visitor Centre, Peebles EH45 8NB ⊘ forestryandland.gov.scot 🐕) Part of the Tweed Valley Forest Park, Glentress is a gateway to glorious wilderness, home to herons and red squirrels. An undulating landscape of forested hills, this is great walking territory, just 4km east of Peebles, where well-behaved dogs can enjoy off-lead adventures (keep an eye and ear out for mountain bikes). Five walking trails start from the Glentress Peel Visitor Centre (🕙 09.00–16.00 Mon–Fri, 09.00–17.00 Sat–Sun), ranging from a short kilometre-long stroll to a hike of nearly 10km that takes in an Iron Age fort. The visitor centre café welcomes dogs.

TRAQUAIR HOUSE (Innerleithen EH44 6PW ⊘ traquair.co.uk 🕙 11.00–17.00 daily; adult/child £6/£5) Selling itself as Scotland's oldest inhabited house, imposing Traquair – a 10-minute drive southeast of Glentress – dates back to 1107 and has been the family home of the Stuarts since 1491. With the dog you can explore its expansive grounds and visit the pottery studio, gift shops and the Garden Café.

ABBOTSFORD (📍 TD6 9BQ ⊘ scottsabbotsford.com 🕙 10.00–17.00 daily; house & gardens adult/child £11.70/£5.10, gardens only £5.90/£3.10 🐕) The first real example of Scottish Baronial architecture, and the building that inspired the royal summer palace in Balmoral, Abbotsford was the home of Sir Walter Scott, Scotland's great historian, poet, novelist and playwright. A 30-minute drive

↑ Traquair House. (Duncan2406/S)

east of Traquair, it's all turrets and towers, and the spectacular house overlooks a 48ha estate with planted gardens, wild meadows and native woodland, all on the banks of the Tweed. Dogs can roam everywhere with you except inside the house; providing you're not travelling solo, take it in turns to go inside – it's worth

LET'S GO

GETTING THERE

Some 35km from Edinburgh, the Tweed Valley is easy to reach by road, with the A72 following the river's course and the A68 offering easy connections from north and south. The nearest train station is in Galashiels (Ladhope Vale, TD1 1BP), which sees direct services from Edinburgh (less than 1 hr). Galashiels is around 35 minutes by car from Peebles or 10 minutes from Melrose, to which it is also connected by regular buses (⌾ bordersbuses.co.uk).

EATING

✖ **Abbey Fine Wines** 17 Market Sq, Melrose TD6 9PL ⓕ abbeywines.rhymersfayre ⊙ 09.00–17.00 Mon–Sat. A buzzing café-cum-wine seller serving sandwiches and cheese platters; there's no corkage on wines bought from the shop.

✖ **Loulabelles** 12 High St, Innerleithen EH44 6HA ⌾ loulabelles.business.site ⊙ 10.00–15.00 Mon–Wed & Fri, 10.00–16.00 Sat–Sun. In the middle of Innerleithen, just north of Traquair House, this place serves excellent salads, bagels and sandwiches; the baked goods are incredibly tempting. Dogs are welcomed with open arms (and treats).

✖ **The Tontine** High St, Peebles EH45 8AJ ⌾ tontinehotel.com ⊙ noon–14.30 & 18.00–19.45 daily. Expect local ingredients like smoked salmon, North Sea haddock and beef from the Scottish Borders in the stylish but relaxed bistro of this dog-loving hotel.

↑ Aerial view of Dryburgh Abbey. (SergeBertasiusPhotography/S)

a look for the eccentric gargoyles in the armoury alone. Dogs kept under control are allowed off-lead in the meadows and by the river on the wider estate; they're also permitted (on leads) in the café.

MELROSE ABBEY (Abbey St, Melrose TD6 9LG *∂* historicenvironment.scot ◷ 10.00–17.00 daily; adult/child £3/£1.80) Just 4km or so east of Abbotsford, Melrose Abbey, founded in 1136, was the first Cistercian monastery in Scotland, home to an order of monks for more than 450 years. Over the centuries important figures such as King Alexander II – and the heart of Robert the Bruce – were honoured with burial at this great church, and the crumbling but extensive ruins still give an idea of its former grandeur. Dogs can join you everywhere except inside the museum.

DRYBURGH ABBEY (St Boswells TD6 6RQ *∂* historicenvironment.scot ◷ 10.00–16.00 daily; free) Established in the 12th century, Dryburgh was a quiet centre of monastic life until the 1560s, when the Protestant Reformation changed religious communities across Britain and Europe. Today, its ruins remain peaceful and it makes a tranquil spot for a dog walk. Dryburgh is just a 15-minute drive southeast of Melrose Abbey; on the way you can stop off at Scott's View (**♀** TD6 9DW) on the B6356 for gorgeous views of the surrounding hills.

SLEEPING

Burts Hotel Market Sq, Melrose TD6 9PL *∂* burtshotel.co.uk 🐾 2. A lovely family-owned hotel with cosy bedrooms – self-catering also available – and a delightful beer garden. The Sunday roasts are excellent and whisky menu extensive. *From £148/night B&B.*

Dryburgh Abbey Hotel St Boswells TD6 0RQ *∂* petspyjamas.com 🐾 3. All red brick and chimneys, this gorgeous hotel sits next to the ruins of Dryburgh Abbey. Dogs can dine with you in the lounge area, and the 4½ha estate is great for walks. *From £155/night B&B.*

The Park Peebles 2 Innerleithen Rd, Peebles EH45 8BA *∂* parkpeebles.co.uk 🐾 2. A large, handsome hotel near the river in Peebles with stylish bedrooms, an in-house bakery and a good grill restaurant. The big lawn is perfect for your dog's morning toilet trips. Its sister hotel, Peebles Hydro, has a spa and pool, and extensive grounds for walking. *From £95/night B&B; dogs from £20/night.*

OTHER PRACTICALITIES

Tourist information The Hub gift shop in Innerleithen (33 High St, EH44 6HD ◷ 10.00–18.00 Mon–Sat) has information maps produced by Go Tweed Valley tourism (*∂* gotweedvalley. co.uk).

Pet supplies There's a Pets at Home in Galashiels (Gala Water Retail Park, TD1 3AP *∂* petsathome. com ◷ 09.00–20.00 Mon–Fri, 09.00–19.00 Sat, 10.00–18.00 Sun).

Veterinary practices Galedin Vets (Melrose Rd, Galashiels TD1 2UH *✆* 01896 753759) offers 24-hour emergency care.

43 FUN & FESTIVITIES IN A CREATIVE CITY

WHERE	Edinburgh, Scotland
WHEN	Year-round
HIGHLIGHTS	Striking architecture, electric festivals and spectacular walks with cityscape views.

There is so much to love about Edinburgh. Its dynamic festival scene draws many, largely thanks to the summer Fringe and International Festival with its world-famous Military Tattoo and endless comedy, drama and live music performances – many of which are outdoors and free of charge, ideal for soaking up culture with the dog. The Science, Jazz and Storytelling festivals draw in smaller but equally enthusiastic crowds, and the Hogmanay celebrations over New Year are a spectacular city-wide party culminating, for some hardy souls, in a chilly 1 January swim in South Queensferry (equally hardy dogs welcome).

Beneath the rich programme of arts and culture lies an historic city bubbling with stories. The medieval Old Town is packed with narrow alleys and closes where whispers of gruesome tales bounce off the

↑ View of Edinburgh from Calton Hill. (Richie Chan/S)

walls – it's here that the notorious Burke and Hare committed their murders, and where *Strange Case of Dr Jekyll and Mr Hyde* inspiration Deacon Brodie terrorised the city. Then there's that castle: the vast medieval fastness that looms over Edinburgh from its volcanic perch, unmissable and spellbinding when taken in from Princes Street Gardens beneath its northern side.

Edinburgh is gratifyingly dog-friendly, too, with ample walking opportunities, from its famous Royal Mile to Holyrood Park, where you can scale the peak of an ancient volcano. On the former, stop in at shops like Marchbrae (375 High St, EH1 1PW ⌂ marchbrae.com ⊙ 10.00–19.00 daily) to try on Harris Tweed jackets and Arran wool scarves, or stock up on shortbread and whisky at the innumerable gift shops. There's fun to be had by the sea, too, especially at Portobello where a large beach welcomes dogs year-round and a long promenade offers breezy walks. Meanwhile, you can get your fix of art, culture and creative silliness at a few dog-friendly city-centre attractions like Summerhall and the Camera Obscura & World of Illusions.

Out on the Firth of Forth, dog-friendly boat tours offer an alternative perspective on Edinburgh's skyline and a glimpse of the country's wild side, with seals, porpoises and many a bird to spot out at sea. There may be no other city in Britain with the breadth of appeal of Edinburgh.

SANDEMANS WALKING TOUR (130 High St, EH1 1TB ⊘ neweuropetours. eu ⊙ 11.00 & 14.00 daily; free) Get to grips with Edinburgh's history while walking the dog on the Sandemans free walking tour. You'll meet on the Royal Mile and be guided by one of Sandemans's energetic storytellers for up to two and a half hours. Tours pass some of the major and minor sights of the Old Town, including the statue of Greyfriars Bobby – the Skye terrier who famously guarded his owner's grave for 14 years. It's customary to tip your guide at the end.

CAMERA OBSCURA & WORLD OF ILLUSIONS (Castlehill EH1 2ND ⊘ camera-obscura.co.uk ⊙ 08.00–22.00 daily; adult/child £18/£14 ☂) A ludicrously fun museum in the heart of the Old Town, the Camera Obscura & World of Illusions is set across five floors in an old townhouse near the castle entrance. Expect mirror mazes, optical illusions and clever bits of tech to play with, and don't miss the dizzying vortex tunnel. The staff love dogs and will happily bring them water when they need it.

SUMMERHALL (1 Summerhall, EH9 1PL ⊘ summerhall.co.uk ⊙ 10.00–22.00 daily; admission fee varies ☂) A 20-minute walk south of the city centre, on the site of the old Royal (Dick) School of Veterinary Studies, Summerhall is now a cultural hub. Home to exhibitions – often associated with the city's festivals – and artist workshops, the whole space is dog-friendly, including the pub and café. Stop by to see what's on and have a G&T at The Royal Dick pub, where the local Pickering's Gin is on tap (the distillery lives just next door).

ARTHUR'S SEAT (📍EH16 5HX 🐕) Just 2km southeast of the city centre is a rather surprising geological feature: an ancient, extinct volcano rising 250m above sea level. The craggy rock formation, which last erupted around 340 million years ago, is also home to a more than 2,000-year-old fort built by the Votadini tribe. Today, it's the highest point of Holyrood Park and presents brilliant views over Edinburgh from its rocky top. The ascent to the peak is only 5km but will likely take around 2½ hours. It involves some steep sections and, if you choose to cross the Salisbury Crags, rough terrain; the peak is also very steep and rocky, not suitable for older, less mobile dogs. That said, it's well worth the effort for the views throughout. Check ⊘ walkhighlands.co.uk for route instructions.

PORTOBELLO BEACH (📍 EH15 2DX 🐕) Most people don't think of Edinburgh as a coastal city, but 5km east of its centre – 15 minutes by bus 25 – is a north-facing coastline with long stretches of golden sand and bustling promenades. Portobello Beach is the most enticing section, with its esplanade

of cafés, pubs and restaurants – many of which place water bowls outside for passing dogs. Dogs can safely roam off-lead, swim in the sea or chase the surf (though do be mindful if the beach is busy with picnicking families; it gets packed in high summer).

FORTH TOURS (Port Edgar Marina, EH30 9SQ ⊘ forthtours.com; ⊙ multiple departures daily; adult/child £16/£9, dogs £1 🐾) Boat trips with Forth Tours provide an opportunity to see Edinburgh from the water and to get up close to

LET'S GO

GETTING THERE

Unsurprisingly for a capital city, Edinburgh is well connected. Trains arrive at its central Waverley Station (Princes St, EH1 1BB) from across Britain, including the pet-friendly Caledonian Sleeper which wends its way up from London daily (⊘ sleeper.scot). There are direct connections to Aberdeen, Glasgow, Dundee, Newcastle and Manchester, too. The coach station, in the New Town (N St Andrews St, EH1 3DQ), connects with major cities in Scotland and northern England. Driving from the south, you'll likely take the A68 or A1, or the M74 and the A702. From Glasgow it's an easy 70km or so along the M8, and the M9 and M90 connect the city with the north of Scotland.

EATING

✖ **BABA** 130 George St, EH2 4JZ ⊘ baba. restaurant ⊙ noon–22.30 daily. Brilliant Mediterranean small plates served in a warren of a restaurant in the New Town, just 500m north of Princes Street Gardens, filled with antiques and old maps. Don't miss the blackened sweet potato or the slow-cooked lamb shoulder.

✖ **Cold Town House** 4 Grassmarket, EH1 2JU ⊘ coldtownhouse.co.uk ⊙ noon–midnight daily. An Old Town-based micro-brewery with a restaurant serving stone-baked pizzas and burgers. Views of the castle from the roof terrace are fantastic.

✖ **The Ensign Ewart** 521–523 Lawnmarket, EH1 2PE ⊘ ensignewartpub.co.uk ⊙ noon– midnight Fri–Sat, noon–23.00 Sun–Thu. Lots of Edinburgh's pubs are dog-friendly, at least in the bar area, but none is quite as handsome as this. Wood-beamed ceilings, exposed stone walls and an enviable whisky collection complete the experience.

✖ **The Huxley** 1–3 Rutland St, EH2 4JZ ⊘ thehuxley.co.uk ⊙ noon–22.30 Tue–Fri, 10am–10.30pm Sat–Sun. Great comfort food from morning 'til night, just west of Princes Street Gardens: fry-ups, boozy brunches and steak and chips in the evening.

✖ **Whighams Wine Cellars** 13 Hope St, EH2 4EL ⊘ whighams.com ⊙ noon–22.30 Mon–Wed, noon–midnight Thu–Sun. A New Town wine cellar with resident Cairn terrier. Good dogs can sit with you in the bar area while you sample Loch Fyne oysters and wines from around the world.

SLEEPING

🏠 **3 Lynedoch Place** 📍 EH3 7PX ⊘ petspyjamas. com 🐾 2. Get a taste of the Edinburgh high life in this lovely Georgian townhouse (sleeping two),

some of its most famous infrastructure. Departing from South Queensferry, around 13km northwest of the city centre, the 90-minute tours cruise the Firth of Forth, taking in the three iconic bridges that cross the body of water, connecting the capital to the Kingdom of Fife. Along the way, you may well spot seals and plenty of seabirds, including gannets, guillemots and all manner of gulls, and if you're lucky there might be a porpoise or two dancing in the water. The boats have indoor and outdoor seating. It's a 30-minute train ride from Edinburgh Waverley station to Dalmeny, a few minutes' walk from the marina.

a 20-minute walk from Waverley Station in central Edinburgh. Cosy down by the fireplace at night, and rest easy knowing the enclosed patio will keep your dog safe outdoors. *From £510/week*.

🏠 **The Four Sisters Boatel** Lochrin Basin, EH3 9QP ⚲ thefoursisters.co.uk 🐾 2. For something different, book one of these beautiful barges on the Lochrin Basin, just a 10-minute walk from the centre. The barges, *Four Sisters* and *Camillia*, sleep four and six respectively; each has a fully equipped kitchen, fluffy bathrobes and an outdoor deck with seating. *From £540/two nights*.

🏠 **Kimpton Charlotte Square** Charlotte Sq, EH2 4HQ ⚲ kimptoncharlottesquare.com. By far Edinburgh's most dog-friendly hotel, New Town-based Kimpton goes out of its way to welcome your pets. Rooms are spacious with quirky retro touches and unusual artworks; best of all is its access to the private gardens on Charlotte Square, where you can enjoy a stress-free game of fetch on the fenced lawn. From £130 B&B.

🏠 **Norton House Hotel** Newbridge EH28 8LX ⚲ handpickedhotels.co.uk 🐾 2. A picturesque country house just 12km from the city centre (an easy bus ride or 30-minute drive), this hotel is for dog owners who prefer a bit more space to roam. Morning walks can be taken in the extensive grounds, and dogs can join you for all meals in the lounge. Dog beds, blankets and bowls provided. *From £120 B&B, dogs £35/night*.

OTHER PRACTICALITIES

Tourist information centre 249 High St, EH1 1JY ✆ 0131 4733820 🕘 09.00–17.30 Mon– Sat, 10.00–16.00 Sun.

Pet supplies In the centre, Dofos (69 Raeburn Pl, EH4 1JF ⚲ dofos.co.uk 🕘 09.30–17.30 Mon–Fri, 09.00–17.00 Sat–Sun) stocks treats, chews and more, while on the coast, Harry's Gourmet Treats (212 Portobello High St, EH15 2AU ⚲ harrystreats.co.uk 🕘 11.00–16.00 Wed–Thu, 11.00–17.00 Fri, 10.00–17.00 Sat, noon–16.00 Sun) stocks homemade dog treats, natural chews and accessories – it's also the only store in the UK where you can have your dog fitted for an Equafleece coat.

Veterinary practices Dick Vet General Practice (Easter Bush Campus, EH25 9RG ✆ 0131 650650, out of hours ✆ 0131 6507883) is on the site of the Royal School of Veterinary Studies.

↑ Portobello Beach. (LG)

44 AN ACTIVE ADVENTURE IN A SCOTTISH WILDERNESS

WHERE	Loch Lomond & The Trossachs National Park, Scotland
WHEN	May–Sep
HIGHLIGHTS	Majestic munros, glassy lochs for swimming and lots of messing about in boats.

Driving to Loch Lomond and The Trossachs from Glasgow or Stirling and hitting the single-track lanes that criss-cross the park, it seems almost impossible that so much wilderness and beauty could exist so close to a city. As the suburbs give way and the hills of the Trossachs loom closer, you'll find yourself in thick forest where ferns blanket the floors and moss clings to the tree trunks, or alongside glistening lochs where the still waters resemble a vast window into the underworld.

As the name suggests, there are two sides to this national park. Loch Lomond sits in the west, stretching over 32km from tip to tip and plunging more than 182m deep, its shores punctuated by small towns and villages and its centre peppered with wild, uninhabited islands, with Ben Lomond, Scotland's southernmost munro, looming above at 873m high. To the east lie the Trossachs, the name given to the forested glens, lochs and mountains that spread out towards Stirling, where you'll find perfect wild swimming – even for beginners – and excellent hiking trails.

With an area so vast – 1,150km, in fact – you're not going to see it all on a weekend, so it's best to choose a base and strike out from there for day trips. On Loch Lomond's western shore, Luss is by far the prettiest place to stay, with its row of quaint, single-storey cottages and lochside beaches where you can hire boats or canoes to get out on the water. On the other side of the loch, with access to the

hugely popular, 154km West Highland Way hiking route (⊘ westhighlandway.org), Inversnaid has a brilliant budget-friendly bunkhouse and a kilometre-long trail down to the pretty Inversnaid Falls (♀ FK8 3TU). It's a long drive on winding, single-track roads to reach Inversnaid, but worthwhile for the feeling of being almost alone in the wilderness – a ferry runs here from Inveruglas Visitor Centre (♀ G83 7DP ◷ 10.00–17.00 daily) on the western side of the loch, so a day trip is possible, too. Alternatively, head to Aberfoyle, a 30-minute drive east of Inversnaid, to explore the Trossachs side of the park – and don't miss the shortbread from Maggie's Aberfoyle Kitchen on the main street (♀ FK8 3UG ⊘ maggiesaberfoylekitchen.co.uk ◷ 09.00–17.00 daily).

LOCH LOMOND LEISURE (Luss G83 8NZ ⊘ lochlomond-scotland.com ◷ Apr–Oct 09.00–18.30 daily; from £20) One of the best ways to enjoy Loch Lomond is from the water – especially on sunny summer days, when its shores and beaches get crowded. With a shoreline of 153km surrounded by hills cloaked in verdant forest, and several small islands in its centre, there's plenty to explore. Keep an eye out for salmon and brown trout in the water, or head towards Inchconnachan Island – 1½km from Luss – to see a population of wallabies thought to have been introduced by the island's owner in the 1950s. Located right on Luss beach, Loch Lomond Leisure hires out canoes, rowing boats and kayaks – and the dog can join you on all paddle vessels. They also run private speedboat tours (from £70/boat for 30 mins); well-behaved dogs are welcome to hop on board.

BALLOCH CASTLE COUNTRY PARK (Drymen Rd, Balloch G83 8LX ⊘ west-dunbarton.gov.uk 🐾) On the southern shore of Loch Lomond, just a 20-minute drive from Luss, this 80ha parkland offers a few marked trails for leisurely strolls with the dog. A derelict 19th-century castle stands within the grounds and there's a small walled garden and Chinese garden to explore.

LOCH ARKLET (📍 FK8 3TX) A 10-minute drive east of Inversnaid, there's not a great deal to see or do at Loch Arklet, but the swimming is spectacular. Park in the lay-by on the B829 on the loch's eastern shore and head down the track towards the dam; you'll find a shingle-and-mud beach that offers easy access to the water. You might well be the only ones here, and on a clear day you'll swim with the peak of Beinn Ime in the distance – glorious.

LOCH KATRINE CRUISES (Trossachs Pier, FK17 8HZ ⊘ lochkatrine.com ⊙ hourly 10.00–16.00; adult/child £14/£8.50, dogs £2 🐾) Loch Katrine – a 15-minute drive north of Aberfoyle – is another of the region's vast and wild bodies of water, peppered with islands and surrounded by native woodland and impressive hills. On these cruises, which vary in length from 45 minutes to 2 hours, commentary offers insight to the loch's history, nature and wildlife – look out for ospreys circling in the skies. There are indoor and outdoor decks and hot drinks and snacks available on board.

LET'S GO

GETTING THERE

The A82, the main road that runs along the western side of Loch Lomond, offers direct and easy access from Glasgow or the Highlands in the north. Take the A811 if coming from Stirling way or the A85 from Perth. Public transport is minimal, so a car is necessary.

EATING

✖ **Aberfoyle Bike Hire & Café** Main St, FK8 3UQ ⊘ aberfoylebikehire.co.uk ⊙ 10.00–17.00 daily. Excellent little café inside a bike hire shop, serving the town's best coffee and deliciously crispy bacon sourdough sandwiches with a small decked seating area out the back.

✖ **The Forth Inn** Main St, Aberfoyle FK8 3UQ ⊘ forthinn.com ⊙ noon–20.00 daily. A traditional Scottish inn serving brilliant steaks, pork and haggis burgers, and pies. Dogs are welcomed heartily with treats and water bowls; bag a seat in the beer garden when the sun's shining.

✖ **The Village Rest** Pier Rd, Luss G83 8NY ⊘ the-village-rest.co.uk ⊙ 10.00–20.00 daily. A tiny but lovely café serving breakfast, lunch and dinner. Expect hearty Scottish breakfasts and black pudding fritters with meat from the local butcher.

SLEEPING

🏠 **Inversnaid Bunkhouse** FK8 3TU ⊘ inversnaid.com 🐾 1. A fairly basic hostel inside

an old church just up the hill from Inversnaid Falls. Dogs are allowed in private rooms and in the upstairs bistro, which serves excellent home-cooked evening meals – the vegetarian options are brilliant. *From £45/night B&B.*

🏠 **Loch Katrine Eco Lodges** Trossachs Pier, FK17 8HZ 🖱 lochkatrine.com 🐾 **1**. On the Loch Katrine shore, these wooden huts sleeping up to four make a good, low-key self-catering option if you want to base yourself near Aberfoyle. *From £100/ night; dogs from £10/stay.*

🏠 **Loch Lomond Arms** Old Luss Rd, Luss G83 8NX 🖱 lochlomondarmshotel.co.uk 🐾 **2**. While the pub's rooms aren't dog-friendly, they have self-catering cottages that welcome dogs; some sleep up to six people. The pub itself serves great comfort food and decent salads and has a vast garden with lawns and patio. *From £895/week; dogs from £20/stay.*

OTHER PRACTICALITIES

Tourist information centre VisitScotland has centres in Aberfoyle (Trossachs Discovery Centre, Main St, FK8 3UQ ⊙ 09.30–17.00 Mon–Sat, 10.00–16.00 Sun) and Balloch (The Old Station Building, G83 8SS ⊙ 09.30–17.00 Mon–Sat, 10.00–16.00 Sun).

Pet supplies Wright for Pets (150 Main St, Balloch G83 0NZ 🕾 07703 980525 ⊙ 11.00– 15.30 Mon–Tue & Thu–Fri, 11.00–14.00 Sun) sells the essentials.

Veterinary practices McKenzie Vets (26 Gilmour St, Balloch G83 0DA 🕾 01389 751182) is a reliable practice with an out-of-hours service.

↑ Balloch Castle Country Park. (IR Stone/S)

45 A FAMILY-FOCUSED CITY BREAK BY THE SEA

WHERE	Dundee, Scotland
WHEN	May–Sep
HIGHLIGHTS	Hands-on museums, watery adventures and breezy beach days will have the kids begging to return.

Sitting at the mouth of the River Tay on the east coast of Scotland, Dundee has an industrious past. In the 1700s, as Scotland's second-most important city and a major jute processing hub, Dundee was rich. Decline came with the railways in the 19th century, though, and investment in the area stunted during the world wars. Today, however, Dundee is very much back on the map, this time as a fantastic cultural destination.

Start your journey at **The Waterfront** (♥ DD1 4EZ), most famously home to the striking V&A Dundee. While you won't be able to take the dog inside to

↑ The V&A Dundee. (Joe Dailly/S)

explore its galleries, it's well worth a walk around the Japanese-designed, cliff-like structure that looks out over the River Tay. From here, you can also see the RRS *Discovery*, the 120-year-old, three-masted ship, built in Dundee, that took Scott and Shackleton to Antarctica in the early 20th century.

Head 500m east from the V&A along The Waterfront and you'll come to Victoria Dock, where the rather unusual **HMS *Unicorn*** (♥ DD1 3BP ⟳ frigateunicorn.org ⊙ 10.00–16.00 Tue–Sun; adult/child £7.25/£3.50) is moored. At almost 200 years old, it's astonishing this frigate is still floating, let alone that it contains a dog-friendly museum charting its history in the Royal Navy. A few minutes' walk away across the dock, you can reward the kids with an hour at the **Wild Shore Dundee Aqua Park** (♥ DD1 3JP ⟳ wildshoredundee. co.uk ⊙ 09.00–dusk daily; £15), an inflatable obstacle course where dogs are welcome to wait with you on the shore.

Around 1½km east, the **Dundee Transport Museum** (Market Mews, Market St, DD1 3LA ⟳ dmoft.co.uk ⊙ 10.00–16.30 daily; adult/child £6.80/£3.60) is another family favourite – kids can sit (sometimes with the dog) in many of the vintage cars, buses, trams and train carriages that make up its vast collection, and get up close with Chitty Chitty Bang Bang.

A second day in Dundee could easily be spent enjoying the beach. Six kilometres from the centre, **Broughty Ferry** is a lovely well-to-do neighbourhood with great pubs, a big play park and a long, sandy strand that looks over the Firth of Tay (the eastern section is dog-friendly year-round; summer restrictions apply on the western end).

For off-lead walks, there are trails in the city's **Balgay Park** (♥ DD2 1SR 🐾) and leafy **Crombie Country Park and Reservoir** (♥ DD5 3QL 🐾), 19km northeast, which also has wildlife hides.

LET'S GO

Dundee is 30km from the M90. The train station (S Union St, DD1 4BY) sees direct trains to London King's Cross, Edinburgh, Aberdeen and Inverness.

Birchwood Food Emporium (28 Commercial St, DD1 3EQ ⟳ birchwoodemporium.com ⊙ 09.00–17.00 Mon–Sat, 10.00–17.00 Sun) is a lovely spot for breakfast or lunch in the city, while Broughty Ferry's **The Ship Inn** (121 Fisher St, DD5 2BR ⟳ theshipinn-broughtyferry.co.uk ⊙ noon–midnight daily) has the finest seafood and local beers, right by the water. For boozy brunches and cocktails where the dog always gets served first (with a bowl of water), try **Bird & Bear** (2 Whitehall Cres, DD1 4AU 🖪 birdandbeardundee ⊙ 11.00–midnight Sun–Thu, 11.00–01.00 Fri–Sat).

Accommodation is somewhat limited to hotels. **Malmaison** (44 Whitehall Cres, DD1 4AY ⟳ malmaison.com 🐾 1; from £60 B&B, dogs £20/night) is a favourite for dog owners, while **Staybridge Suites** (Lower Dens Mill, DD4 6AD ⟳ ihg.com 🐾 2; from £70 B&B, dogs £25/night) has kitchenettes and is great for families.

46 A WILD ISLAND GETAWAY WITH FABULOUS FOOD

WHERE	Isle of Mull, Scotland
WHEN	May–Sep
HIGHLIGHTS	Exploring the coast on thrilling boat trips, lazing on pristine beaches and savouring the astonishing local produce.

Separated from the mainland by the almost 30km-long Sound of Mull, Mull is a wonderfully remote and wild island off the west coast of Scotland. It's not huge – measuring around 40km from north to south – but the variety of landscapes is impressive, with linen-white sandy beaches lining its coastline and towering munros with rocky peaks rising up in its centre.

Tobermory, Mull's capital, makes a great base. Sitting on the northeast tip of the island, it's most famous for its starring role in children's TV show *Balamory*, which used the colourful houses overlooking the ocean as a backdrop for its wholesome entertainment. A working harbour town, it's a bustling place with a couple of fun attractions, but the real highlight is the food and drink. Gin and whisky drinkers should make a beeline for the Tobermory Distillery (Ledaig, PA75 6NR ⌂ tobermorydistillery.com ⊙ 11.00–16.00 Mon–Sat, noon–16.00 Sun) to pick up a tipple that's been made here for over 220 years. Those with a sweet tooth will need to stop at the nearby Isle of Mull Ice Cream kiosk (Main St, PA75 6NT ⌂ isleofmullicecream.co.uk ⊙ noon–15.00 daily) for unusual and refreshing cones, or Tobermory Chocolate (57 Main St, PA75 6NT ⌂ tobermorychocolate.com ⊙ 09.00–17.00 Mon–Sat) to sample handmade sweets. Spectacular local seafood abounds in the local pubs and restaurants; if you're here on a Monday, make sure to head to the Open Air Producers' Market (♀ PA75 6NR ⊙ 11.00–14.00), on the harbour, to try the scallop wraps with seaweed chutney from the Tobermory Fish Company. The local farmhouse cheeses from Isle of Mull Cheese are also highly recommended.

In the northwest of the island, around a 40-minute drive west of Tobermory, spectacular Calgary Bay, where a scythe of white sand separates grassy dunes from an astoundingly blue sea, is a gorgeous spot, and makes a great alternative base if you want beach time.

You could easily spend an entire weekend in the north of the island, but south Mull is where things get a bit wilder, so make an effort to get down here – it's an almost 2-hour drive from Tobermory but the views along the way will have you mesmerised, and you'll be richly rewarded with steep hikes up Ben More (1,174m; see ⌂ walkhighlands.co.uk) or quiet beaches like Knockvologan (♀ PA66 6BN). Also in the south is the Fionnphort ferry terminal (♀ PA66 6BH ⌂ calmac.co.uk ⊙ multiple departures daily), the gateway to neighbouring Isle of Iona, a car-free island community where you can visit a ruined abbey and find yet more wonderful beaches on a day trip from Mull.

MULL MUSEUM (Main St, Tobermory PA75 6NY ⌂ mullmuseum.org.uk ⊙ 10.00–16.00 Mon–Sat; free ☂) This tiny museum is packed with interesting artefacts and engaging displays that show how life on Mull has changed over the centuries. See old farming tools, cooking equipment and model kitchens, and find out about the island's military history. Small and medium dogs are welcome (large dogs are impractical in such a small space); the museum is entirely run by volunteers and donations are welcome.

← Arty enjoying the beach at Calgary Bay. (LG)

TOBERMORY AQUARIUM (1 Ledaig, Tobermory PA75 6NR ⊘ mullaquarium.co.uk ⊘ 10.00–16.30 Mon–Thu, 12.30–16.30 Sun; adult/child £5.50/£4 🌂) Billing itself as 'Europe's first catch and release aquarium', meaning each creature stays in their exhibits for no longer than four weeks, this is a small but surprisingly exciting little attraction on Tobermory Harbour, a 10-minute walk south of the Mull Museum. Everything here is caught in Tobermory Bay by local fishing boats, so you might see giant crabs, anemones, langoustines or sea slugs – some of which you'll get to handle in the 'get your hands wet' sessions.

CALGARY BAY (📍 PA75 6QT 🐕) By far Mull's most popular beach, though still never too busy, Calgary is a fine sweep of coarse white sand lapped by astonishingly clear seas and backed by grassy dunes. On a warm, sunny day the water might look tempting, but even in the height of summer it only warms to around 10°C, so if you're a keen swimmer you'll want a wet suit. Come early in the morning so the dog can race around off the lead without disturbing the picnicking families that descend by lunchtime.

CALGARY ARTS (Calgary PA75 6QQ ⊘ calgary.co.uk ⊘ 10.30–16.00 Tue–Sun 🌂) Creativity abounds in this arty complex, less than 1km from the beach, which has a workshop, gallery and café (up for sale at the time of writing), plus a nature walk with sculptures and unusual constructions along the way. Browse the ceramics, woodwork, soft furnishings and paintings by local artists in the shop before spending an hour or so on the Art in Nature trail, encountering such pieces as carved tree trunks, handmade oyster catchers, a woman made from rope and a life-sized stag woven from sticks and branches. While the shop and gallery close at 16.00, the nature walk can be enjoyed any time, seven days a week, with guides for sale at an honesty box at the start of the trail.

STAFFA TOURS (Taigh Solais, Ledaig, Tobermory PA75 6NR & Fionnphort, PA66 6BH ⊘ staffatours.com ⊘ multiple departures daily; adult/child £30/£15) Between April and October, whales, dolphins, porpoise and basking sharks roam the waters around Mull, and on a boat trip with Staffa Tours you might be lucky enough to see them all. Launching either from Tobermory or Fionnphort in the southwest, the guided trips take in Staffa Island, with its dramatic hexagonal basalt columns and the vast Fingal's Cave; those from Tobermory also land in the Treshnish Isles, where you can see the remains of Viking and medieval settlements. Whichever tour you take, expect to see golden eagles, guillemots and puffins. Tours last between 3 and 4½ hours; during the summer nesting season, dogs must be kept well away from the puffins on land, so note that there may be some areas that are off limits to you.

LET'S GO

GETTING THERE

CalMac Ferries (⊘ calmac.co.uk) offers multiple services daily to Mull from mainland Scotland: either from Oban (Alma Cres, PA34 4LE; book online in advance) to Craignure (A489, PA65 6AZ) or from Lochaline (Morvern, PA80 5XP; just turn up on the day) to Fishnish (A884, PA65 6BA). If you're coming without a car, Oban train station (Railway Pier, PA34 4LW) is your best bet, with connections to Glasgow; the ferry terminal is a short walk from the station. Getting around Mull without a vehicle is slow, but West Coast Motors (⊘ westcoastmotors.co.uk) runs buses between the Tobermory and Calgary ferry ports.

EATING

✖ **The Craignure Inn** Craignure PA65 6AZ ⊘ craignure-inn.co.uk ⊙ noon–22.00 daily. Pub classics like pies and burgers, plus pizzas and fish and chips, served in the dog-friendly bar area and outdoor benches opposite the Craignure ferry terminal on the southeast coast of the island.

✖ **The Creel Shak** 8 A849, Fionnphort PA66 6BL ✆ 01681 700312 ⊙ 09.30–20.00 daily. Located right on the ferry dock at Fionnphort, this little shack sells proper home-cooked chips with whatever the owner has managed to catch that day – often mussels, lobster, scallops, prawns and oysters. Outdoor seating only.

✖ **Mishnish** Main St, Tobermory PA75 6NU ⊘ themishnish.co.uk ⊙ 11.00–01.00 daily. A lovely restaurant with a dog-friendly bar area where you can order haggis nuggets, local oysters, seafood chowder and pizza. Don't miss the homemade sticky toffee pudding for dessert.

✖ **The Taste of Mull** Hawthorn Cottage, PA72 6JB 🅵 ⊙ 16.30–20.30 daily. On the east coast, 20 minutes south of Tobermory, this little takeaway shack serves hearty home-cooked food incuding beef chilli, mussels in white wine sauce, fish and chips and burgers – all of which can be devoured sitting next to their open fire pit.

✖ **The Tobermory Scullery** 10 Main St, Tobermory PA75 6NU ⊘ thetobermoryscullery. co.uk ⊙ 08.00–17.00 Mon–Sat. A family-run café serving Scottish breakfasts, local fish and shellfish, and homemade cakes. The staff here love dogs, so expect a fuss and water bowl on arrival.

SLEEPING

🏠 **Calgary Arts** Calgary PA75 6QQ ⊘ calgary. co.uk. Just a 10-minute walk from the beach,

↑ Sound of Mull. (Beachy Photography/S)

these self-catering cottages are only available by the week, which is just as well as Calgary Bay is the sort of place you'll want to linger for longer than a weekend. There are two dog-friendly options within the complex, sleeping two and four people. *From £400/week; dogs £20/week.*

🏠 **Glengorm Castle** PA75 6QE 🐾 glengormcastle. co.uk. Small and medium-sized dogs are welcome at Glengorm Castle, a rather majestic property around 15 minutes north of Tobermory. All turrets and towers, this magnificent castle overlooks the Atlantic and is surrounded by green lawns and woodland, ideal for morning walks. *From £165/ night B&B.*

🏠 **Isle of Mull Hotel & Spa** Craignure PA65 6BB 🐾 crerarhotels.com. By far the largest and most luxurious hotel on Mull, this place is incredibly dog friendly. It has spectacular sea views over the Craignure ferry terminal, lovely gardens for your dog's morning loo trips and direct access to a small beach. There are water bowls and dog-mess bins dotted throughout the property, and your dog can dine with you at the restaurant. *From £190/night B&B; dogs £20/night.*

🏠 **Sunset Cottage** Balmeanach PA65 6BA 🐾 petspyjamas.com 🐾 **1**. A simple but smart single-storey self-catering cottage just 5 minutes from Fishnish ferry terminal on the island's east

coast. It has an enclosed garden with gorgeous sea views and sleeps up to four people. *From £145/night.*

🏠 **Western Isles Hotel** 64 A848, Tobermory PA75 6PR 🐾 westernisleshotel.com. This handsome 19th-century property overlooking Tobermory Bay is perfect for a stay in Mull's capital. Dogs are permitted in all public areas, meaning you can eat with them at breakfast and dinner. Speaking of dinner – the views from the restaurant are sensational but the food is even better, while the cocktail list is packed with local gins and, of course, whisky. *From £198/night B&B.*

OTHER PRACTICALITIES

Tourist information centre VisitScotland Craignure iCentre, The Pier, Craignure PA65 6AY 🐾 visitscotland.com 🕘 09.15–10.15 Mon–Sat, 10.00–17.00 Sun.

Pet supplies Oban, on the mainland, has a Pets at Home (3 Lochavullin Dr, PA34 4BW 🐾 petsathome. com 🕘 09.00–18.00 Mon–Sat, 10.00–17.00 Sun) with all the usual essentials.

Veterinary practices A 40-minute drive south of Tobermory, Mull and Iona Vets (Lagganulva Farm, Ulva Ferry PA73 6LT 🐾 01688 500139) offers routine appointments and 24-hour emergency help for medical issues.

47 MAGICAL MOUNTAINS & GLORIOUS GLENS

WHERE	Glencoe & the Nevis Range, Scotland
WHEN	Mar–Sep
HIGHLIGHTS	Awe-inspiring Highlands scenery that can be savoured on glorious railway trips and from easy-to-reach mountain viewpoints.

There may be no more famous a glen in Scotland than Glen Coe – not to be confused with Glencoe, the village, which sits at the western end of the valley – and that's for good reason. Spectacular views are rife in this part of the southern Scottish Highlands: you only have to stand outside the **National Trust Scotland visitor centre** at the glen's western end (♀ PH49 4HX ⊘ nts.org.uk ☉ 09.30–16.30 daily) to feel the power of the towering mountains that surround this lush, green valley. Start your exploration here, learning about the region and fuelling up with a bacon sandwich at the café before you set off on one of the many fantastic walks this area has to offer.

There's a lovely 1½km woodland walk from the visitor centre, or you can follow the 5km forestry road out the back and up to the summit of Am Meall,

↑ The Jacobite Steam Train on the Glenfinnan Viaduct. (travellight/S)

a 414m-high munro with brilliant views over Loch Leven. For longer walks you'll need to be comfortable with an OS map or similar, though there are a few signposted trails around the somewhat hidden **Glencoe Lochan** (♥ PH49 4HT) – a small, glassy loch with sensational views of the Pap of Glencoe and Beinn a' Bheithir. See ⌀ walkhighlands.co.uk for more inspiration.

For those without the inclination to romp for hours on the mountain trails, there are some more sedate options near Fort William, 25km north of Glencoe and another convenient base. Fifteen minutes from the town centre is the **Nevis Range Mountain Gondola** (♥ PH33 6SY ⌀ nevisrange.co.uk ☉ 09.00–16.30 daily; adult/child £22/£12.50 ☂), a cable car that takes you 550m up the side of Aonach Mòr, Scotland's eighth highest mountain. Originally built to ferry skiers up the slopes, it's an equally exciting summer attraction with a couple of viewpoints worth walking to from the station (allow around 30 minutes for each). On the way up, you'll spot mountain bikers hurtling down the face of the mountain beneath you. The on-site café is a great stop for hot drinks with a view.

The other star attraction around here is the famous **Jacobite Steam Train** (Tom-na-Faire, Station Sq, Fort William PH33 6TQ ⌀ westcoastrailways.co.uk ☉ multiple departures daily; adult/child £49/£28 ☂). The 135km return trip, from Fort William to remote Mallaig on the west coast, chunters over the iconic Glenfinnan Viaduct overlooking Loch Shiel. Grab fish and chips in Mallaig and watch the ferries come and go before heading back to Fort William.

LET'S GO

The A82 and A86 are the main roads in this part of the Highlands. Fort William's train station (Tom-na-Faire, Station Sq, PH33 6TQ) has good connections with Edinburgh, Glasgow, Inverness and London, including via the Caledonian Sleeper (⌀ sleeper.scot). Scottish City Link (⌀ citylink.co.uk) and Shiel (⌀ shielbuses.co.uk) buses connect the town with Glencoe and the Nevis Range Gondola.

The most popular pub in Glen Coe is the **Clachaig Inn** (Old Village Rd, PH49 4HX ⌀ clachaig.com ☉ 11.00–23.00 daily), which serves hearty dinners for hungry hikers. In Glencoe, the casual **The Gathering** pub (A82, PH49 4HP ⌀ crerarhotels.com ☉ noon–21.00 daily) offers local seafood, pizza and burgers next door to the area's best hotel, the **Glencoe Inn** (A82, PH49 4HP ⌀ crerarhotels.com 🐾 2; from £185/night B&B, dogs £20/night). Bedrooms are cosy, with complimentary Tunnock's snacks, and excellent breakfasts and dinners are served at the dog-friendly, residents-only restaurant.

In Fort William, try **The Garden Flat** (♥ PH33 6SP ⌀ petspyjamas.com 🐾 2; from £125/night), a self-catering cottage for two with an enclosed suntrap of a garden garden, around 10 minutes' drive east of the centre.

Call **Crown Vets** (Glen Nevis Pl, Croft Rd, PH33 6DA ✆ 01397 702727) for medical advice and head to **Pet & Gardenstop** (8B Blar Mor Ind Estate, PH33 7PT ✆ 01397 700715 ☉ 10.00–17.00 Tue–Sat) for supplies.

48 MOUNTAIN ADVENTURES BIG & SMALL

WHERE	Cairngorms National Park, Scotland
WHEN	May–Sep
HIGHLIGHTS	Munros to bag, mountains passes to drive and plenty of watery adventures in or on the lochs.

A vast landscape of rotund, heather-clad hills, pine forests and sweeping mountainsides often cloaked in snow (even in summer), the Cairngorms National Park is an adventure playground for humans and dogs alike. And while its lofty summits might intimidate some, a visit here is not all about scaling peaks. Glistening lochs, royal estates and mountain railways offer a soft adventure experience that's accessible for all.

Most of the infrastructure lies in the northern part of the national park, with towns like Aviemore and Grantown on Spey attracting the bulk of the attention thanks to the area's concentration of attractions and accommodation. The likes of Loch Morlich and the Rothiemurchus Estate are magnets for families, offering watersports, sandy beaches and safe swimming spots.

↑ Cairngorms National Park. (Duncan Andison/S)

But base yourself further into the park's mountainous belly (around 90 minutes' drive south of Aviemore) and you'll find lovely little low-key villages like Braemar, Crathie and Ballater. There's a far more peaceful vibe here, and it's in this area where the royal family has spent many a summer staying in their not-so-modest holiday home, Balmoral Castle. Follow in their footsteps for a day by exploring the gardens and grounds, which are open to the public from April through July.

Connecting Braemar and Aviemore is the Old Military Road, one of Scotland's most spectacular mountain drives. Its two hours of twists and turns and steep climbs are well worth tackling in the car – providing your dog doesn't get motion sickness – and you'll be rewarded with glorious views of the Lecht Pass, a popular ski resort in winter. Stop off at the various viewpoints for a picture or picnic, or stretch your legs on the 1½km-long walk through a pretty glen to the former Lecht Mine (look out for the Well of Lecht car park (♥ AB37 9ES) just north of the Lecht ski centre).

Of course, if you and your dog do have the energy for a good mountain hike, there's many a munro to be bagged in the Cairngorms. The excellent Walk Highlands (⊘ walkhighlands.co.uk) website has myriad suggestions for hikes of all kinds. It's important to be aware of the wildlife you might encounter in the national park; especially ground nesting birds between April and August.

STRATHSPEY RAILWAY (Grampian Rd, Aviemore PH22 1PY ∂ strathspeyrailway.co.uk; adult/child £16.75/£8.40, dogs £1 🐾) Spending some 2 hours on a steam train from Aviemore station is a delightful way to pass an afternoon. You'll travel through Boat of Garten village, watching the moors whizz by the window before stopping at Broomhill station where you can hop off to get a picture of the locomotive with the Cairngorm Mountains in the background. The train heads back along the same line, but if you're feeling active, you could alight at either Boat of Garten or Broomhill and walk back 9½km or 16km respectively, along the Speyside Way.

LOCH AN EILEIN (♀ PH22 1QT ∂ rothiemurchus.net 🐕) Surrounded by ancient pine forests where red squirrels leap from tree to tree and crested tits nest in summer, Loch an Eilein is, as Sir David Attenborough once said, 'one of the glories of wild Scotland'. The beautiful loch is part of the Rothiemurchus Estate, and on an island along its northern shore lies a ruined 14th-century castle. Despite being a mere 8km south of Aviemore it feels gloriously remote, and the swimming is superb, though you'll need water shoes to get over the rocky bed. You could also follow a fantastic 7km trail (allow 2 hrs) all the way around the shore. Dogs should be kept on leads unless under very close control; there's a fenced-in exercise meadow where they're allowed to run free.

LOCH MORLICH WATERSPORTS (♀ PH22 1QY ∂ lochmorlich.com; 1hr £25) Its spectacular location in the shadow of Cairngorm Mountains, just a

20-minute drive southeast from Aviemore, makes Loch Morlich one of the most enchanting places in the national park. Floating around on its deep blue waters in a canoe is a serene way to enjoy it, especially on sunny days, when its single sandy beach gets packed with families. Dogs can join you in a canoe while you paddle out to other areas of the lake to escape the crowds; they are also allowed on the beach, though best kept on a lead if it's busy. With water temperatures of around 18–19°C, the loch is a balmy spot for a swim.

BALMORAL CASTLE & ESTATE (♀ AB35 5TB ⊘ balmoralcastle.com; adult/child £16/£6) Located in the southern section of the national park, 15 minutes east of Braemar, the Queen's summer residence is open to the public between April and July each year, during which time you and your dog are welcome to explore the grounds and gardens that surround this striking Scottish baronial castle. The 1.2ha of formal planted gardens include glasshouses and a kitchen garden installed by Prince Philip, the Duke of Edinburgh, while beyond the castle's immediate surroundings lies the 20,000ha Balmoral Estate, where you can hike over hills and through pine forests. The 9½km circular Balmoral Cairns walk (⊘ walkhighlands.co.uk) is a spectacular trail with excellent views of Her Majesty's summer home; it starts at the Crathie Visitor Centre (♀ AB35 5UL), 1km east of the castle.

CAMBUS O'MAY WOODLAND (♀ AB35 5SD ⊘ forestryandland.gov.scot 🐾) A 15-minute drive east of Balmoral brings you to this peaceful woodland nature reserve, a tranquil place for a picnic and a stroll along one of its three

↑ Balmoral Castle. (Bas Meelker/S)

↑ Loch an Eilein (chromoprisme/S)

trails. Ranging from 1km to 4km, the routes are easy enough even for older dogs. Each one takes in something different, but the favourite is the Two Lochans trail (2½km; approx 1 hr), which passes handsome Douglas fir trees and a pair of lochans where butterflies flit among the ferns.

MUIR OF DINNET NATURE RESERVE (♀ AB34 5NB ♂ nature.scot 🐾)

The Muir of Dinnet, just a 5-minute drive northeast of Cambus O'May, encompasses wetlands, woods and moors. For a short, pleasant walk, take the trail to the Vat Gorge (just short of 1½km; about 45 mins), where you can clamber up a gentle waterfall that was carved out during the last Ice Age, before continuing through pine woodland for views over Loch Kinord.

LET'S GO

GETTING THERE

The Cairngorms are best tackled in your own vehicle, but it is possible to travel here by train: Aviemore station (Grampian Rd, PH22 1PY) is on the main line between Perth and Inverness. Roads-wise, the A9 from Edinburgh gets you straight up to Aviemore, connecting with the A86 for drivers coming from the west. From Aberdeen, it's an enjoyable drive on the A93 which runs through Braemar and connects to the A939 and Old Military Road towards Aviemore.

EATING

✕ The Barn Rothiemurchus Centre, Aviemore PH22 1QH ♂ rothiemurchus.net ☉ 10.00–16.00 daily. A fantastic café at the Rothiemurchus Estate Visitor Centre with plenty of indoor and outdoor seating. There are breakfast rolls for early morning snacks, hearty burgers made from the estate's own Highland beef, and that Scottish classic, Cullen skink. The farm shop next door is well worth a visit if you're self-catering.

✕ The Boat Inn Charleston Rd, Aboyne AB34 5EL ♂ theboatinnaboyne.co.uk ☉ 09.30–22.00 daily. An 18th-century coaching inn on the banks

of the River Dee just outside the boundaries of the Cairngorms National Park, the Boat Inn serves top-quality food in a relaxed setting. Expect excellent salads, great pub grub and brilliant veggie options. Dogs are well looked after with bowls and biscuits.

✕ The Explorer Café Aviemore Retail Park, Grampian Rd, Aviemore PH22 1AF ♂ explorercafe. co.uk ☉ 09.00–19.00 Mon–Wed, 09.00–20.00 Thu–Fri, 09.00–18.00 Sat, 10.00–18.00 Sun. A great little café inside the Tiso Outdoor Experience kit shop, with brilliant views of the mountain ranges. Expect classics such as fish and chips, burgers, sandwiches and cooked breakfasts. There's a dog watering station and you can even treat your pet with a plate of sausage.

✕ The Flying Stag Mar Rd, Braemar AB35 5YN ♂ thefifearms.com ☉ noon–20.00 daily. Perhaps not one for vegetarians (or those on a budget), this pub inside the luxurious Fife Arms hotel (see opposite) has serious character, largely thanks to the taxidermy flying stag that lords over its bar. Expect haggis, neeps and tatties and Highland steaks, and prepare to pay upwards of £25 for a Sunday roast.

✖ **The Winking Owl** 123 Grampian Rd, Aviemore PH22 1RH ⌂ thewinkingowl.co ⊙ noon–23.00 daily. A craft ale pub in the centre of Aviemore offering good, hearty food and – as you might expect – an excellent range of local beers. There's a dog-friendly seating area downstairs.

SLEEPING

🏠 **Banchory Lodge** Dee St, Banchory AB31 5HS ⌂ banchorylodge.com 🐾 2. A handsome Georgian property with a mix of antique furnishings and quirky, colourful décor. Dogs are welcomed with open arms (and biscuits) and they're allowed to join you for meals in the bar. *From £209/night B&B.*

🏠 **Coire Cas** Coylumbridge PH22 1QN ⌂ petspyjamas.com 🐾 2. This homely cottage (three bedrooms; sleeping up to six people) just outside Aviemore is an excellent self-catering base for outdoor adventures. There's an enclosed garden, and even a hot tub and sauna. *From £210/ night, minimum four-night stay.*

🏠 **The Fife Arms** Mar Rd, Braemar AB35 5YN ⌂ thefifearms.com 🐾 2. Dating back to the 1800s, The Fife Arms is brimming with style and intriguing stories. Rooms are furnished with Scottish antiques, the public spaces are packed with unusual works by local artisans, and the hotel even has its own house tweed and tartan. *From £250/night B&B; dogs £25/stay.*

🏠 **Macdonald Aviemore Woodland Lodges** Aviemore PH22 1PN ⌂ macdonaldhotels.co.uk 🐾 2. This hybrid hotel-meets-self-catering property has a collection of 18 woodland lodges within a pine forest. Lodges, which sleep between four and six people, include a small kitchenette, but breakfast, served in the food court (which has a dog-friendly area), is included in the nightly rate. *From £182/night B&B.*

OTHER PRACTICALITIES

Tourist information centre Grampian Rd, Aviemore PH22 1RH ✆ 01479 810930 ⊙ 09.00– 17.00 daily.

Pet supplies Bark + Ride (Dalfaber Industrial Estate, Highland Home Centre, Aviemore PH22 1NZ ⌂ barkandridesports.com ⊙ 09.00–17.00 Mon–Sat) is primarily an outdoors shop but also stocks leads, collars and treats.

Veterinary practices Strathspey Veterinary Centre (Forest Rd, Grantown-on-Spey PH26 3JJ; 2 Granish Way, Dalfaber Dr, Aviemore PH22 1UQ; both ✆ 01479 872252) offers a 24-hour emergency service.

↑ Muir of Dinnet Nature Reserve. (Pecold/S)

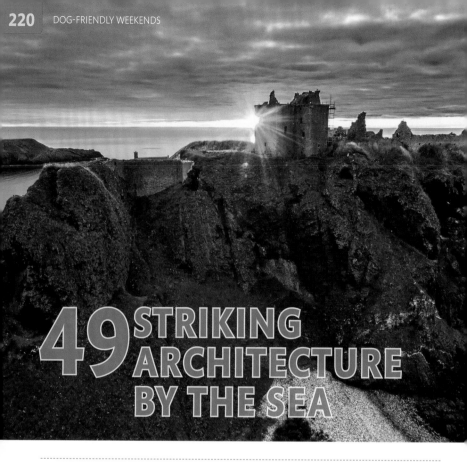

49 STRIKING ARCHITECTURE BY THE SEA

WHERE	Aberdeen, Scotland
WHEN	Mar–Sep
HIGHLIGHTS	Pearly granite buildings sandwiched between vibrant street art displays, plus ancient castles with glorious walks.

Aberdeen's muted grey tones lend this northern Scottish city an elegance you might not expect from a place powered by the North Sea oil industry. Constructed with the region's silvery granite, many of its buildings, some of them dramatically Gothic in style, look as though they have been lifted from fairytales and plonked on to the busy streets.

You'll see most of this splendid architecture around the central neighbourhood of Castlegate. Take it in on the self-guided **Nuart Trail** (⊘visitabdn.com), a street art initiative that sees new works brighten up office blocks and shopping centres each year. Download the map online and start at Union Street, meandering down side roads to check out murals and installations by world-renowned street artists, and looking up at magnificent 19th-century buildings like **Marischal College** (Broad St, AB10 1AB), **Aberdeen Citadel** (28 Castle St, AB11 5BG) and the terrific

↑ Dunnottar Castle. (TatianaStolcova/S)

trio of the theatre, library and St Mark's Church, like a mini St Paul's Cathedral, on Rosemont Viaduct. Look out for **Provost Skene's House** (Marischal Sq, Guestrow, AB10 1AS), a 16th-century stone dwelling with turrets and tiny windows that's the oldest house in the city.

The city's thriving nightlife – Aberdeen has a lively university – is concentrated around Castlegate, too. A few cafés and pubs here are dog-friendly, including Aberdeenshire's own **Brewdog**: stop by one of their pubs (5–9 Union St ⊙ 11.00–midnight daily; 17 Gallowgate ⊙ 16.00–midnight Mon–Thu, noon–01.00 Fri–Sat), for a burger and a pint.

For something leafier, head 3km north to Old Aberdeen and stroll down the pleasingly symmetrical Cathedral Walk and on to the university campus' cobbled High Street. You could also head coastward to **Aberdeen Beach** (Beach Blvd, AB11 5DN 🐾), 1km from Castlegate, for off-lead time.

There are plenty of potential day trips, too. Drive 30 minutes inland to 16th-century **Crathes Castle** (♥ AB31 5QJ ∅ nts.org.uk ⊙ 10.00–16.00 daily; adult/child £14.50/£11) for walks amid manicured gardens; 30 minutes south to Stonehaven Harbour and the dramatic clifftop ruins of **Dunnottar Castle** (♥ AB39 2TL ∅ dunnottarcastle.co.uk ⊙ 09.00–18.00 daily; adult/child £8/£4); or 20 minutes north to **Newburgh Beach** (♥ AB41 6BY) where hundreds of seals bask on the sands (make sure your dog keeps their distance).

LET'S GO

Aberdeen train station (Guild St, AB11 6LX) has excellent connections with Edinburgh, Glasgow and Inverness. The city is easy to reach by car, sitting on the A90 and A92.

Foodstory (11–15 Thistle St, AB10 1XZ ∅ foodstorycafe.co.uk ⊙ 09.00–20.00 Tue–Sat, 10.00–15.00 Sun–Mon) offers light lunches in central Aberdeen, while **The Bobbin** (500 King St, AB24 5ST ∅ pubswithmore.co.uk ⊙ 11.00–22.00 Mon–Fri, 10.00–22.00 Sat–Sun), between Castlegate and Old Aberdeen, includes curries and quesadillas on its eclectic dinner menu. If you head to Crathes Castle, don't miss the cakes at **Ride Coffee House** (46 Station Rd, Banchory AB31 5YA 🅕 ⊙ 09.00–17.00 daily); **The Cock & Bull** (Ellon Rd, Balmedie AB23 8XY ∅ thecockandbull.co.uk ⊙ 11.00–22.00 Mon–

Sat, 11.00–20.00 Sun) makes an excellent post-beach pub stop near Newburgh.

At **Brewdog Kennels** (5–9 Union St, AB11 5BU ∅ brewdog.com; from £109/night), the dog gets VIP treatment with a biscuit on arrival and you get a cheeky half on the house, while at **Malmaison** (49–53 Queen's Rd, AB15 4YP ∅ malmaison.com 🐾 1; from £95/night, dogs £20/night), in a quieter part of town, 2km west of Castlegate, your dog can join you for dinner, drinks or breakfast in the cosy bar.

Ashgrove Vets (10 Belmont Rd, AB25 3SR ✆ 01224 486 444) are available in emergencies. Head to **Pets at Home** (Unit 1B, Beach Boulevard Retail Park, Links Rd, AB11 5EJ ∅ petsathome.com ⊙ 09.00–18.00 Mon–Sat, 10.00–18.00 Sun) for all the essentials.

50 A LOCHSIDE ESCAPE WITH WATERFALLS & WILD LEGENDS

WHERE	Loch Ness, Scotland
WHEN	May–Sep
HIGHLIGHTS	Boat trips, waterfall walks and one of Scotland's best dog-friendly hotels.

Deeper than the North Sea and filled with more water than all of England and Wales's lakes combined, it's hardly surprising that Loch Ness is shrouded in folklore. It's most famous, of course, for that eponymous monster which was first reported in 1933 as 'an enormous animal rolling and plunging on the surface'. Since then, scientists armed with sonar and passionate self-appointed investigators have scoured its waters for any sign of a giant aquatic beast, but no such animal has been found. If you come to Loch Ness you're unlikely to find Nessie, but you will discover a beautifully green landscape surrounding a brooding body of water that's well worth exploring – by boat or on land.

One of the highlights of the Scottish Highlands, skinny Loch Ness is 37km long and around 1½km wide, stretching from the charming city of Inverness in the north right down to low-key Fort Augustus in the south. Its western side is relatively gentle, characterised by rolling green hills and patches of forest, while its eastern edge is fringed with bulbous rocky peaks and unusual geological formations – a landscape more akin to the drama for which the Highlands is usually known.

It's just an hour's drive between Inverness and Fort Augustus, and it's perfectly possible to take in the length of the loch in a weekend. Base yourself in Fort Augustus, where one of Scotland's most dog-friendly hotels provides an ideal base, and you could enjoy walks along the Caledonian Canal (♀ PH32 4BD), which wends its way south after a series of five locks and a swing bridge. Or choose Inverness as your weekend home and enjoy the hubbub of the city and its picturesque riverside location.

DOLPHIN SPIRIT INVERNESS (Inverness Marina Pier, IV1 1FF ⊘ dolphinspirit.co.uk ☉ 10.00, noon, 14.00 & 16.00 daily; adult/child £19.50/ £12 ☂) Forget Nessie spotting: strike out on to the Moray Firth to look for otters, dolphins and porpoise. Cruises last around 75 minutes, sailing around the Beauly Firth and Munlochy Bay, and a guide is on hand to help you spot and learn about the wildlife and local folklore. The upper deck has the best views, while the lower deck is weatherproof.

JACOBITE CRUISES (Dochgarroch Lock, IV3 8JG ⊘ jacobite.co.uk ☉ 09.30, noon & 14.00 daily; adult/child £25/£19 ☂) Heading from north to south and back again, Jacobite Cruises offer the best way to see the real extent of Loch Ness, taking in the western shore, and cruising past the ruins of Urquhart Castle and along the Caledonian Canal. Live commentary provides insight into the region's history, as well as that all-important bit of folklore: tales of the Loch Ness monster. Dogs are allowed on the outdoor upper deck and covered indoor areas below. The visitor centre at Dochgarroch Lock, a 15-minute drive south from Inverness, has an excellent dog-friendly gift shop and café.

← Falls of Foyers. (grafxart/s)

DORES BEACH & TORR POINT (📍IV2 6TQ 🐾) One of the best viewpoints for admiring the sea-like expanse of Loch Ness, Dores is a lovely shingly stretch of beach just a 20-minute drive south of Inverness on the eastern side of the loch. Come here to paddle in the achingly cold waters – the loch enjoys a year-round temperature of just 5˚C – and take the kilometre-long footpath out to forested Torr Point: head all the way along the shoreline away from Dores, then turn into the pine woodland to meander around the forest before heading back.

FALLS OF FOYERS (📍IV2 6XX ✐walkhighlands.co.uk) Set within a dramatic gorge on the eastern side of Loch Ness, the spectacular Falls of Foyers can be seen on a beautiful 4½km walk that takes up to 2 hours. The trail starts opposite the car park, a 25-minute drive north of Fort Augustus, and leads down steep steps to a pair of viewpoints from which you can see the main, 50m-high cascade. It then passes through glorious woodland towards the lower, smaller falls, and on to the shores of Loch Ness before climbing back up to the village.

INVERMORISTON FALLS (📍IV63 7YA 🐾) For a sedate, picturesque dog walk head, 15 minutes north of Fort Augustus to the village of Invermoriston, an idyllic little place on the banks of the River Moriston which flows on the western side of the loch. Here, you can walk along the river on a network of trails, passing a picturesque 19th-century bridge that was once the main river crossing and the handsome Invermoriston Falls. Come in October or November, and you might spot salmon jumping out of the water around the bridge.

↑ Boat trip on Loch Ness. (LG) → Dolphins in the Moray Firth. (grafxart/s)

LET'S GO

GETTING THERE

The A82 runs the length of Loch Ness's western shore. From Edinburgh, take the A9 to Inverness; for Fort Augustus, aim for the A86. Inverness railway station (Academy St, IV2 3PY) sees direct trains from Edinburgh and Glasgow and sits at the end of the line for the Caledonian Sleeper from London (♥ sleeper.scot), which has dog-friendly berths.

EATING

✕ **Black Isle Bar & Rooms** 68 Church St, Inverness IV1 1EN ✑ blackislebrewery.com ☺ noon–midnight daily. The city-centre tap room for the organic Black Isle Brewing Company offers their newest beers on tap, guest ales and excellent wood-fired pizza.

✕ **Dores Inn** Dores IV2 6TR ✆ 01463 751203 ☺ noon–21.00 Wed–Sat. This beachside pub on the eastern shore of Loch Ness, 15km south of Inverness, serves great fish and chips and good local ales. Booking ahead recommended.

✕ **The Lock Inn** Canal Side, Fort Augustus PH32 4AU ✑ the-lockinn.co.uk ☺ noon–23.00 daily. A splendid little boozer on the Caledonian Canal in Fort Augustus, dishing up pub classics such as burgers, scampi and fish and chips.

SLEEPING

🏠 **Bridgend House** Drumnadrochit IV63 6TU ✑ sykescottages.co.uk 🐾 2. Ideally situated between Fort Augustus and Inverness, this lovely self-catering house sits on the western edge of Loch Ness. It sleeps up to eight in four bedrooms and you'll have an enclosed garden for the dogs and a bubbling hot tub for chilly nights. *From £708/week.*

🏠 **The Glenmoriston Townhouse** 20 Ness Bank, Inverness IV2 4SF ✑ petspyjamas.com 🐾 2. This upscale riverside property offers cosy rooms with a few tartan touches. Dogs can dine with you in the Piano Bar, which has over 250 whiskies. *From £159/night B&B.*

🏠 **The Lovat** A82, PH32 4DU ✑ thelovat.com 🐾 2. Hotels rarely come more dog-friendly than this excellent place in Fort Augustus. The garden rooms have their own enclosed patios, there's a large fenced-in lawn for off-lead runabouts, and dogs can join you in the restaurant which serves fantastic tasting menus. *From £110/night B&B; dogs from £20/night.*

OTHER PRACTICALITIES

Tourist information centre Drumnadrochit car park, IV63 6TX ✑ lochnesstravel.com ☺ 09.30–17.00 daily.

Pet supplies Inverness has a Pets at Home (8 Eastfield Way, IV2 7GD ✑ petsathome.com ☺ 09.00–20.00 Mon–Fri, 09.00–19.00 Sat, 10.00–18.00 Sun).

Veterinary practices Crown Vets (58 Argyle St, Inverness IV2 3BB ✆ 01463 237000) is a reliable practice with an out-of-hours service.

Hiking the Derwent Fells, Lake District. (Duncan Andison/S)

INDEX

Page numbers in **bold** indicate main entries; those in *italics* indicate maps.

A

Aberdeen 220-1

accommodation, dog-friendly xvi

Aldeburgh 108-9

Anglesey 144-7

Areas of Outstanding Natural Beauty

   High Weald AONB 54-5

   Nidderdale AONB 160-3

   Shropshire Hills AONB 114-17

   Wye Valley AONB 92-5

B

Bamburgh 180-7

Bath 62-3

beaches *see* coastal breaks

Berkshire

   Pangbourne 78-83

Beverley 158-9

birdwatching *see* wildlife watching

booking dog-friendly accommodation

   xvi

Brecon Beacons National Park 104-7

Bury St Edmunds 112-13

C

Cairngorms National Park 212-19

Cardiff 72-7

city breaks

   Aberdeen 220-1

   Bath 62-3

   Cardiff 72-7

   Dundee 202-3

   Edinburgh 192-7

   Lincoln 138-43

   Liverpool 156-7

   London 64-71

   Nottingham 128-9

   Portsmouth 34-5

   Royal Tunbridge Wells 54-5

   Salisbury 52-3

   Wells 56-61

   Winchester 50-1

Clovelly 48-9

coastal breaks

   Aldeburgh 108-9

   Anglesey 144-7

   Bamburgh 180-7

   Clovelly 48-9

   Dundee 202-3

   Hastings 32-3

   Holkham & Wells 124-7

   Isle of Mull 204-9

   Isle of Wight 28-31

   Isles of Scilly 2-9

   Pembrokeshire 84-91

   Roseland Heritage Coast 10-17

   South West Coast Path 10-17, 26-7

   Weymouth 26-7

control, keeping your dog under xi, xiii

Corbridge & Northumberland National

   Park 174-7

Cornwall

   Isles of Scilly 2-9

   Roseland Heritage Coast 10-17

Cotswolds 96-103

countryside breaks

   Brecon Beacons National Park 104-7

   Cairngorms National Park 212-19

   Corbridge & Northumberland

      National Park 174-7

countryside breaks *continued*
   Cotswolds 96–103
   Dartmoor National Park 18–25
   Forest of Dean 92–5
   Glastonbury 57–61
   Glencoe & the Nevis Range
     210–11
   High Weald AONB 54–5
   Lake District 170–3
   Loch Lomond 198–201
   Loch Ness 222–5
   Ludlow 114–17
   Midhurst 40–7
   New Forest National Park
     36–9
   Nidderdale AONB 160–3
   North York Moors 164–9
   Peak District 148–55
   Rutland 118–23
   Shropshire Hills AONB 114–17
   Snowdonia National Park 130–7
   South Downs National Park 40–7
   Thames Path 78–83
   Trossachs National Park 198–201
   Ullswater 170–3
   Wells 57–61
   Wye Valley AONB 92–5
Countryside Code xi

D
Dartmoor National Park 18–25
Derbyshire
   Peak District 148–55
Devon
   Clovelly 48–9
   Dartmoor National Park
     18–25
Dorset
   Weymouth 26–7
Dundee 202–3

E
East Midlands
   Lincoln 138–43
   Nottingham 128–9
   Rutland 118–23
East Sussex
   Hastings 32–3
Edinburgh 192–7
equipment, useful xv–xvi

F
first aid kit for your dog xv
forests *see* woodland & forests
Forest of Dean 92–5

G
Galloway Forest Park 178–9
Glastonbury 57–61
Glencoe & the Nevis Range 210–11
Gloucestershire
   Cotswolds 96–103
   Forest of Dean 92–5
   Wye Valley AONB 92–5

H
Hampshire
   Isle of Wight 28–31
   New Forest National Park 36–9
   Portsmouth 34–5
   Winchester 50–1
Hastings 32–3
Herefordshire
   Wye Valley AONB 92–5
High Weald AONB 54–5
hills & mountains
   Brecon Beacons National Park 104–7
   Cairngorms National Park 212–19
   Glastonbury 57–61
   Glencoe & the Nevis Range 210–11
   Ludlow 114–17

hills & mountains *continued*
    Nidderdale AONB 160–3
    North York Moors 164–9
    Peak District 148–55
    Shropshire Hills AONB 114–17
    Snowdonia National Park
      130–7
historical breaks
    Bath 62–3
    Cardiff 72–7
    Lincoln 138–43
    Portsmouth 34–5
    Salisbury 52–3
    Stratford-upon-Avon 110–11
    Winchester 50–1
Holkham & Wells 124–7

I
Isle of Mull 204–9
Isle of Wight 28–31
Isles of Scilly 2–9

K
Kent
    Royal Tunbridge Wells 54–5

L
Lake District 170–3
legal issues xi
Lincoln 138–43
Liverpool 156–7
Loch Lomond 198–201
Loch Ness 222–5
London 64–71
Ludlow 114–17

M
maps xii
Merseyside 156–7
Midhurst 40–7

Monmouthshire
    Wye Valley AONB 92–5
mountains *see* hills & mountains

N
national parks
    Brecon Beacons 104–7
    Cairngorms 212–19
    Corbridge & Northumberland
      174–7
    Dartmoor 18–25
    New Forest 36–9
    North York Moors 164–9
    Snowdonia 130–7
    South Downs 40–7
    Trossachs 198–201
    Yorkshire Dales National Park
      160–3
New Forest National Park 36–9
Nidderdale AONB 160–3
Norfolk
    Holkham & Wells 124–7
North York Moors 164–9
Northumberland
    Bamburgh 180–7
    Corbridge & Northumberland
      National Park 174–7
Nottingham 128–9

O
Oxfordshire
    Cotswolds 96–103
    Wallingford 78–83

P
Pangbourne 78–83
Peak District 148–55
Pembrokeshire 84–91
Portsmouth 34–5

R
river breaks
Pangbourne 78–83
Stratford-upon-Avon 110–11
Thames Path 78–83
Tweed Valley 188–91
Wallingford 78–83
Wye Valley AONB 92–5
Roseland Heritage Coast 10–17
Royal Tunbridge Wells 54–5
rural areas *see* countryside breaks
Rutland 118–23

S
safety concerns xiv
Salisbury 52–3
Scilly Isles 2–9
Scotland
Aberdeen 220–1
Cairngorms National Park 212–19
Dundee 202–3
Edinburgh 192–7
Galloway Forest Park 178–9
Glencoe & the Nevis Range 210–11
Isle of Mull 204–9
Loch Lomond 198–201
Loch Ness 222–5
Trossachs National Park 198–201
Tweed Valley 188–91
Shropshire
Ludlow 114–17
Shropshire Hills AONB 114–17
Snowdonia National Park 130–7
Somerset
Bath 62–3
Glastonbury 57–61
Wells 57–61
South Downs National Park 40–7
South West Coast Path 10–17, 26–7
Stratford-upon-Avon 110–11

Suffolk
Aldeburgh 108–9
Bury St Edmunds 112–13

T
Thames Path 78–83
Trossachs National Park 198–201
Tweed Valley 188–91

U
Ullswater 170–3

W
Wales
Anglesey 144–7
Brecon Beacons National Park 104–7
Cardiff 72–7
Pembrokeshire 84–91
Snowdonia National Park 130–7
Wye Valley AONB 92–5
Wallingford 78–83
Warwickshire
Stratford-upon-Avon 110–11
Wells 57–61
West Sussex
Midhurst 40–7
South Downs National Park 40–7
Weymouth 26–7
wildlife watching xii, 2–9, 28–31, 36–9,
78–83, 84–91, 96–103, 108–9, 124–7,
144–7, 178–9, 180–7, 198–201, 204–9,
222–5
Wiltshire
New Forest National Park 36–9
Salisbury 52–3
Winchester 50–1
woodland & forests
Forest of Dean 92–5
Galloway Forest Park 178–9
New Forest National Park 36–9

woodland & forests *continued*
  Snowdonia National Park 130–7
  Tweed Valley 188–91
Worcestershire
  Cotswolds 96–103
Wye Valley AONB 92–5

Y
Yorkshire
  Beverley 158–9
  Nidderdale AONB 160–3
  North York Moors 164–9

INDEX OF ADVERTISERS

Charley Chau xx
Dicky Bag 1
PetsPyjamas 1
Karma St Martin's 236
Needles Pleasure Cruises 235

Runswick Bay Cottages 169
The Bird Bath 235
The Lygon Arms inside-front cover
The Old Bell Hotel inside-back cover

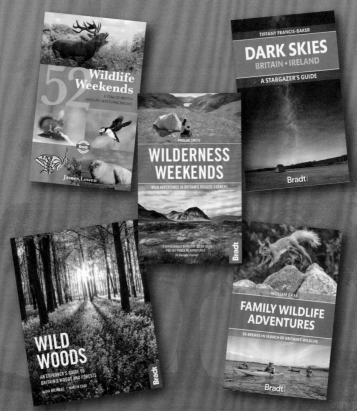

The award-winning
Slow Travel series from
Bradt Guides

Over 20 regional guides across Britain.
See the full list at bradtguides.com/slowtravel.

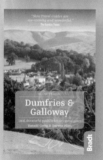

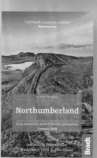

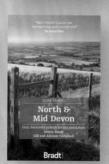

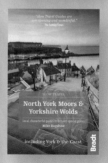